MODERN CHINA: APPROACHES TO GLOBAL GOVERNANCE AND INTERNATIONAL COOPERATION

Written by Carsten Boyer Thøgersen et al.

Prunus Press USA

This edition is published by Prunus Press USA.

Modern China: Approaches to Global Governance and International Cooperation

Copyright © China National Publications Import and Export
(Group) Co., Ltd.

Written by Carsten Boyer Thøgersen et al.

First Edition 2025
ISBN: 978-1-61612-169-3

Prunus Press USA

Contents

Carsten Boyer Thøgersen

Former Danish ambassadorial-level diplomat posted in China for twenty years as Consul-General in Shanghai and Guangzhou, at the Embassy of Denmark in Beijing, at the Delegation of the European Union in Beijing and five years in the China Office of the European Commission in Brussels, member of the Executive Committee of International Confucian Association. Since 1976, he has written about China's foreign policy and Chinese affairs including: *A Leap into the Twenty-First Century*, Introduction in *China in the 1980s – and Beyond, To Point at the Moon – Only to See Your Own Finger, From a Strong Past to a Dynamic Present, Danes and Danish Companies in the Greater Shanghai Region 1846 to 2006, Xi Jinping: My Road into Politics*, first translation into a Western language of an interview by the Governor of Fujian Province in 2000, *Three Chinese Writers On Cultural Differences Between the East and the West, The Origin of the 1871 Chinese Telegraphic Code Book, List of Danish and Chinese Scholars and Professionals.*

China's Economic, Social and Political Development: As Observed by a European

"China wants to become the world's richest, most environmentally friendly, most democratic, and most civilized nation", a young official in the Shanghai Municipal Government told me in 2006. As Consul-General of Denmark in Shanghai, I met with him from time to time and whenever the opportunity arose, we always talked about Chinese national politics and international relations.

"It is very ambitious," I said. The young official replied that for China – the world's oldest uninterrupted civilization – there was a special responsibility. It was China's obligation to be an inspiration to other cultures in the world, he said.

I sympathized with the young official's beliefs, but at the time, I found that his wishes would only come true in the distant future.

Hope for the Economy

In 2006, five years after China entered the World Trade Organization (WTO), China's economy was rapidly developing. In the 1980s, profound structural economic changes took place in the countryside after China introduced its Reform and Opening-up Policy in 1978.

From 1988 to 1992, I travelled extensively in China. I was the EU principal project coordinator of an EU-China agricultural co-operation project worth 330 million EURO covering 20 large Chinese municipalities. In the countryside, new residential houses were built on an impressive scale to replace the old ones that had often lacked basic facilities. Some years later development of urban areas started for real.

In the 1990s, China opened up for more foreign investment, and large multinational companies set up representation offices in China while some started to build their own production facilities. After 2001, a new wave of foreign companies entered the Chinese market. Thousands of foreign companies started doing business with China and set up offices in China. But in 2006, China was, despite its large population, still only the fifth largest economy in the world.[1]

No one expected continued and even stronger economic growth in China after 2006. After 2008, China quickly succeeded in curbing the effects of the global financial crisis that had started in the United States. After 2010, China's domestic market became still more important to foreign exporters.

By 2022, 16 years later, China had become the world's second-largest economy[2], the largest recipient of foreign investment, was deeply integrated into global value chains, and on its way to becoming the world's largest economy within a few years. Although consumers and businesses in the U.S. and the EU prospered intensely in trade with China, China's robust economic development also fostered concern. In a way, it is simple. If we look at the development of China's GDP from 1997 to 2022, a period of 25 years, it increased by 18 times.[3] In history, this is unprecedented for a large country like China. In the same period, the GDP of the U.S. increased by 2½ times. Obviously, people in the U.S. would ask themselves how to address this change in world economic power relations. One choice for the U.S. would have been to continue to benefit economically from trading in the flourishing Chinese market. However, some people in the U.S. started to feel threatened by China's

---

[1] After the U.S., Japan, Germany, and France and measured in nominal terms.

[2] Measured in nominal terms. Measured in PPP (purchasing power parity) China became the largest economy of the world already in 2014.

[3] https://data.worldbank.org/country/CN

development. From 2010, the U.S. policy towards China changed step by step.

The U.S. Response to the Rise of China

The first pivot came about in 2010, when U.S. Secretary of State Hillary Clinton, in a speech at a regional ASEAN meeting in Hanoi, Vietnam, introduced a new global focus of the United States, later called the "Pivot to Asia". Ms. Clinton raised the question about the South China Sea and stated that the United States would be willing to facilitate a collaborative process for addressing the various territorial claims.[4] The United States, thereby, for the first time, intervened in the ongoing regional negotiations on the territorial borders of the South China Sea.[5]

During the Arab Spring from 2010 to 2012, the Obama administration supported a democracy campaign in the Middle East, using the latest digital technology and social media.[6] The United States brought the concept to East Asia and became involved in various regional conflicts that lurked under the surface and had their local background. In 2011, organizations based in the United States tried from their websites to promote a democratic spring in China.[7] The Jasmine Revolution, as it was called, did not happen. There were no protesters; only Western journalists appeared for the announced events. The aim was not to contain China – China's economy was already too large to contain by 2010 – but to slow down China's economic and technological development.

China and Japan had agreed in 1972 that the sovereignty of the Diaoyu Islands in the East China Sea would have to wait and be settled by future

---

[4] The American Pivot to Asia, Kenneth G. Lieberthal, December 21, 2011. https://www.brookings.edu/articles/the-american-pivot-to-asia/

[5] 2002 Declaration on the Conduct of Parties in the South China Sea. https://cil.nus.edu.sg/wp-content/uploads/2017/07/2002-Declaration-on-the-Conduct-of-Parties-in-the-South-China-Sea.pdf

[6] The digital road to Egypt's revolution, *New York Times*, February 10, 2012. http://archive.nytimes.com/www.nytimes.com/interactive/2012/02/12/opinion/sunday/20120212-tahir-timeline.html?_r=1

[7] "The US-based Chinese pro-democracy website Boxun last week urged citizens to gather for subtle "strolling" demonstrations each Sunday afternoon at designated locations in cities across China." https://www.dw.com/en/china-fears-jasmine-revolution-of-its-own/a-14881020

generations. In 2011, China protested when the islands were made the subject of a public Japanese real estate deal while the islands' sovereignty remained unresolved. China's protest prompted the United States to declare that the U.S.-Japan Security Treaty covered the islands for the first time.[8]

In 2012, President Obama launched the formation of a trade and investment agreement for the countries around the Pacific, the Trans-Pacific Partnership Agreement (TPP). The deal, which did not include China, was finalized in 2016. The following year, President Trump withdrew U.S. support for the TPP.

The "umbrella" demonstrations[9] in Hong Kong in 2014 had distinct local causes. But foundations under the U.S. Congress financially supported the protests, and members of the US Congress later received the movement leaders.[10]

The second pivot come about after 2017 when the dialogue between China and the U.S. diminished.

Under Presidents George W. Bush and Barack Obama, the U.S. administration had ongoing and close contact with the Chinese leadership. It continued in the first year of President Trump's presidency. In April 2017, three months after Trump's inauguration as president, China's President Xi Jinping traveled to Florida and met with Trump. Later that year, Trump paid an official visit to China, receiving the most impressive reception in the Forbidden City that no other foreign head of state had received in China since 1949.

In December 2017, just after President Trump's return from his visit to China, the White House published the "National Security Strategy of the United States of America," making China the main adversary of the U.S.[11]

In 2018, Trump began levying significant tariffs on U.S. imports from the EU, Mexico, and Canada before imposing extremely high tariffs on imports

---

[8] TheDiaoyu Dispute: U.S. Treaty Obligations, U.S. Congressional Research Service. https://sgp.fas.org/crs/row/R42761.pdf.

[9] 占中运动 ("Occupy Central with Love and Peace").

[10] https://www.nytimes.com/2014/10/11/world/asia/some-chinese-leaders-claim-us-and-britain-are-behind-hong-kong-protests-.html and https://www.ned.org/region/asia/

[11] https://trumpwhitehouse.archives.gov/wp-content/uploads/2017/12/NSS-Final-12-18-2017-0905.pdf

from China. At the same time, the United States began to exclude Chinese tech companies like Huawei and ZTE[12] from the U.S. market. In October 2018, Vice President Mike Pence took the U.S. confrontation with China to a new level. In a speech on China in the neoconservative think tank, the Hudson Institute, Pence stated that China was the United States' primary adversary and that the United States was working for a change in China's political system. The speech was rhetorical, had few facts, and laid the foundation for the following years' American narrative about China.[13] Subsequently, many U.S. allies embraced the American narrative about the global threat posed by China.

The third pivot came about in 2020 when China-US confrontation became even more intense.

President Joe Biden continued President Trump's China policy but handled it far more professionally, assisted by a team of experienced officials. Biden set up special China offices across the administration to better coordinate his China policy. The CIA set up a China Mission Centre to "further strengthen our collective work on the most important geopolitical threat we face in the 21st century, an increasingly adversarial Chinese government."[14] In May 2021, the proposal "Act on Strategic Competition"[15] was presented in the U.S. Senate. The bill was 281 pages long and a comprehensive catalogue of the threats that U.S. lawmakers saw coming from China. In the years 2022 to 2026, the bill would annually allocate between USD 110-150 million to non-military activities to counter threats from China. Under President Biden, NATO was now pointing to China as a security threat to NATO member states.[16]

China's increased economic and technological strength – regardless of China's political system – is a challenge for the West, the rest of the world, and

---

[12] 中兴通讯股份有限公司 (ZTE)

[13] Vice President Mike Pence's remarks on the administration's policy towards China，https://www.hudson.org/events/1610-vice-president-mike-pence-s-remarks-on-the-administration-s-policy-towards-china102018

[14] CIA's New China Mission Center: How To Do It Right. https://breakingdefense.com/2021/10/cias-new-china-mission-center-how-to-do-it-right/

[15] S.1169 - Strategic Competition Act of 2021. https://www.congress.gov/bill/117th-congress/senate-bill/1169/text

[16] Madrid Summit Declaration, issued by NATO Heads of State and Government participating in the meeting of the North Atlantic Council in Madrid 29 June 2022, https://www.nato.int/cps/en/natohq/official_texts_196951.htm

for China itself. It is telling that the United States – pragmatically and through negotiations – has chosen an ideological and value-based conflict instead of addressing these challenges within international organizations.

Since 2018, the U.S. has developed a new narrative about China: China is an authoritarian regime, aggressive in the South China Sea, breaking international trade rules, committing genocide in Xinjiang, violates democracy and international agreements in Hong Kong, oppresses human rights in Tibet and wants to attack a democratically self-governing Taiwan. The U.S. goal is a regime change in China.[17]

This new U.S. narrative about China, which continued under President Joe Biden, did not particularly criticize China's international behavior. China has no troops outside China, overseas military bases, military alliances, overseas colonies, or client states. The new U.S. narrative focused on China's border regions, Xinjiang, Tibet, the South China Sea, Hong Kong, and Taiwan, and criticized these places' internal situation. However, safeguarding sovereignty and defending its own territory, borders, and political system is crucial for any country. In China, it is called "core interests." In Western countries, we call it red lines.

It is not new that the United States is putting pressure on China. What is new is the scope and intensity. Today, relations between the United States and China are the most confrontational since 1969, when the United States and China – after Richard Nixon's inauguration as U.S. President in January 1969 – initiated a rapprochement, which was confirmed by President Nixon's historic visit to China in February 1972. While the United States still maintains all official relations with China, it opposes China – or, as the United States says: competes robustly – in most other areas. Collaboration takes up little space, while competition is dominant. What is the content of this new U.S. narrative about China?

---

[17] U.S. Secretary of State Mike Pompeo says free world must change China or 'China will change us'. The Guardian, July 24, 2020. https://www.theguardian.com/world/2020/jul/24/mike-pompeo-says-free-world-must-change-china-or-china-will-change-us

The U.S. Critique of China – Case by Case

The South China Sea

The Spratly Islands[18] are the largest and most disputed archipelago in the South China Sea. Both China, Vietnam, the Philippines, Malaysia, and Brunei make claims in the Spratly archipelago, which consists of well over a dozen islands, small sandbanks, and over 100 flooded reefs.

China claimed sovereignty over the archipelago as early as 1936 and again in 1947. Later, other countries did the same. From 1980 on, they began to occupy, enlarge, and fortify several islands. China continued to demand sovereignty over most of the Spratly Islands but occupied none of the islands – except for a single island in 1988 after a controversial clash with Vietnam. In 2002, China entered into an agreement with Vietnam, the Philippines, Malaysia, and Brunei to negotiate the islands' future. The starting point was that disagreements were recognized and that these should be negotiated bilaterally between the countries involved. In 2011, the countries reaffirmed the dialogue.

In 2010, the United States launched its "Pivot to Asia" policy and engaged in the issue of the future of the Spratly Islands. A regional negotiation process was replaced by geopolitical confrontation. Since 2014, China responded by occupying and expanding six islands. The original area of the archipelago was less than 2 km². Later, China added 10 km² by embankment after the other countries had already expanded the islands they occupied by 2 km². Today, 26 of the islands and reefs are controlled by Vietnam, ten by the Philippines, seven by China, and seven by Malaysia.

In 2016, the UN Convention on the Law of the Sea, UNCLOS, headquartered in Hamburg, Germany, stated that none of the islands could

---

[18] https://www.britannica.com/place/Spratly-Islands

be called islands and, therefore, the rule of a coastal state's exclusive economic zone of 200 nautical miles applied to the area. From the beginning, China opposed the intervention of UNCLOS. The South China Sea had a long history before UNCLOS was established in 1982. Since 1946, the Republic of China (Taiwan) has controlled Taiping, the archipelago's largest island, and has claims on islands in the Spratly archipelago identical to the claims of the People's Republic of China.

The Spratly Islands in the South China Sea have no indigenous people. They are just sandbanks. With the presence of its navy, the United States wants to assert the right of freedom of navigation. No country – including China – disputes that right. The area is one of the world's busiest for merchant ships, though not directly through the archipelago, but 200 km to the west. But clashes occurred when U.S. warships sailed within the 12 nautical miles' maritime territorial zone of Chinese-controlled islands.

The conflict in the South China Sea is symbolic and is a test of strength between the United States and China. China wants the United States to stop patrolling the coastline of China, 12,000 km off the west coast of the United States. The United States sees it as its national interest to be present. Should clashes occur, they will only involve military units. There is no civilian population in the area, and the regular traffic of civilian merchant ships has never been threatened.

Xinjiang, China

From 1995 to 2022, China had more than 1,000 casualties and more than 2,000 wounded from terrorist actions.[19] In 2014, China's central government launched the "Strike Hard Campaign against Violent Terrorism."

Two tracks are important for understanding the situation in Xinjiang also because the two tracks often are mixed up in testimonies from Uyghurs in

---

[19] Various sources. See e.g. Wikipedia.

exile. The Chinese central government is fighting terrorism, and separatism. Suspects are interrogated, their cases are processed within the Chinese judicial system, and sentenced people are imprisoned to serve their sentences. It is basically what is happening in Western countries as well.

The second track is China's poverty alleviation campaign. In 2020, China declared it had achieved its national goal of fighting extreme poverty across the country. The campaign also included the Uyghur ethnic minority in Xinjiang. They have lived their traditional lives for centuries with agriculture and sheep farming in the area between Urumqi and Kashgar. Should they be brought into a modern world, learn new skills, and learn China's national language, Mandarin, which allows for higher education and better jobs, or should they continue to live in ethnic reserves?

It is an often seen social and economic development issue with well-known challenges. Training centers were established, where over one million Uyghurs were trained in crafts and service sector skills and then offered job opportunities.

There has been no Chinese attempt to eliminate the ethnic Muslim minority in Xinjiang. For 1400 years, Islam has been part of China's cultural history, with many Muslims in prominent public positions, such as the famous 15th-century seafarer Admiral Zheng He. Outside of Xinjiang, in other parts of China, over 12 million Muslims live peacefully as part of their local communities. No Muslim countries have turned against China's policy in Xinjiang.

Many reports on Xinjiang are American-sponsored and convey statements from Uyghurs living outside China and with connections to groups fighting for an independent Xinjiang. In August 2022, the Office of the UN High Commissioner for Human Rights (OHCHR) published its assessment of human rights concerns in the Xinjiang Uyghur Autonomous Region primarily based on these reports.[20] Hard-core evidence based on reliable sources was not

---

[20] https://www.ohchr.org/sites/default/files/documents/countries/2022-08-31/22-08-31-final-assesment.pdf

presented to validate the serious allegations of genocide, torture, and forced labor.[21]

Since 2020, U.S. sanctions on imported goods manufactured in Xinjiang have been imposed, adding a mercantile aspect to the U.S. policy.

Hong Kong, China

From March 2019 to the outbreak of the COVID-19 pandemic in early 2020, Hong Kong went through massive protests, initially against the proposed "Anti-Extradition Law Amendment Bill"[22] and later against the Hong Kong SAR government in general.

Although the demonstrations were massive and almost daily for almost a year, sometimes developing into riots like wrecking the local parliament, the Hong Kong Legislative Council on July 1, 2019, and a few times with bombs being thrown,[23] the Hong Kong police force was disciplined and behaved well. Only one person lost his life, hit by a stone thrown by a protester. Like in 2014, during the "umbrella" demonstrations, protesters in 2019 received financial support from U.S. Congress organizations and other U.S. organizations.

In July 2020, China's Central Government imposed the National Security Law for Hong Kong, making activities advocating terrorism, subversion, secession, and collusion with foreign forces illegal.

Today, it is a Western narrative that China's Central Government has abolished the agreed principle of "Two Systems" for Hong Kong, ended democracy in Hong Kong, suppressed freedom of speech, imposed strict supervision, and broken international agreements.

The concept of "One Country, Two Systems" was designed by China in 1960 for future Chinese mainland and Taiwan relations and applied in 1997

---

[21] Phrases often used in the report were "maybe, seems to indicate, possible." The assessment was critical and its release had its own controversy.

[22] https://www.legco.gov.hk/yr18-19/english/bills/b201903291.pdf

[23] https://www.nytimes.com/2019/10/14/world/asia/hong-kong-bomb-ied.html. Not including petrol bombs or "Molotov cocktails" which were often used.

for Hong Kong. It is a simple concept, but often not fully understood. So, what does "One Country, Two Systems" mean?

The concept has two principles. For Hong Kong, "One Country" means that China's sovereignty of Hong Kong was reconfirmed when the United Kingdom withdrew from Hong Kong in 1997. "Two Systems" stipulates that the overall administrative and political systems of Chinese mainland and Hong Kong will remain different, shall stay so for fifty years and that Hong Kong shall enjoy a "high degree of autonomy and executive, legislative and independent judicial power."

In short, there are two red lines: 1) Hong Kong is a part of China. That is not up for discussion. 2) China's central government shall not interfere whatsoever in Hong Kong running its own internal affairs. One deal – two clear principles.

In 1984, Deng Xiaoping met in Beijing with a group of Hong Kong business people and gave a razor-sharp explanation of the concept of "One Country, Two Systems."[24] This is probably one of the best explanations given by a Chinese leader.

Deng Xiaoping said that Hong Kong's administration and public institutions could employ foreigners, advisers, and others well but that Hong Kong's senior officials should be patriots. A patriot, Deng continued, is one who supports Hong Kong's return to China and works for Hong Kong's prosperity and stability. Those who meet those requirements are patriots, regardless of whether they believe in capitalism, feudalism, or slavery. "We do not demand that they support China's socialist system."

"Feudalism or slavery" was probably added to emphasize that the political system that the people of Hong Kong might choose was not important to China's central government. If the people of Hong Kong wanted democracy, Hong Kong could have democracy all day long. At least for fifty years. In China's long history, fifty years is like a click of a finger. China could sit back,

---

[24] This speech by Deng Xiaoping also reflects the opinion of China's Government. http://www.china.org.cn/english/features/dengxiaoping/103372.htm.

wait, and assess the situation fifty years later.[25]

Did the "One Country, Two Systems" work in Hong Kong? Yes and no. Until 2019, the concept worked well in Hong Kong. China's sovereignty over Hong Kong was not challenged, and China's central government did not interfere in Hong Kong's internal affairs. From 2019, however, the "high degree of autonomy," including "freedom of speech, the press, and publication; and freedom of association, assembly, demonstration, communication, and movement," was used to promote the independence of Hong Kong, even with documented foreign financial, political, and organizational support. These actions disregarded and negated the first principle of the "One country, Two systems" deal that Hong Kong is a part of China, the fundamental principle that Deng Xiaoping stressed in 1984.

The U.S., the United Kingdom, and other Western countries argued that the National Security Law violated the Sino-British Joint Declaration signed in 1984, with its basic principles included in the Hong Kong Basic Law in 1990, allowing for "freedom of speech, of the press, of demonstrations, etc."

However, the National Security Law only prohibits activities that oppose China's sovereignty over Hong Kong. The National Security Law is not about democracy, freedom of speech, and local governance in Hong Kong but about China's sovereignty over Hong Kong. The right to promote democracy and address and debate current political issues in Hong Kong remain intact and fall outside the scope of the National Security Law – if such activities do not challenge the "One Country" concept.

In 1997, China was handed its part of the Hong Kong deal with Britain – sovereignty over Hong Kong – on a silver platter. Hong Kong was again – de facto and de jure – part of China. For the first twenty years after 1997, China was laid back in relation to Hong Kong until 2019, when China's sovereignty over Hong Kong was challenged.

---

[25] The Report to the 20th National Congress of the CPC stated in chapter XIII: "We will ensure that the capitalist system and way of life remain unchanged in Hong Kong and Macao in the long run," meaning beyond fifty years.

Many people in Hong Kong have issues with the Hong Kong Government regarding housing, education, social welfare, income distribution, and the governance of Hong Kong in general. The space to raise these issues peacefully has not changed. Freedom of the press and other freedoms in Hong Kong stipulated in the Basic Law are unaffected – again, except for promoting the independence of Hong Kong.

Today, there are more democratic procedures in Hong Kong than ever before, but there is no democracy in Hong Kong in a Western sense, and there has never been since Hong Kong became a British Crown Colony in 1842. But a process towards full suffrage for all was written into Hong Kong's constitution. China's demand that only patriots in the sense of Deng Xiaoping can be elected to the absolute top posts has been contested by groups in Hong Kong who want greater independence for Hong Kong than granted in the constitution. The groups in Hong Kong that want democracy have gathered considerable support, but the groups are divided, lack practical visions, and are without a program.[26]

In 1997, the people in Hong Kong got a window of opportunity for fifty years to develop a strong local civil society of their own liking, including creating what all of China's provinces and regions attach great importance to – a robust defense of their own local interests against China's central government, which locally has always been seen as a troublesome albeit necessary evil. As a diplomat working in China, I have met with government officials in all provinces and autonomous regions.[27] Their views, policies, and priorities were all different. But they had one thing in common: their own province, their region, or their city was the most important place in China's history, in

---

[26] In 2017, the conflict in Spain between the regional Catalonian Government and the National Spanish Government was in many ways similar to the situation in Hong Kong in 2019. Most importantly, the two conflicts were not about democracy, but sovereignty. In Catalonia, a democratically elected regional government held a regional referendum about Catalonia's independence from Spain. A majority in this democratic election voted for independence. The referendum was not accepted by the National Spanish Government and nine democratically elected leaders of the Catalonian Government were sentenced up to 13 years in jail. The National Spanish authorities have acted more severe than what we have seen in Hong Kong so far. European media covered the situation in Hong Kong intensively while being mostly silent about Catalonian.

[27] Over a period of 30 years and excluding Taiwan. However, visiting Taiwan in 2018, I met with representatives of the Guomindang at the Guomindang Headquarters in Taipei.

China's current economic and social development, and they were all working hard in numerous ways to secure optimal favorable policies from the central government while upholding their own regional autonomy. How much and how wisely did the people in Hong Kong plan for the future after fifty years to secure maximum and continued favorable policies for Hong Kong? The people of Hong Kong still have the opportunity – in the next 25 years leading up to 2047 – to build a strong local government according to their own wishes and with the concept of "One Country" as the basis.

Taiwan, China

The Chinese Civil War from 1946 to 1949 ended with the establishment of the People's Republic of China, while the military elite and senior officials of the Republic of China, about 2 million people, relocated to the island of Taiwan that Japan had handed back to China in 1945 as the Province of Taiwan. During President Nixon's visit to China in 1972, the United States and China signed a declaration called the Shanghai Communiqué, in which the United States declared:

The United States acknowledges that all Chinese on either side of the Taiwan Strait maintain there is but one China and that Taiwan is a part of China. The United States Government does not challenge that position.[28]

After 1972, almost all Western countries severed "diplomatic relations" with the Taiwan authorities and established diplomatic relations with the People's Republic of China. A handful of Western countries, including Denmark, had previously established diplomatic relations with the People's Republic of China.

Today, 76 years after the actual end of the Chinese Civil War, with its official conclusion still pending, Taiwan's status remains unresolved. Under the Trump administration and now more strongly under President Biden, the

---

[28] https://digitalarchive.wilsoncenter.org/document/joint-communique-between-united-states-and-china

narrative of Taiwan has changed from a historical, constitutional narrative to a value-based narrative. The People's Republic of China is an authoritarian government, while Taiwan, for the past 25 years – rightly – can be called a well-functioning democracy in a Western sense. The United States supplies arms to Taiwan, builds state-to-state-like relations with Taiwan, and promotes Taiwan's position as an independent nation, detached from the Chinese mainland. This is new and will cross one of China's red lines. No Chinese leadership will survive giving up Taiwan as a part of China.

Seen from China, the question of Taiwan's status is not about Taiwan's political system but about China's sovereignty. China's model for Taiwan is simple: Following an official ceremony on Taiwan's return to China, Taiwan continues as before with its own political system, its own elected government, its own public institutions, and full self-government. China's goal is Taiwan's formal status as part of the Chinese nation and the absence of foreign interference. After that, Taiwan can develop according to its people's wishes and its local leaders' capabilities. But Taiwan must remain part of China.

In 2008, cross-strait relations changed when Ma Ying-jeou, from the Guomindang (KMT), was elected the leader of Taiwan[29], succeeding Chen Shuibian of the Democratic Progressive Party. In 2008 in his inaugural address, President Ma said he would deal with cross-strait relations during his tenure as the leader based upon the "three no's": "no reunification, no independence, and no use of force."[30]

Eight years of Chinese mainland-Taiwan tensions under Chen Shuibian were followed by eight years of the closest cooperation between the Chinese mainland and Taiwan since 1949. From 2008 to 2016, no less than 23 cooperation agreements were signed between the Chinese mainland and

---

[29] In December 1946, China's Constituent National Assembly Session in Nanjing ratified the Constitution of the Republic of China (中华民国宪法) and adopted it one year later in December 1947. This is still the constitution of the present-day government located in Taipei including later amendments. Another reason why I use the term "Republic of China" is that China's civil war between 1946 and 1949 has not yet found an official end. According to the constitutions of both the People's Republic of China and the Republic of China, Taiwan is a part of China.

[30] 不统, 不独, 不武. https://china.usc.edu/ma-ying-jeou-%E2%80%9Cinaugural-address%E2%80%9D-may-20-2008

Taiwan authorities.

In 2014, the mainland of China and the Taiwan authorities held their first official talks since 1949.

In 2015, China's president Xi Jinping met with Ma Ying-jeou, the leader of Taiwan, in Singapore. The meeting was the first between the political leaders of the two sides of the Taiwan Strait since 1949.[31] It was also the third high-level meeting between leaders of the Communist Party of China and the Guomindang (KMT),[32] with the first taking place in 1945 in Chongqing between Mao Zedong and Chiang Kai-shek and the second in 2005 in Beijing between Hu Jintao and Lien Chan.[33]

After Tsai Ing-wen was elected the leader of Taiwan and after the election of Donald Trump as U.S. President, the United States has, in practice, if not in words, changed its one-China policy. U.S. government members have paid official visits to Taiwan, and U.S. military planes landed there. The U.S. has military advisers stationed on the island, and the U.S. Navy is massively present in the waters around. Recently, a U.S. nuclear submarine crashed in the South China Sea without the U.S. authorities informing the international community about the damage's time, place, cause, and extent. In 2021, Taiwan's unofficial representative in the United States was invited to Joe Biden's inauguration as president.

In October 2021, U.S. Secretary of State Antony Blinken said Taiwan's exclusion from UN forums "undermines the important work of the UN and its related bodies, all of which stand to benefit greatly from its contributions. That is why we encourage all UN member states to join us in supporting Taiwan's robust, meaningful participation throughout the UN system and in

---

[31] The two leaders did not use official titles to address each other but "mister"(先生). No agreement was signed, and no joint communique issued. The purpose of the meeting was to enhance trust, consolidate common political ground, and advance peaceful development. https://america.cgtn.com/2015/11/06/xi-jinping-and-ma-ying-jeou-to-hold-face-to-face-talks-in-singapore

[32] In 2014, Ma Ying-jeou had resigned as chairman of the Guomindang/KMT. https://thediplomat.com/2015/11/who-is-mr-xi-jinping/

[33] https://english.president.gov.tw/Page/88

the international community."[34] In 1971, the UN General Assembly decided that the Government of the People's Republic of China was the only legitimate representative of China to the United Nations while regarding Taiwan as a province of China. In 2007, UN General Assembly reconfirmed this position.[35]

Under the predecessor of the Taiwan leader Tsai Ing-wen, Taiwan had an observer status in several U.N. specialized agencies under the name "Chinese Taipei". That was because Taiwan at the time recognized the 1992 Consensus between the mainland of China and Taiwan[36], in which both parties agreed that there was only one China but left its definition open.

When Tsai Ing-wen failed to confirm the 1992 Consensus, China no longer supported Taiwan's participation in U.N. organizations because it would signal the existence of "two Chinas." If Tsai Ing-wen confirmed the 1992 Consensus, Taiwan could assume its former observer status in UN specialized agencies. But Tsai Ing-wen's authorities does not want to confirm the "one-China" formula.

According to Western sources, China's response to the U.S.'s step-by-step attempt to change Taiwan's international status has been massive military overflights into the airspace around Taiwan. It is true that China, unlike in the past, has allowed military aircraft to show China's presence.

The U.S. officially supports the status quo for Taiwan, has diplomatic relations with the People's Republic of China, formally recognizes the "one-China policy," and has no official "diplomatic ties" with Taiwan. I believe that China might respond by severing diplomatic relations with the United States

---

[34] https://www.reuters.com/world/blinken-urges-all-un-member-states-support-taiwan-participation-2021-10-26/

[35] From United Nations press release on September 21, 2007: "With 140 speakers taking the floor during a day-long meeting, delegations overwhelmingly agreed that Taiwan's latest application to join the United Nations was not acceptable for legal reasons linked to General Assembly's resolution 2758 (1971) that gave China's seat in the Assembly to the People's Republic of China. Most delegations strongly supported the "one-China" policy and stressed that the "Taiwan question" was an internal affair of China and should, therefore, only be resolved by the Chinese people themselves." https://www.un.org/press/en/2007/ga10617.doc.htm

[36] The 1992 Consensus (九二共识). In November 1992, representatives from the Association for Relations Across the Taiwan Strait (ARATS) based in Mainland China and representatives from Strait Exchange Foundation (SEF) based in Taiwan met in British Hong Kong. The semi-official representatives from Mainland China and Taiwan agreed upon the consensus of "one China, different interpretations (一中各表，一个中国各自表述), i.e. that Mainland China and Taiwan agreed that there is one China, but disagreed about what China meant.

if the latter should further its cooperation with Taiwan, especially militarily, and establishes de facto state-to-state ties with it based on the view that it is historically not part of China. A diplomatic break between China and the U.S. will have unforeseeable global consequences – in terms of trade, economics, and all international cooperation.

The Speaker of the U.S. House of Representatives is the highest-ranking legislative official in the U.S. government and next in line after the President and Vice President. In August 2022, the then Speaker of the House, Nancy Pelosi, visited Taiwan semi-officially. Following the visit, China performed a five-day unprecedented military exercise around the island of Taiwan.

Will China attack Taiwan? I think not. During a meeting in Beijing in 1984 with businessmen from Hong Kong, Deng Xiaoping explained China's principle of "One Country, Two Systems":

"The concept of 'One Country, Two Systems' has been formulated according to China's realities. China has not only the Hong Kong question to tackle but also the Taiwan question. What is the solution to these questions? Is it for socialism to swallow up Taiwan, or for the 'Three People's Principles' of Taiwan to swallow up the mainland? No one should swallow the other. If the problem cannot be solved by peaceful means, then there is only force left to solve the question, but neither side would benefit from that. Reunification of the motherland is the aspiration of the whole nation. If it cannot be accomplished in 100 years, it will be in 1000 years. As I see it, the only solution lies in practicing two systems in one country."[37] (Bold script added).[38]

Deng Xiaoping's position in 1984 was also China's official position and is still valid today. China cannot, as a matter of principle, waive the right to use force within a region that China considers part of China. But it emphasizes peaceful reunification, knowing that reunification may lie far ahead.

97% of the population in Taiwan are Han Chinese, who have emigrated to Taiwan from the Fujian and Guangzhou provinces since the 18th century.

---

[37] http://www.china.org.cn/english/features/dengxiaoping/103372.htm.
[38] http://hk.ocmfa.gov.cn/chn/jb/yglz/zyjh/200402/t20040219_6742806.htm

China's demand for Taiwan is a formal return to China and assurance of self-government in Taiwan without posting officials or soldiers from the mainland of China. Negotiations can lead far towards a mutually acceptable agreement.

Tibet, China

Since China re-established its governance of Tibet in 1950, the West, particularly the U.S., has upheld a long and sustained critique of Chinese policies and presence in Tibet. Although the question of Tibet has been reported less by Western media over the past decade, myths about Tibet's history still exist.

Tibet has never been a sovereign nation nor recognized as such by any other country or international organization. The 14th Dalai Lama was appointed by the central government of the Republic of China. On February 5, 1940, the central government of the Republic of China officially endorsed a five-year-old soul boy with the birth name Lhamo Döndup as the reincarnation of the 14th Dalai Lama. The Chairman of the Commission for Mongolian and Tibetan Affairs at that time, Wu Zhongxin, traveled all the way from Chongqing via India to Lhasa to personally approve the appointment and preside over the enthronement ceremony of the Dalai Lama. The central government of the Republic of China appropriated 400,000 yuan as the expenses for this ceremony.[39] Although Japan occupied China at the time, the central government of the Republic of China was careful about its governance of Tibet as a part of China.

Tibetans are not a minority in the ethnic Tibet. More than 90 percent of the people living in the Tibetan Autonomous Region are ethnic Tibetans.[40]

---

[39] http://un.china-mission.gov.cn/eng/zt/xzwt/200310/t20031014_8413335.htm

[40] In 2021, the total Tibetan population in China was 6.3 million. In 1950, the Tibetan population in the ethnic Tibet (now Tibet Autonomous Region) was 1 million. Today, it is 3 million people. In 1990, the Tibet Autonomous Region had 46% of all Tibetan population in China. Other concentrations of Tibetans were in Sichuan Province (24%), Qinghai Province (20%), Gansu Province (8.0%), and Yunnan Province(2%). Outside China, 200,000 are living in India, Nepal, and Bhutan. 25,000 Tibetans are living outside Asia, mainly in the U.S. https://pubmed.ncbi.nlm.nih.gov/12319208/.

In the 1980s and 1990s, reports in the Western media claimed that 1.2 million Tibetans had perished in Tibet since the 14th Dalai Lama, Tenzin Gyatso, at the age of 24 years old, left Lhasa in 1959. In 2008, the former director of the Free Tibet Campaign in London visited the "Tibetan Government-in-Exile" in Dharamsala, India, to study their archives. He found no documentation. The number of 1.2 million Tibetans killed would no longer be used, the former director wrote in an article in the *New York Times*.[41]

Over the years, the U.S. Congress has continuously supported the exiled Tibetan community. In December 2020, the "Tibetan Policy and Support Act" authorized the use of sanctions for Chinese officials who interfere in recognizing reincarnations or the succession of Tibetan Buddhist leaders, including the future 15th Dalai Lama.[42] Recalling that in 1940, the Chairman of China's Commission for Mongolian and Tibetan Affairs went to Lhasa to authorize the appointment of the 14th Dalai Lama and preside over his enthronement, this U.S. Congress act is remarkable.

In 1949, poverty in Tibet was manifest. Over the last 40 years, an enormous development has occurred in Tibet's economy, education, health care, and social life. In 2021, Tibet had a GDP of USD 7,562 per capita. This is three times more than in countries neighboring Tibet, such as Myanmar, Bhutan, Nepal, India, and Bangladesh.

I visited Lhasa twice, in 1991 and 2001. The unique culture of Tibet and Tibetan people, warm and welcoming, left a strong impression. Tibetans and Uyghurs are probably, I believe, the ethnic groups in China who culturally are most different from Han-Chinese culture. It shows the cultural diversity in China. The Dalai Lama is an institution, a tradition, and the DNA of Tibetan culture. It was a misfortune that the 14th Dalai Lama left Tibet in 1959 and did not stay with his people. But geopolitics interfered and reduced the Tibetan culture's exchange with the rest of the world for decades. Today, Tibetan culture

---

[41] He May Be a God, but He's No Politician, by Patrick French, *New York Times*, March 22, 2008. https://www.nytimes.com/2008/03/22/opinion/22french.html

[42] https://www.cecc.gov/media-center/press-releases/chairs-welcome-passage-of-the-tibetan-policy-and-support-act

is as strong as ever and has thrived under the economic and social development of China over the last decades. Sometime in the future, when geopolitics are different, the Western world will have a better chance to learn from and interact with the old and unique culture of Tibet.

Hope for Democracy and Civilization

Now let's turn to the young Shanghai government official's last two wishes – China as the most democratic and civilized nation.

It is not an easy discussion. You can objectively measure wealth and economy. Likewise, you can measure pollution. How to measure democracy, human rights, humanity, and civilization? Should democracy be measured on principles and words or by practice and reality? Where does humanity, taking care of the well-being of a people, fit in? And where does the freedom to pursue own interests fit in? Of course, if you disregard diversity, choose one single measurement you call universal, and if you emphasize words, regulations, and not reality, humanity is easy to measure. Who are to define absolute humanity and the highest level of civilization?[43]

Three older and one contemporary views on civilization

In the following, I will quote three Chinese essayists, writing in 1884, 1915, and 1935 and one contemporary former Chinese official, in 2019, on the question of democracy, humanity, and civilization. It will give a perspective of 140 years to reflect on continuity and consistency in Chinese thinking.

---

[43] In February 2012, in a speech in Washington D.C. to President Joe Biden, President Xi Jinping said: "When it comes to human rights, there is no best, only better. "(人权问题上没有最好,只有更好). http://finance.sina.com.cn/china/20120216/072911388980.shtml

Lin Yutang[44]

In 1936, the Chinese writer Lin Yutang[45] differentiated between the "machinery" or "principles" of democracy and the "spirit" or "practice" of democracy like this:

"For we must distinguish between democracy as a method and democracy as an end in itself, between the machinery and the spirit of democracy. In China, the Western democratic machinery will be grafted upon the old spirit of democracy that is as old as China itself. The machinery of democratic government will be new. In contrast, the broad base of liberal, generous, democratic views of mankind and a government existing only for the welfare and benefit of the people is as old as Mencius and Shujing[46] (Book of Documents), the most archaic of the Confucian Five Classic. It is as old as the theory of Chinese historians, based on the Shujing, that a dynasty ruled the people in trust as a "mandate from Heaven" and that as soon as the government misruled, it forfeited that mandate. The people had the right to revolt."[47]

Lin Yutang also added what I find is a reminder to some democracies in the West today:

"The most perfect outward conformity with an established democratic pattern cannot prevent a democracy from degenerating, in fact, into a plutocracy."[48]

What is the "spirit of democracy" when it includes "a democratic view of mankind" focusing on the welfare and benefit of the people? Lin Yutang wrote:

---

[44] Partly based upon my essay on Lin Yutang, Chen Jitong and Gu Hongming in Three Chinese Writers On Cultural Differences Between the East and the West (书写东西方文化差异的三位中国作家), by Carsten Boyer Thøgersen (曹伯义), Consul-General (Ret.) , published in December 2013 in World Sinology, Renmin University of China, Beijing.

[45] Lin Yutang, 林语堂 (1895–1976) was a Chinese novelist, philosopher, and translator with a long list of publications, changing in topics and attitudes over the years. In this context, Lin Yutang is quoted as a Chinese writer with a sense of the long perspective of Chinese culture and history.

[46] 书经 (尚书).

[47] Lin Yutang, *My Country and My People*. Shanghai February 1936. Quote from revised edition May 1939, p. 395f.

[48] Lin Yutang, ibid. p. 395.

"For the Chinese are a hard-boiled lot. There is no nonsense about them: they do not live to die, as the Christians pretend to do, nor do they seek a Utopia on earth, as many seers of the West do. They only want to order this life on earth, which they know to be full of pain and sorrow, so they may work peacefully, endure nobly, and live happily. Of the noble virtues of the West, nobility, ambition, zeal for reform, public spirit, sense for adventure, and heroic courage, the Chinese are devoid. They cannot be interested in climbing Mont Blanc or exploring the North Pole. But they are tremendously interested in this commonplace world. They have indomitable patience, indefatigable industry, a sense of duty, level-headed common sense, cheerfulness, humor, tolerance, pacifism, and the unequaled genius for finding happiness in hard environments ... And the chief of these is pacifism and tolerance, which seem to be lacking in modern Europe.[49]

Indeed, it seems at times, on watching the spectacle of present-day Europe, that she is suffering less from a lack of smartness or intellectual brilliance than from the lack of little mellow wisdom. It seems barely possible for Europe to outgrow its hot-headed youthfulness and intellectual brilliance. After another century of scientific progress, the world will be brought so close together that the Europeans will learn to take a more tolerant view of life and each other (...) Perhaps the West will learn to believe less in self-assertion, and more in intolerance, for tolerance will be direly needed when the world is closely knit together. They will be a little less desirous of making progress and a little more anxious to understand life. And the voice of the Old Man of Hangu Pass[50] would be listened to more widely.

From a Chinese point of view, pacifism is not 'noble'; it is simply 'good' because it is common sense. If earthly life is all we can have, we must try to live in peace if we want to live happily. From this point of view, the self-assertion and the restlessness of the spirit of the West are signs of its youthful rawness.

---

[49] Lin Yutang, ibid. p.55.

[50] 函谷关. According to the Chinese legend, Laozi wrote his work *Dao De Jing* (道德经), at the Hangu Pass on the south bank of the Yellow River in Shaanxi Province.

The Chinese, steeped in his Oriental philosophy, can see that that rawness will gradually wear off at Europe's coming of age. For, strange as it may seem, out of the extremely shrewd philosophy of Taoism, there always emerges the word 'tolerance'. Tolerance has been the greatest quality of Chinese culture, and tolerance will also become the greatest quality of modern culture, when that culture matures.[51]

Pacifism, too, is a matter of high human understanding. If man could learn to be a little more cynical, he would also be less inclined toward warfare. That is perhaps why all intelligent men are cowards. The Chinese are the world's worst fighters because they are an intelligent race, backed and nurtured by Taoistic cynicism and the Confucian emphasis on harmony as the ideal of life. An average Chinese child knows what the grey-haired European politicians do not know, that by fighting, one gets killed or maimed, be it an individual or a nation. That mellow, old roguish philosophy, which teaches the Chinese patience and passive resistance in times of trouble, also warns them against momentary pride and assertion at the moment of success. It is merely a matter of culture, or hanyang,[52] as we call it.

To the Chinese, the Versailles Treaty was not only unfair, but it was also merely vulgar or lacking in hanyang. If the Frenchman had been imbued a little with the spirit of Taoism at the moment of his victory, he would not have imposed the Versailles Treaty, and his head would rest more easily on his pillow today. But France was young, and Germany would certainly have done the same thing, and no one realized the extreme silliness of two nations like France and Germany, each trying to keep the other permanently under its iron heels.[53] But (neither) had read Laotse."[54]

---

[51] Lin Yutang, ibid. p.56.

[52] 涵养. Well behaved, prudence, and empathic.

[53] In 2022, this reminds of the history leading up to the Ukraine crisis in 2022. That said, the politicians behind the Versailles Treaty were not responsible for Germany's policies under Adolph Hitler, of which Lin Yutang did not know much in December 1935 when he finished his manuscript. Likewise, NATO policies were not directly responsible for Russia's invasion of Ukraine in February 2022.

[54] Lin Yutang, ibid. p.56.

Chen Jitong

Chen Jitong[55] (1851-1907) was a Chinese diplomat, general, and scholar during the late Qing Dynasty. Chen was born in Fujian Province. At eighteen years old, he studied French at the school attached to a French-controlled Fuzhou shipyard. In 1876, he was selected to accompany a high-level official of the Qing Dynasty, Shen Baozhen[56], to Europe. Chen subsequently served in several important positions in the Qing foreign service.

While serving as a military attaché at China's diplomatic mission in Paris, Chen wrote a number of works in French, including the book *Les Chinois Peints par eux-mêmes* from which I shall quote in the following.[57]

Chen Jitong finds Europeans uninformed about China, although he suggests that a distinction should be made between childish misunderstandings, errors, and prejudice. Chen wishes to describe China as it is, based on his knowledge about China as a Chinese. But he will talk, write and think like a European. In other words, Chen Jitong would think like a European if he only knew what Chen knew about China. Together with the reader, Chen will travel to Chinese provinces. On their way, they will chat in French, English, and German, and the reader will get a better idea of the Chinese civilization. If there should be something to criticize – one should remember that nothing is perfect in this world, and one must keep hope for future improvement. Here and there, criticism of European manners will also be found: Chen will use a steel pen, not a Chinese ink brush, because he has learned to think and write

---

[55] 陈季同 also written as Tcheng Ki-tong. In 1891, he was dismissed from all official positions and settled in Shanghai. Following China's defeat in the First Sino-Japanese War, he served as foreign minister of the short-lived Republic of Formosa.

[56] Shen Baozhen （沈葆桢) was born in Fujian Province and obtained the highest degree, *jinshi*, (进士) in the imperial examinations in 1847 and was soon after appointed to the Hanlin Academy. His administrative abilities attracted the attention of his superiors, who enlisted him in the effort to suppress the Taiping Rebellion. Following the suppression of the rebellion in 1864, Shen became actively involved in the Self-strengthening Movement and later worked at the shipyard in Fuzhou. He utilized the skill of French technicians and workers to construct modern warships for the Imperial Navy. Shen was married to Lin Puqing （林普晴, 1821–1877), the third daughter of Lin Zexu.

[57] *Les Chinois Peints par eux-mêmes*, par Tcheng Ki Tong, Paris 1884. English edition: *The Chinese Painted by Themselves*, by Tcheng-Ki-Tong, translated from the French by James Millington, London, 1885. Edition used: RareBooksClub.com, USA, 318890LV00005B/99/P. Chinese edition: 陈季同,《中国人自画像》.

in a European way. Criticism is the salt of discourse, and one cannot always be admiring. However, criticism will have no other pretension than to add variety to his text. If he becomes too positive towards his native land, he will apologize and hope for understanding from those who love their country, too.[58]

Chen Jitong discusses subjects such as the family, religion and philosophy, marriage, divorce, women, the Chinese language, social classes, Chinese scholars, journalism, public opinion, pre-historic time, education, worship of ancestors, European society, and the East and the West.

Chen's style is elegant and humorous, and he never forgets to include the reader in his story. To no surprise, Chen's narrative on Chinese affairs is positive. He said so himself from the beginning. His strength is his constant comparison with European society and his ability to make Chinese life understandable and familiar to the European readers through this comparison with European affairs.

To Chen Jitong, the family is the foundation upon which China is built, much more so than one will find in Europe. In fact, China is a society made up of many families. The Chinese family is like a cooperative society. All family members must live in one community and give mutual assistance. All its resources are united in a single fund, and all contributions are made without distinction more or less. The family is subject to an "equality" and "fraternity" regime. These are great words,[59] Chen concedes. But in China, they are written in the heart and not as elsewhere upon the walls. Still, the chief authority of the family rested in the hands of the oldest family member. Also, every family member must conduct himself to maintain harmony. It is a duty, Chen emphasizes and admits that perfection is always difficult to find.[60]

Chen also wishes to introduce Confucius to his European readers. Chen starts to write about religion because Europeans are familiar with religion, but Confucianism is no religion. Chinese people do not envy the Europeans for

---

[58] Tcheng-Ki-Tong, ibid. p. 2

[59] "Liberté, égalité, fraternité ou la Mort" was a slogan during the French 1793 revolution.

[60] Tcheng-Ki-Tong, Ibid. p. 3-4.

having a religion. Chinese people have different beliefs. Chen does not wish to dwell much on the difference between the various religions: man is only a tiny creature, and it is not important to know in which specific way he serves God. God understands every language and sees the silent inner reflection of every soul. In China, too, some silently follow the spirit and truth of God and worship God with their lips in an earthly religion that is manifested through ceremonies. The two of them have nothing in common. The difference is between genuine devotion and hypocrisy. In China, people follow the religion of the most enlightened people in society, the scholars. It is the philosophy of Confucius. Confucius was the founder of a school of which moral principles to follow. Confucius never contemplated the fate of man or the nature of God. Confucius only recommended showing respect for moral traditions. Herein one will find the true simplicity of believing without dogmas. Confucius never referred to any vision of a God, nor did he mention priests, only some ceremonies which never were of much importance anyway.[61]

Writing about the Chinese woman, Chen feels obliged to mention the concubinage during his time.[62] Chen writes that hardly anyone will be impartial because much bad is attached to the word "concubinage". On the other hand, Chen argues that if the word mistresses had been used instead, and not concubines, no one in Europe would have noticed. The mistresses or concubines in China differed from those in Europe because they were recognized as "legitimate mistresses" in China. In Europe, men easily found themselves mistresses, and *double ménage* was not an unknown institution in the Christian world. But in China's social system at that time, where the future of the rising generation was a main concern, the dispersion of children born out of wedlock would not be acceptable. It was the reason for concubinage, Chen claims. Chen fully understands that to Europeans, the improper institution

---

[61] Ibid. p. 5-7.

[62] In this paper concubinage – read with a distance of 125 years – is not the focus for debate. Neither is Chen's late Qing Dynasty view of the woman. Chen's comments – not forgetting time and place – show a practical Chinese attitude without moral condemnation, weaving together and comparing the East and the West.

of concubinage was difficult to tolerate. But under the cloak of discretion, much greater crimes were committed when children born of illicit unions were thrown upon the world with a lifelong stain upon them and found themselves with neither resources nor family. Chen finds these evils graver than the brutality of concubinage. Chen's final argument he takes from the Bible: Sarah, Abraham's wife, bore no children. Hence Sarah introduced her husband to Hagar, her handmaid, who eventually bore Abraham a son. "Is this the horrible example that we have copied in China?" Chen exclaims, making his point. But to be truthful, Chen quickly adds, the concubinage had many drawbacks and problems. Still, the concubine could only enter a family with the consent of the legitimate wife, whom the concubine was bound to obey. And children born by a concubine had the same rights as legitimate children.[63]

During his time in Europe in the 1880s, Chen Jitong was introduced to the European concepts of democracy and a bourgeois parliamentarian practice. These concepts and thinking must have been new to a Qing Dynasty official. Wishing to emphasize the similarities between the East and the West, Chen finds that these concepts can also be found in China.

Chen argues that all Chinese are admitted to participate in the competitive examinations that determine degrees and open government positions. This right in itself is precious; in no other part of the world there is a more democratic institution. "If you are poor, can you by study alone obtain a place within the state administration? Can you rise by the credit of science alone?" Chen asks. In China, yes. In Europe, no, Chen replies. He argues that Chinese practices are more liberal and more just and useful. During ten years in Europe, studying its institutions, Chen has never found any principle which deserves to be called democratic or liberal, like the right that every Chinese enjoys regardless of background, namely the right to participate in public examinations. In Europe, the celebrated *Immortal Principles and Declaration of the Rights of Man and of the Citizen,*[64] Chen claims, have not yet created the best

---

[63] Ibid. p. 11-12.

[64] The French *Déclaration des droits de l'homme et du citoyen de 1793*

governments and the least imperfect social conditions. Chen's meritocratic view is seen in his observation: "If someone suggested that members of the French Academy[65] should be elected by universal suffrage, he would be laughed at. Yet the members of a national legislature are chosen by such a system."[66]

In Europe, exposed to newspapers, the freedom of the press, and public opinion, Chen Jitong does not like what he sees, maybe because Chen was a representative of the Qing Dynasty, which had a different political and social structure.

To his readers, Chen readily admits he is an admirer of European newspapers. One will always spend a pleasant time reading newspapers when traveling or waiting. But this is all that Chen can say about newspapers on the good side. Chen finds that the influence of the newspapers is smaller than one thinks. Newspapers are good at keeping one updated on developments. Usually, newspapers only report on facts. Sometimes newspapers write reports on what has not happened. The following day such news will be called back. On the part of the readers, it is difficult to see what they like and dislike. They change their opinion all the time. Few people only read serious articles, Chen observes.

After the freedom of the press was introduced in Europe, newspapers developed there. This freedom does not exist in the Heavenly Kingdom. Chen argues that when writing about history, the emphasis should be on the truth, which does not go with the freedom of the press.

Chen reports that when Chinese harbors were forced open by the Europeans, newspapers were established in the Chinese harbor cities by the Europeans. Chinese people studied this and founded their own newspapers. But the Government decided to implement control and censorship, and the newspapers ceased to exist. China had only foreign newspapers, Chen writes.[67]

---

[65] *L'Académie française*, founded in 1635.

[66] Tcheng-K-Tong, ibid. p. 15.

[67] Tcheng-Ki-Tong, ibid. p. 17-21.

Nevertheless, Chen finds that China still had a strong public opinion. Scholars from all over the country represented the people's voices. They had the right to put forward petitions in the name of the people, and often the petitions were heard and followed. The scholars were, in a way, China's national representatives. Suppose China ever were to introduce national assemblies or parliaments like in Europe. In that case, Chen hopes that China would only give the right to vote and the right to be elected to "those distinguished by study and virtue." Chen argues that the Qing Dynasty was perfectly well suited to accommodate such a wish if that day came when a public opinion or "the voice of the people" wanted a political or institutional change. Chen expects that a change could happen without unrest or revolution. Not just for the change itself but for the wish to keep stability, peace, and development in the provinces while making the change.

Chen emphasizes peace, the stability of society, and what he sees as the quality of governance and decision-making. Government promotions should be based upon education and merits instead of universal suffrage.[68]

Chen Jitong turns to the power of the press and notes that the Chinese were criticized because they were not responsive to inventions and new ideas promoted by the press. Chen maintains that a newspaper could not convince Chinese people about the good use of an invention. In a country that does not give into the power of the press, new inventions are only welcomed if they have proven to progress. In the eyes of Europeans, it was a crime that the Chinese did not take on the inventions suggested by newspapers. It is not an easy subject to discuss. Chen writes and apologizes that he does not conceal his view on a matter that the Europeans admire.

In the 1880s, China's technological backwardness compared to the West was obvious. Why doesn't Chen Jitong suggest China open to the West and welcome foreign technology? Probably because Chen expected that most foreign countries would be in control of that technology. Probably also because

---

[68] In 1884, universal suffrage in Europe was still restricted by gender, age, and income.

Chen was uneasy about the power of the press, which Chen had observed while in Europe.

It opens for Chen's criticism of European dominance. The main characteristic of the European civilization is that it expands into new territories, the good and bad. Looking back into history, uncivilized tribal people expanded using power, not to bring new blessings unto other civilizations but to plunder and destroy flourishing societies. The European pioneers of civilization go in the same direction but with the difference that they call their move forward the extension of happiness on earth. But their expansion is based upon violence. In China, people wish for happiness on earth. The only acceptable progress is what promotes peace and reduces poverty. War and poverty are the enemies of humankind, Chen emphasizes.

In China, people are convinced that China will be happy to join any universal worldwide cooperation if the new spirit from Europe – with all its innovations that are the pride of all Europeans – understands the secret to promoting peaceful coexistence between peoples of different nationalities to enhance their livelihood. Chen argues that those who know the Chinese people have never doubted this.[69]

Chen moves on to criticize the occupation of China by European powers. Today, this is a fact of history, and Chen's early critique has become part of world history. The reading today of Chen is interesting partly because Chen presents the critique directly in French to European readers and partly because Chen's critique was so obvious already in 1884. Chen's basic narrative about foreign dominance in China includes most of the elements of a critique of foreign powers used in the following years and until today. Still, Chen suggests an open door for dialogue, but on equal terms. Today, we know such equal terms between China and foreign countries were many years away after Chen wrote his book.

---

[69] Ibid.

Did the Europeans convince China that peace and cooperation were their goals, Chen asks? What kind of commodities did the Europeans export to Chinese harbors, which were made into international harbors assisted by treaties[70] forced upon China? China hoped for "Peace Machinery" but was instead sold "War Machinery." China is against everything which shall destabilize peace and promote unrest. Would it ever be good to see four hundred million Chinese people carrying weapons on their shoulders, Chen asks.

European weapons were not the only commodities exported to China. Ask any Chinese what he called an Englishman, and he would answer an opium dealer. A Frenchman he called a missionary. The first thing ruined his health, and the other made him confused. These were only facts, Chen argues. Of course, there is a possibility that opium and new religions are important to human progress. Chen concludes with sarcasm that it is up to the reader to decide for himself.

All foreigners coming to China have only one goal: to do business. One could hardly blame Chinese people for being a bit suspicious. On the other hand, there are also foreigners coming to China who behave in a decent and civilized way. The diplomats are usually civilized and pay respect to Chinese culture. Some scholars come to China to study the Chinese language and culture. Such people are not foreigners but friends with whom Chinese people are proud to exchange their thinking. China is happy to talk with the civilized representatives of humanity about new ideas and share common dreams about progress and civilization. With that, Chen concludes his critique of European powers.[71]

As an example of Europeans with a cooperative attitude to China, Chen mentions the Jesuit missionaries who went to China three hundred years ago. They were excited by what they saw. Every human being in China seemed to be happy, they wrote. God had given this country and its people so many gifts, various skills, and all kinds of products. The Jesuits, Chen writes, wished

---

[70] The Treaty of Nanjing, 1842 and the Treaty of Tianjin, 1860.

[71] Ibid.

to learn more about this country and sent their best people to China. They realized they first had to obtain confidence and friendship with the Chinese people, study their thinking and forget about their European mindset. They respected Confucius and were careful not to offend rooted convictions upon which the empire's political structure was built. Only then could the Jesuits start to talk about the Bible and their own God, Chen writes.[72]

The views of Chen Jitong were written at another time. Chen Jitong was a Qing-dynasty official writing about new foreign concepts such as democracy, freedom of the press, and public opinion. Still, many of his observations ring through as contemporary. He should be credited for his initiative to establish a dialogue and communicate in the French language.[73]

Gu Hongming

Gu Hongming[74] (1857-1928) was born in Penang, Malaysia. His father was an overseas Chinese who had immigrated from Fujian Province. His mother was Portuguese. In 1867, at the age of ten years, Gu Hongming was sent to a boarding school in Scotland and later enrolled in the University of Edinburgh, where in 1877, he graduated with an M.A. Before returning to Malaysia in 1880, Gu studied civil engineering at the University in Leipzig and law in Paris. In 1880, Gu Hongming joined the British colonial civil service in Singapore.[75] In 1885,[76] he went to China and served in the following twenty

---

[72] Ibid.

[73] One wonders why Chen Jitong's book from 1884 has remained largely unnoticed. In China maybe because Chen Jitong after 1911 was seen as associated with the Qing Dynasty. In the West one reason could be that the only English translation of Chen's book was by J. Millington's in 1885, as far as the writer of this article was informed. This translation is a poor translation of Chen's book in French, failing to translate Chen's vivid style of writing. The Danish translation of Chen Jitong's French book was of a remarkably high standard. But Danish is only read by few Europeans. Cf. Tcheng Ki Tong, *China and the Chinese (Kina og Kineserne)*, Copenhagen, 1886, translated by M. Ottesen.

[74] 辜鸿铭

[75] As an assistant secretary for the Straits Government.

[76] While in Singapore, Gu met with Ma Jianzhong, (马建忠, 1845–1900), a Chinese scholar and member of Qing-dynasty official Li Hongzhang's secretariat. Ma himself had for three years studied international law in Paris. Their conservation was in French. Ma Jianzhong probably spotted the young talent. Gu Hongming on his side was awakened by Ma Jianzhong and realized the importance of the Chinese language, culture, and his Chinese heritage. And probably also saw a good job opportunity. In 1883, Gu resigned from his post in Singapore and started learning the Chinese language. In 1884, he went to Hong Kong for

years as an advisor on Western affairs to the high-ranking Qing Dynasty official Zhang Zhidong.[77] From 1905 to 1908, he was the director of the Huangpu River Authority in Shanghai.[78] He served in the Imperial Foreign Ministry from 1908 to 1910, then as the president of Nanyang Public School in Shanghai.[79] He resigned from this post in 1911. He kept wearing a queue as a sign of his loyalty to the fallen imperial government. In 1915 he became a professor at Peking University. From 1924 to 1927, he was a guest lecturer on oriental cultures in Japan. He died in Beijing in 1928.[80]

Gu Hongming was perhaps the first Western-educated Chinese intellectual in Modern China[81] after the fall of the Qing Dynasty. His upbringing was truly international – or cosmopolitan with a Chinese father and a Portuguese mother living in Penang, Malaysia, where his father was a manager at a British plantation. Ten years old, he was sent to Scotland, supported by the British owner of the plantation. Gu did not return to Malaysia until he was 23 years old. Perhaps he spoke some Southern Fujian dialect (*Minnanhua*), learned from his father, but not Mandarin. His knowledge of Chinese characters must have been poor, if any at all. Twenty-five-year-old Gu Hongming decided to identify himself as Chinese and started to learn Chinese. At twenty-eight years old, he moved to China, where he worked and stayed for the rest of his life. Because of his unusual background, he catapulted into an important position in the Chinese government. Gu Hongming probably quickly and loyally absorbed the essence of and identified himself with Chinese thinking during the late Qing Dynasty, to which he stayed devoted also after 1911.

---

further Chinese studies.

[77] Zhang Zhidong (张之洞, 1837-1909) was one of the Four Famous Officials of the Late Qing Dynasty (四大名臣). The others were Zeng Guofa (曾国藩, 1811-1872), Li Hongzhang (李鸿章, 1823-1901) and Zuo Zongtang (左宗棠, 1812-1885).

[78] 上海浚治黄浦江河道局

[79] The forerunner of Shanghai Jiaotong University.

[80] Gu Hongming was a talented linguist fluent in English, German, French, Latin, Greek, Italian, and many other languages. In particular, he commanded excellent skills in writing and speaking English, German, and French. But his Chinese handwriting and use of the brush were never good. Before Gu Hongming's departure for Scotland in 1867, his father had taken his son to the ancestral tablets and said: "Wherever you go, whether you are together with British, German or French people, do not forget, you are a Chinese." (不论你走到哪里，不论你身边是英国人，德国人还是法国人，都不要忘了，你是中国人）。http://www.guoxue.com/master/guhongming/ghm007.htm

[81] Liberal Cosmopolitan: Lin Yutang and Middling Chinese Modernity, Qian Suoqiao (钱锁桥), Leiden, 2011, p. 38.

In 1915, Gu Hongming published *The Spirit of the Chinese People*,[82] written in English. It is an unusual book today, difficult to categorize, and must have been so in 1915. On most issues, Gu Hongming was a conservative, rooted in and loyal to the thinking of the Qing Dynasty. He did not welcome change in China and wrote against the May Fourth Movement in 1919. But his understanding of European thinking and affairs were always clear. Gu Hongming knew Europe. From his childhood, he had had Europe under his skin. This, combined with his Chinese thinking acquired later in life, makes his book an interesting reading when the focus is the difference between the East and the West. Maybe we find in Gu Hongming's writing better than elsewhere the strong difference – and the contrast as embodied in his own life - between European thinking and Gu's upbringing in Europe on the one hand, and Chinese thinking, which Gu later in life adopted and chose to identify with, on the other hand.

Central words in Gu Hongming's *The Spirit of the Chinese People* are the soul and heart of the Chinese people. Gu knew what most Europeans – at that time – generally thought about Chinese people's spiritual values, humanity, and inner life of thinking. Or rather their disrespect of the same. Gu must have heard it many times.[83] Brought up in a Chinese-Portuguese family, living in British-controlled Malaysia, and studying in Europe from ten to twenty-three years old, Gu Hongming was, as a young man, probably more European than Chinese. Later on, working in China and identifying with China, Gu Hongming must have been especially sensitive and exposed to Europeans' lack of respect for Chinese culture. Whether the Europeans spoke English, German, French or Italian, Gu would always understand.

---

[82] *The Spirit of the Chinese People* (春秋大义). With an Essay on *"Civilisation and Anarchy"*, by Gu Hongming, M.A. (Edin.). Quote on the title page: "Es gibt zwei friedliche Gewalten: das Recht und die Schicklichkeit", Goethe, published by the Commercial Press, Work Ltd, Peking, 1922. First edition published by the *Peking Daily News*, Peking in 1915.

[83] For Gu, the Englishmen's sense of superiority was revealed in a casual remark made to Gu by an Englishman in Shanghai: "You Chinese are very clever, but still, we Englishmen consider you Chinese as an inferior race". Quoted from *Liberal Cosmopolitan*, Qian Suoqiao, ibid. p. 40.

To illustrate typical European thinking about China that Gu Hongming must have encountered when meeting Europeans from 1885 to 1915, one example of a European's thinking ten years before Gu started working in Shanghai is quoted below. At first, this text appreciates the qualities of Chinese people in a thoughtful and cultured way. But its indirect and ostensibly reflected conclusion is, in fact, negative, if not offensive.

In 1893, after working for more than twenty years in Shanghai, a European businessman, Jacob Henningsen, a Dane[84] and managing director of one of the largest foreign companies in Shanghai, published his second of several books about China[85]. He spoke and read Chinese and was probably one of the relatively few foreigners in Shanghai with a long and intimate knowledge of Chinese affairs.[86] Henningsen starts his book by describing the difference between the Eastern and Western types of characters. He compares the Chinese to the evergreen bamboo plant. It is numerous, appreciated, sometimes just an insignificant straw, sometimes a large tree several feet wide. It is light, strong, tough, durable, and thrives everywhere. Like bamboo, the Chinese thrive everywhere, and there will be no place where the Chinese would not be useful and welcomed.

Henningsen writes that you can produce simple products and fine handicrafts from bamboo. Likewise, the Chinese are good at hard work

---

[84] Cf. *From a Strong Past to a Dynamic Present. Danes and Danish Companies in the Greater Shanghai Region 1846 to 2006*（从光耀灿然的昨天到生机盎然的今天-大上海地区的丹麦人和丹麦公司，1846-2006）by Carsten Boyer Thøgersen and Hans Jørgen Hinrup, Shanghai Bookstore Publishing House, 2008.

[85] *Djung Rhua Dji* (中华记), by J. Henningsen (恒甯生), Copenhagen, 1894. Mr. J. Henningsen (1849-1913) was a Dane posted in China from 1871 to 1900 by the Great Nordic Telegraph Company (大北公司). From 1885 to 1900 Henningsen was head of the company's East Asian office, covering China and Japan and located in Shanghai. In its heyday, Great Nordic managed most of the telegraph communication in the Far East and may be called the "Microsoft Company" of its time.

[86] Henningsen's obvious disrespect of Chinese culture – probably shared with many fellow Europeans at that time – is perfectly illustrated by this other quotation from his book: "There are intelligent Europeans who have spent half of their lives in Beijing and who find life in Beijing so exiting that they prefer Beijing to the "too-civilized" Europe. The sinologists are such people. Men who have made the study of the Chinese language the mission of their life and who do not find any nobler or more worthwhile challenge than studying whether the Chinese character CHOU was written with eight or nine strokes during the Tang Dynasty. They do not see the manure in the street; they do not smell the open sewers. They do not hear the noisy Chinese yelling and screaming. They delude themselves and others into thinking that the dust in Beijing that fills your eyes, your nose and your mouth are only good for your lungs. The same has happened to them as to the Manchurians, the Mongols, and other intruders, who from time to time invaded in China: They have become so Chinese that they only lack the queue to be a complete Chinese. The sinologists' slanted perspective on things, they already had before coming to China." *Djung Rhua Dji*, by J. Henningsen. Ibid p. 38-39

and excel in the finest spiritual delicacies. Henningsen finds the greatest resemblance in their flexibility, toughness, and endurance. When the wind blows, the bamboo bends. When the wind's pressure has ceased, it stands intact in its former position. Unchanged, with every trace of the former burden gone. It yields, bends, and sometimes lies flat on the ground but does not break into pieces. China's civilization was already in full flower at the time of Babylon and has remained unaffected until today, Henningsen notes. While the storms of the world may break out, upset the roots, and destroy even the strongest trees in the forest, they will accomplish nothing against the small, tough grass that continues to set fresh shoots without delay and the slightest change in its original form and shape, Henningsen observes.

However, bamboo has another characteristic, Henningsen suggests. Although invisible, but not less important – and this characteristic the bamboo shares perhaps even more with the Chinese people – it is hollow inside, Henningsen argues.

"The hollowness in the Chinese national character, a lack of content, is one of its greatest shortcomings. It lacks the marrow that makes other plants and nations less flexible and more prone to shatter during great changes. But it also gives them a weight and a strength that makes them into the timber of a much sounder nature, timber that is used for larger and more significant building structures than the light bamboo," Henningsen concludes.

Hollowness? After so many years in China? What does Henningsen mean? I think the answer is simple. Henningsen was a true European of his own time. He was insensitive to Chinese culture. In China, Henningsen did not find any European values or Christianity.

This hollowness, lack of marrow and substance, which the European Henningsen – and probably with him many other Europeans in China – did not see, was a European statement with which Gu Hongming must have been familiar. It is exactly this subject that Gu writes about. Gu writes about what Europeans like Henningsen see as "hollowness" and what, to Gu, is the soul and heart, the core of Chinese culture.

Gu Hongming writes that he wishes to interpret the spirit and demonstrate the value of Chinese civilization.[87] The level of civilization cannot be measured in great cities built,[88] fine products manufactured, and not even in what institutions, art and science have been invented. The value of civilization is what type of humanity and what kind of men and women a civilization has produced.[89] That is a civilization's essence, personality, and soul. Gu then mentions three cases that will illustrate the spirit and value of the Chinese civilization: "the Real Chinaman, the Chinese woman, and the Chinese language." To understand China and its civilization, one must have a sense of the three main characteristics of Chinese thinking and civilization: depth, broadness, and simplicity. Plus, its chief characteristic, namely delicacy. Foreigners analyzing China, Gu writes, are confined in their ability to understand Chinese civilization because of a lack of sense for some of these characteristics caused by constraints in their own nationality and culture.

American people, Gu claims, find it difficult to understand China because they are – generally speaken – broad, simple, but not deep. The English are deep and simple but lack broadness in their thinking. Germans are deep and wide but do not know simplicity. The French, Gu finds, are the ones who better understand the Chinese civilization. The French may not have the same depth of nature as the Germans, the broadness of mind of the Americans, and the simplicity of mind of the English. However, the French have another quality, failing the other nationalities – the quality of delicacy.[90]

One may ask how useful this classification – or stereotypes – by Gu Hongming is today and even one hundred years ago. As a reflection on the difference between nationalities, it is too general. As a reflection on attitudes chosen when analyzing cultures in general, Gu's categories may be worthwhile for a quick glance.

---

[87] Gu Hongming, *The Spirit, ibid.* Preface.

[88] Like Henningsen wrote above.

[89] Qian Suoqiao, *Liberal Cosmopolitan.* , ibid. p. 42.

[90] Gu Hongming refers to the French say of literary composition: *Le style, c'est l'homme.* Ku Hung-ming, *The Spirit,* ibid. Preface.

Although the modern civilization of Europe today has succeeded in conquering nature, previously not seen by any other civilization, it is obtained by physical force. Gu claims and finds that the harm physical force can do to mankind is only small compared to the harm that human passion can do. Therefore, without the regulation and control of human passion, there can be no civilization. Gu argues that to control human passion, you need moral force, not physical force.

In European civilization, civil order was kept, and human passion was controlled by religion and law. That is by "Fear of God" and "Fear of Law". Fear implies the use of force. Many idle and expensive priests were engaged to keep up with the Fear of God. Gu writes that with the Reformation and the coming of the modern age, priests lost their moral power.[91] When Christianity's strength of moral force collapsed, the European civilization introduced the Law. To keep up with the Fear of the Law, another group of idle and expensive persons were hired – police officers and soldiers. By 1915, this had in Europe developed into a strong militarism, which caused the outbreak of the Great War, Gu argues.

Gu Hongming believes that the people of Europe can find the morals needed to sustain the civil order in the Chinese civilization. The moral force in the Chinese civilization which will make militarism unnecessary is the Religion of Good Citizenship, Gu claims. The first principle of the Religion of Good Citizenship is to believe that the Nature of Man is good.[92] The unsoundness of the civilization of Europe lies in the wrong concept of human nature that human nature is evil. Because of this wrong concept, the structure of society in Europe has always rested upon force. Therefore, if the people of Europe want to get rid of religion and militarism and priests and soldiers, which have caused them so much trouble and bloodshed, they shall use the Religion of Good Citizenship from China.

---

[91] Ibid. P. 42

[92] Gu Hongming, *The Spirit*, ibid. pp. xx.

Gu warns the people of Europe and America not to destroy the Chinese civilization and change or spoil the "Real Chinaman" as they are now trying to do with their "New Learning." If Europe and America succeed in destroying the Real Chinaman, destroying Chinese humanity, and succeed in transforming the Chinaman into a European or an American – a person who will require priests or soldiers to keep them in order – then this will increase the militarism of the world. On the other hand, changing the European or American type of humanity to that of a Chinese one will not require priests and soldiers – "just think what a burden will be taken off from the world", Gu claims.

In another chapter[93] on foreigners in China, Gu writes that all economic and practical wisdom is an extension of the formula "2 plus 2 equals 4". Every philosophical proposition has the more general character of the expression "a plus b equals c". John Smith Senior[94] came to China to sell his goods and make money, and he got on very well with the Chinese because both he and the Chinese understood and agreed upon the formula 2 plus 2 equals 4. John Smith Junior, who now ruled the British Empire, Gu writes, came to China with his mind filled with a plus b equals c formula. He wanted more than to sell his goods. He wanted to civilize the Chinese and "spread Anglo-Saxon ideas." The result is that John Smith Junior got on very badly with the Chinese.

Is there any truth in Kipling's dictum that East is East, and West is West? Gu asks. Of course, Gu replies. However, as long as one sticks to the formula 2 plus 2 equals 4 formula, there will be no problems. When you engage in the formula a plus b equals c, there is a great difference between the East and the West, and you will have problems. Gu Hongming's *The Spirit of the Chinese People* can be read as a direct reply to what he must have heard: The human spirit and values and the soul and heart of the Chinese people were different from European values, which might not exist at all. He must have heard that continuously as a child among foreigners in Malaysia, during the 13 years of studying in Europe and China, working as a secretary for foreign affairs in the

---

[93] Gu Hongming, *The Spirit*, "John Smith in China", ibid. pp. 107-114.

[94] A fictional person

office of a Qing-dynasty official – Gu's dramatic suggestion to Europeans is that they better learn from the "Real Chinaman" to save their own civilization. Gu made his point.[95]

Teng Wensheng[96]

China's views on its history and culture, the international situation, and the country's role are expressed in many contexts. In 2019, one of China's "chief ideologues" – my expression – gave a lecture at a conference in Copenhagen. It was the 79-year-old Teng Wensheng. From 1975 to 1997, Teng worked at the Policy Research Office of CPC Central Committee for the last eight years as the Head of the office.[97] From 2002 to 2012, Teng was one of the Party's Central Committee's nearly 300 members. Teng represents the political thinking that has characterized the Communist Party of China for 30 years and more. Continuity is normal in China.

In his lecture,[98] which he gave in his capacity as President of the International Confucian Association, Teng Wensheng highlighted the historical contributions of the East and the West to the cultures of the world. Next, Teng discussed the major global challenges over the last 50 years and finally decided on what a new collaborative global world could look like.

East Asian culture is based on Confucius' teaching, "Harmony is the sum of diversity." The foundation of society is the individual family. Governance must be peaceful, and the goal must be to promote living conditions, safety, and good neighborhood among people. People need to be convinced. Winning

---

[95] That said Gu's writing comes across as rather intellectual and constructed. Gu did not grow up in a Chinese environment. 43 years in China did not change that. Apparently, Gu never went back to Europe after 1880 for any longer period. Gu's European experience stopped when he was 23 years old. Gu did not comprehend the fall of the Qing Dynasty and failed to see the change which the May Fourth Movement signified. Indeed, the May Fourth Movement was the starting point of China's modern development. Even today – 100 years later – the energy and enthusiasm embodied in the May Fourth Movement give rise to inspiration. Gu did not see that. For most of his life, wherever he was, it is fair to say that Gu Hongming remained an outsider.

[96] 滕文生

[97] Teng Wensheng's successor was Wang Huning (王沪宁), who had joined the office in 1995.

[98] *Between Eastern and Western Civilizations: Mutual Learning and Joint Building of a Community of Shared Future for Mankind,* by Teng Wensheng, President of the International Confucian Association, August 26, 2019, Copenhagen.

over others by force creates resistance, and punishment and sanctions must be applied with caution. A compromise must be sought. The highest and most brilliant goal is reached by taking the middle road. Man must be in harmony with nature. Man can overcome and exploit nature, but the laws of nature must be respected. The world is a shared world for all the people. Discoveries and innovation for the benefit of society must be promoted.

According to Teng, the merits of Western culture included the industrial revolution and the economic and social development created by capitalist democratic civilization, including human rights, personal freedom, humanism, and equality. Market competition and innovation created material progress in the West. The market economy was an economic miracle. At the same time, Western civilization gained important experience in macro-control and market adjustment to promote social equality and welfare and solve problems created by the pure market mechanism. Legislation and democracy secured the rights and property of the individual. Analytical and scientific thinking and method developed society rationally as opposed to mysticism and empiricism.

According to Teng, both Eastern and Western cultures had strengths and weaknesses. Bringing cultures together would increase wisdom and benefit all of humanity. No civilization can develop in isolation.

Teng said that globalization had dominated the world for the past 50 years and was critical of the neoliberalism introduced in the 1970s. It wanted less public regulation, free capitalist markets, and tax cuts for big businesses and the wealthy. At the same time, it created speculative financial products, reduced public investment in welfare and infrastructure, weakened unions, and privatized former public enterprises. The result was financial bubbles, debt crises, and increased inequality. Neoliberalism did not lead to wealth and socially balanced societies, and hampered the development of Western capitalist civilization. In the United States, neoliberalism led to unilateralism, protectionism, sanctions, tariffs, technical blockades, trade disputes, and old-fashioned nationalism.

Teng saw among European centrist parties a movement away from neoliberalism and towards increased public regulation of the market to promote economic development and adjustment of the income distribution. If reforms of Western capitalism succeeded, they would make progress, and the positive experiences must be studied in developing countries and China.

Globalization was positive, economically, culturally, innovatively, and internationally and could not be stopped. But there were also disadvantages and problems. The international system was locked in and dominated by developed capitalist countries. Their previously constructive role needed to be reaffirmed so that they once again could contribute to the common international regulation. Economic globalization must be inclusive for the benefit of all and ensure peace, democracy, and welfare for all.

According to Teng Wensheng, climate change and technological development were the world's biggest challenges. Excessive industrialization and the over-consumption of natural resources had created unbalanced economic growth and destruction. Pollution and destruction of natural resources and ecological systems threaten sustainable development. The world's biggest challenge was the rational use of natural resources and the protection of the environmental system.

Although the rapid technological and industrial development was positive, it was also challenging. Results in IT, biology, new energy, and new materials meant that we were in the middle of a new technological and industrial revolution with new industries, standards, and management methods. IT, artificial intelligence, big data, and cloud computing changed people's thinking, lifestyle, and socializing. It required reforms, new concepts, and new rules, which required international cooperation.

Today, the Western world does not live up to the responsibility of pursuing the best in its culture, history, and tradition and ensuring a balanced, sensible capitalist system based on the best of the West's values. The world needed responsible Western political leadership. If the West failed, it would weaken the world's diversity and threaten its overall harmony. Teng concluded that the world's global center was moving towards Asia in these years.

How to practice democracy?[99]

Westerners may see the traditional Chinese desire for stability and continuity as contrary to a development towards Western-style democratic and look like stagnation.

Throughout history, Western culture has been different from Chinese culture. China has not attempted to spread the values of Chinese culture to unenlightened barbarians. China lived with its own values, reclusive and introverted. Resources were better used to build a great wall to keep strangers away than to build an offensive army and navy to conquer other nations. If unrest existed outside the empire's borders, the neighboring countries would fight among themselves. Chinese people called uninformed strangers what they believed they were – barbarians. [100]

Our Western culture has been a culture of conquest, in which trade, new markets, military control, and the Christian missionaries have all played a role. We felt obliged to convert heathens worldwide to the Christian faith, and to spread what we ourselves perceived as a universal principle. The goal of American and European missionaries was to report the number of souls saved for God from our crusade on the Christian mission field – from the war on the ideological battlefield. This was the task of the missionaries.

What social and economic conditions the converted Christians in faraway countries lived under and how Christianity could work together with other cultures were less important. It was none of our business or the business of the converted Christians. It was in the hands of God, preferably with the Vatican and other Christian institutions in the West as intermediaries.

---

[99] Carsten Boyer Thøgersen, *To Point At the Moon – Only to See Your Own Finger* (因指而见月), Copenhagen, 2001.

[100] Naturally, Western people saw this as insulting. In the Treaty between Denmark and China, signed in Tianjin on July 13th, 1863, Article LL stipulated: "It is agreed that the character 夷 (barbarian) shall not be applied to government and subjects of His Danish Majesty in any official document issued by Chinese authorities, either in the capital or in the provinces".
https://books.google.at/books?id=bRtYAAAAcAAJ&printsec=frontcover&hl=de&source=gbs_ge_summary_r&cad=0#v=o nepage&q&f=false

Today, we Westerners may wonder what drove our fellow Westerners, the Christian missionaries one hundred and fifty years ago, and find it difficult to understand all the hardships they went through to preach God's word.

But the goal of Christian missionaries to win over foreign peoples to pursue our way of thinking is continued today through the West's demands on China to introduce a Western democracy for the sake of principle, and regardless of the social and economic consequences it may have. In 1991, I heard a young Chinese intellectual ask a British politician during a meeting at the Delegation of the European Commission in Beijing:

"How do you envisage, in practical terms, that democracy can be introduced in a country as large as China? We have a cultural tradition different from the West?"

"It's very simple: One man, one vote, and at least two independent candidates to vote for. If it can be done in India, the world's largest democracy, it can also be done in China. China is no different at all from other countries."

Introducing democracy is as simple as Christian baptism. It is the enforcement of a principle. Many countries that have formally introduced a democratic system are miles away from China and suffer from instability, social discrimination, and pockets of unbelievable poverty. This has nothing to do with the principle of democracy. The people can just vote for better governments. Destiny lies in the hands of democratic principles, preferably with Western institutions to monitor the implementation of the principles.[101]

| Governance in China

History tells us that when China has a united, stable, peaceful, and central government, China can make use of its full potential – landmass, population, governance experience, education, and innovation – and achieve the common

---

[101] In 1921, the British philosopher Bertrand Russell stayed one year in Beijing and published in 1922 the book *The Problem of China*. Can be recommended. https://www.gutenberg.org/files/13940/13940-h/13940-h.htm

goal of the well-being of the Chinese nation. The Dynasties of Han, Tang, Song, Ming, and Qing are examples.

From history, China has three basic policies:

To keep the Chinese nation together and defend the borders. Without a united China, there will be no China.

To ensure economic progress, people's welfare, stability, and the continuity of China's central government.

Regional separatism and active rebellion against China's central government are not accepted.

Rebellion on small matters gives rise to instability and is not tolerated. Rebellion on big questions is different. Here, Mencius invoked the Mandate of Heaven,[102] which can only be held by a just ruler, and said:

"The people are to be valued most, the altars of the grain and the land (the vitality of the state) next, the ruler least. Hence winning the favor of the common people, you become the Emperor. When the ruler makes a serious mistake, the people will admonish him. If the ruler does not listen to them after repeated admonishments, the people depose the ruler."[103]

Beyond these three basic policies and with Mencius in mind, everything can be negotiated, depending on time and place. "Strong outside, soft inside,"[104] as a Chinese proverb says. Moreover, China and its culture have no mission, no spiritual and religious goal, do not preach to convert other people, and have no colonies.

Ahead of other civilizations, China developed a central administration to govern the empire. Meritocracy and consensus were two key elements. In the Imperial China, officials were selected through exams, and promotions were based on additional exams. In this way, it was ensured that the empire's best

---

[102] 天命

[103] 孟子说："民为贵，社稷次之，君为轻。"
https://iep.utm.edu/mencius/

[104] 外硬内软

talents were at the forefront of the state's administration. Everyone – regardless of social background – could register for the state exams. Titles and honors could not be inherited. This avoided the rise of nobility and families that could assert their influence for generations.

Today, meritocracy is also practiced in China and includes entrance exams to the country's universities. Manuals for the selection and promotion of civil servants have been developed within the state and party apparatus. An official document recently stated that to develop a group of the most talented individuals, officials are selected and promoted based on integrity, ability, and experience, regardless of their personal background.[105] This means that China's top officials have CVs with long and diverse administrative experience, but also, that one will find a few younger people among China's leading officials.

Consensus is another important element of Chinese governance. When, for example, a new five-year economic plan is presented at the National People's Congress – it takes a couple of hours to read the entire text aloud – there is a vote in which virtually everyone votes in favor. In Europe, we ask: Where is the debate? Isn't this top-down management? It has taken two years to make the five-year plan, which results from negotiations at many levels: in the provinces, cities, sectors, and so on. The vote is the end of a long process.

In China, the need for consensus is based on the concept that vital national decisions cannot be founded on a narrow majority. Such decisions may not stand the test of time and can later create confrontation between large and significant political groupings with the danger of subsequent instability. If there is no large and broad support behind a proposal, it is set aside while discussions and negotiations continue. The downside is that urgent and important decisions may be postponed. But it is considered less dangerous than instability and confrontation in the political system.

China has two important governance experiences, different from the European experience. Based upon a history of more than 2000 years as a

---

[105] http://mv.china-embassy.gov.cn/eng/zt/fe/202108/t20210827_8922388.htm

nation, China has the experience of governing the difficult relations between a central government and strong regional power centers with specific regional interests. Important national decisions are based upon consensus among central and regional power players and officials. China has no Western Christian democracy but a tradition of consensus.

How did communism come to China?

In 1911, the Qing Dynasty collapsed, and the central power in China disintegrated. The Treaty of Versailles in 1919 did not allow China to regain control of the German territories in China. Instead, these territories were taken over by Japan. It created a nationalist atmosphere in China and furthered two political movements in China: the already existing Nationalist Party Guomindang/KMT under Sun Yat-sen – later under Chiang Kai-shek – and the Communist Party of China (CPC) founded in 1921. Both parties became inspired by the October Revolution, which had just taken place in Russia. From the early 1920s, both parties cooperated with the Soviet Union. Chiang Kai-shek sent his son to Moscow, where he stayed for 12 years. Cooperation between the KMT and the Communist Party of China was close. Mao Zedong, like many other Chinese Communists, was a member of both parties in the very beginning.

In April 1927, the Shanghai Massacre took place when Chiang Kai-shek arrested and executed over 5,000 members and supporters of the Communist Party of China. After 1927, the KMT and the CPC were at war with each other but negotiated a truce after the Xi'an Incident in 1936. The truce lasted until 1946, when a Civil War broke out. In 1949, the Communist Party of China gained control of Chinese mainland. It established a Chinese national government, now for the first time in more than 100 years, without foreign influence and in control of a unified China – except for Taiwan, whereto the leaders of the KMT had relocated and Hong Kong and Macao, still under foreign control.

Was the governance of New China – the People's Republic of China –
based upon the Chinese reading of the two Europeans Karl Marx and Vladimir
I. Lenin? I think not. China's new government was primarily rooted in China's
history and tradition.

China – a Communist one-party state?

In 2015, during an informal conversation with a Chinese Deputy Minister,
who had also been an ambassador to a European country at an international
conference in Beijing, I suggested China drop the word communist and use
the word "China's party" because "communism" had a negative meaning in the
West.

"Don't forget the word 'one-party state.' It has a negative meaning in the
West, too," the Deputy Minister replied and continued. "Formally, of course,
it is true that the party has the name communist and that only one party is the
leading party. But we understand it differently. The party has over 90 million
members. There are many opinions, interests, and considerations to take,
and the notion of a 'coalition party' fits better. The party is a framework. We
have debates within the party. If no agreement can be reached, the dialogue
continues, and we seek to avoid confrontations. Today, there is no alternative
party in China with a program and vision. In China, a broad debate is taking
place within the party's framework."

"What about the democratic principle of one person, one vote, several
candidates to vote for?" I asked.

"It is an important principle and a vision that many of us share. Our
political system can certainly be improved," the Deputy Minister said. "It is a
process, and we try step by step. But no one has yet proposed a practical model
for how such a principle can be implemented in a country of 1.4 billion people.
Implementing the principle overnight for the sake of the principle itself would
be wrong and throw the country into chaos."

The Deputy Minister continued: "In China, we rarely use the word 'communist,' and when we do, we say 'shared products' party, as it is called in Chinese. We seldom use the Western word 'communism,' and few Chinese know the Western history of that word. Usually, we only say 'the party.' I know the history of the word communism in Europe, but in China, we will not change our own words: 'shared products party.' The party and the People's Republic of China were born with these names. The Ming Dynasty (1368-1644) had 16 emperors, and politics changed along the way. But the word MING was maintained."

China is Chinese – neither communist nor heathen

In the West, "communism" is a negative word. Communism is mainly about political systems, whereas socialism is about policies.

Since World War I, almost all Western European countries have had large center-left political parties, social democratic parties, socialist parties, or labor parties – not allied with the Soviet Union but still with an origin in the writings of Karl Marx. Some of them have been ruling parties for many years.

Das Kapital, written by Karl Marx, is difficult to read in its original language for Europeans, even for many Germans. Today, one will find many references in China to "Marxism" but fewer to the specific terminology of Karl Marx. Few Chinese study and quote the works of Karl Marx, which are deeply rooted in European philosophy, history, and tradition. Even fewer Chinese are familiar with the European scientific and scholarly discussion on the theories and methodologies of Karl Marx. The same goes for many European center-left parties.

I find that integrating Marxism and socialism with the specific national cultural tradition of one's own country is what all governing social democratic, labor, and socialist parties in Western Europe have done over the past one hundred years. China is doing the same today. As stated in the report to the 20th National Congress of the CPC in 2022: "Only by taking root in the rich historical and cultural soil of the country and the nation can the truth of

Marxism flourish here."[106] The following quote summarizes the importance that China places on China's cultural traditions.

"With a history stretching back to antiquity, China's fine traditional culture is extensive and profound; it is the crystallization of the wisdom of Chinese civilization. Our traditional culture espouses many important principles and concepts, including pursuing the common good for all; regarding the people as the foundation of the state; governing by virtue; discarding the outdated in favor of the new; selecting officials on the basis of merit; promoting harmony between humanity and nature; ceaselessly pursuing self-improvement; embracing the world with virtue; acting in good faith and being friendly to others; and fostering neighborliness. These maxims, which have taken shape over centuries of work and life, reflect the Chinese people's way of viewing the universe, the world, society, and morality and are highly consistent with the values and propositions of scientific socialism." [107]

In 2014, Xi Jinping stressed that Confucianism was "the cultural soil that nourishes the Chinese people." "Confucianism," he said, is the key to "understanding the national characteristics of the Chinese as well as the historical roots of the spiritual world of the present-day Chinese." He added that flexibility and openness were important aspects of civilizations' spread and development and that the Chinese civilization had become more diverse through exchanges with other civilizations, referring to the ancient Silk Road and the coming of foreign diplomats to China during the Tang Dynasty (618-907).

"Chinese communists are Marxists, uphold and develop socialism with Chinese characteristics, but Chinese communists are not historical nihilists, nor are they, cultural nihilists. We have always believed that the basic principles of Marxism must be closely integrated with China's concrete reality. We are also convinced that we should scientifically treat traditional national culture and the cultures of all countries in the world and arm ourselves with all the outstanding

---

[106] "Hold High the Great Banner of Socialism with Chinese Characteristics and Strive in Unity to Build a Modern Socialist Country in All Respects", Report to the 20th National Congress of the Communist Party of China, October 16, 2022.

[107] http://my.china-embassy.gov.cn/eng/zgxw/202210/t20221026_10792358.htm

ideological and cultural achievements created by mankind." Urging respect for the diversity of civilizations in the world, Xi Jinping quoted Mencius: "It is an objective fact that all things are different from one another." [108]

"Studying Confucius and Confucianism is an important way to understand the national characteristics of the Chinese people and understand the historical origin of the spiritual world of the Chinese people today." "The Chinese Communists have always been faithful inheritors and advocates of China's excellent traditional culture. From Confucius to Sun Yat-sen, we have paid attention to absorbing the positive nutrients."[109]

I find that the Communist Party of China refers to Karl Marx's general thinking in the same way as many European social democratic parties do. Instead of referring to Confucius and Mencius, European social democratic parties are referring to their cultural tradition, thus integrating Marxism with their national history. The welfare state developed in Northern European countries is a model that has gotten much attention in China. In 2021, China launched the policy concept of "Common Prosperity."[110] It is a policy in the direction of a Northern European welfare state. But North European societies are wealthier and have developed their policies for decades. Western politicians' attempts to describe China as a continuation of a European communist and a Soviet-Russian, Leninist tradition fail in their analysis.

Chinese Buddhism

At the congresses of the Communist Party of China every five years, the use of language is important. Since Xi Jinping became General-Secretary of the CPC, quotes from China's cultural history have increased. During and just after

---

[108] http://english.www.gov.cn/news/photos/2014/09/25/content_281474989289200.htm
http://hk.ocmfa.gov.cn/eng/jbwzlm/xwdt/jzzh/201409/t20140925_7752732.htm
https://china.usc.edu/sites/default/files/forum/Xi%20Commemorates%202565th%20Anniversary%20of%20 Confucius%27%20Birth%20Xinhuanet.pdf

[109] http://www.xinhuanet.com//politics/2014-09/24/c_1112612018_2.htm

[110] https://www.lse.ac.uk/ideas/Assets/Documents/updates/LSEIdeas-Decoding-Chinas-Common-Prosperity-Drive.pdf

the 19th National Congress of the CPC in the autumn of 2017, Chinese media, light boards in cities, and even electronic information boards on highways quoted the slogan, "Never forget why you started, and your mission can be accomplished."[111] I was in Beijing and Shanghai at the time, and I first thought it was the start of a new political campaign. But what was the slogan? It was a saying from the Indian Buddhist sutra around 200,[112] introduced and translated in China during the Eastern Jin Dynasty (317-420). The message was: do not forget the continuity of China's long history.

On September 17th, 2001, the then Chinese President, Jiang Zemin, received the newly appointed ambassador of Denmark to China at the Great Hall of the People to hand over his credentials, followed by a 30-minute conversation. I had the privilege to accompany the Danish ambassador. Six days after the 9/11 terror attack in New York, Washington D.C., Jiang Zemin started the conversation by saying that such violence was against the Buddhist tradition in China. :

There is no Buddhist faction in the Communist Party of China. But Buddhism is part of China's many-sided cultural heritage and is alive today.

Today, some Western opinion leaders argue that China's leadership is advocating reshaping the whole world by imposing its own model on other countries. This claim is true, but in a different way than what the Western observers allege. One should listen to what China says: countries should establish their governance according to their own specific conditions and cultural traditions, like China is doing. This is the message.

Profit and seeking interests versus justice

In 2014, China's Foreign Ministry published several works on China's foreign policy world view.[113] Three objectives were mentioned: 1) To build a

---

[111] 不忘初心，方得始终

[112] https://www.theworldofchinese.com/2017/10/the-ancient-origins-of-xi-jinpings-latest-buzzword/

[113] Yang Jiechi, State Councillor, *Innovations in China's Diplomatic Theory and Practice under New Situations*, 2014. Wang Yi,

new major-country relationship between China and the United States;[114] 2) Mutual respect for each other's social systems, core interests, and concerns; 3) Win-win cooperation and considering the other's interest while pursuing one's one.

The last objective was explained as putting forth the right approach between upholding justice and seeking own interests to enhance friendship and cooperation with neighbouring countries and developed countries.[115] "In China's traditional culture, it is important to handle the relationship between justice and profit and stress the value of morality and responsibility. It is a living characteristic of China's diplomacy. The Chinese nation has studied moral benchmarks and a code of conduct for thousands of years. It means to value justice above profit, profit after justice, and use a proper way to gain your profit."

It was followed up by referring to classical Chinese thinking. Mencius said: "Life is my desire; justice is my desire, too. When I cannot have both of them at the same time, I will uphold justice at the expense of my life." Morality is "heavy," and self-interest is "light." First morality, second self-interest.[116]

I read Mencius like this: We take good care of our own family and fortune – this is our first and overall obligation; We deal fairly and in good faith with other people – that is win-win and good for everybody. However, if there is a conflict between justice and fairness on the one side and our personal interests on the other, justice shall prevail.

The saying of Mencius is part of China's cultural DNA and is known to most Chinese people. When explained, most foreigners would understand, and many agree with the saying of Mencius.

Foreign Minister, *Exploring the Path of Major Country Diplomacy with Chinese Characteristics*, June 27, 2013. Wang Yi, Foreign Minister, *Adhering to the Right Approach to upholding Justice and Seeking Interests, Playing an Active Role as a Responsible Major Country*, 2014.

[114] 中美新型大国关系

[115] http://ke.china-embassy.gov.cn/eng/zxyw/201308/t20130826_6816022.htm

[116] 孟子说，"生，亦我所欲也；义，亦我所欲也。二者不可得兼，舍生而取义者也。"重义轻利，先义后利。

When the Foreign Ministry of China introduced this valuable thinking and stressed the words "justice" and "profit," it was not understood in the West for good reasons. Although the thought was presented in good faith and is familiar to Chinese people, the cultural barriers between the East and West are many. To explain Mencius to foreigners is not easy for Chinese people, and understanding Mencius is not easy for Western people.

| East and West

The U.S. has chosen to launch an ideological and cultural fight with China on human and social values and formed an alliance of democratic countries against an "autocratic" China. The primary focus is not what China is doing outside its borders to other people and other nations but how China is behaving in its own country, within its own family.

Remarkably, the U.S. has decided on an ideological and cultural showdown with China, challenging its values and thoughts. The U.S. has been the world's largest economy for 125 years and the number-one superpower for 75 years, with four percent of the world's population and a history of 233 years as a nation. On the other hand, China has 18 per cent of the world's population, with an uninterrupted history of 4000 years and a governance tradition practiced for 2250 years.

Formally, the focus of critique of the U.S. is not Chinese culture or the people themselves but the political leadership currently in power in China, the Communist Party of China. This opinion only makes sense if China's ruling party was a small, isolated group without popular support. China's leadership today has broad support throughout China. There is no alternative party with a name, program, or vision inside or outside China.

The cultural challenge from China

The West is aware of the economic and technological challenges posed by China. But the cultural challenge from China – which is less a challenge and more should be about inspiration – is rarely mentioned. Instead, the West attributes to China concepts such as communism which originated in Europe, dictatorship, and the absence of European values. A 4000-year-old Chinese civilization does not fit into the concepts that Western culture has developed over the last 200 years. China is an old civilization that, after 150 years of decline, is back in good shape and draws on the experiences and wisdom of its own culture through the millennia and from the rest of the world. Today, Chinese people, well-educated and studying hard, have access to massive information on digital databases with writings and records on China's old culture, long history, and scientific inventions through the centuries. China's cultural hard disk drive is huge and does not require translation by linguists. The Chinese characters are today the same as they were 3000 years ago.

Europe and the U.S. have only had close contact with the Chinese civilization for less than 200 years. The classical Chinese works of Lao Tzu, Mencius, Zhuangzi, and Mozi were first tentatively translated into a European language some 180 years ago. Confucius was translated partly 100 years earlier, while the first comprehensive European translation of the *Book of Changes*, or *I Ching*, was published in German in 1924.

In our European culture, we have only read and studied Sun Tzu for plus hundred years. In 1910, the British sinologist Lionel Giles translated Sun Tzu's full text into a European language for the first time.[117] We are at the beginning of our understanding of Sun Tzu. We translated the title of Sun Tzu's work,

---

[117] Sun Tzu, *The Art of War, the Oldest Military Treatise in the World*. Translated from the Chinese with introduction and critical notes by Lionel Giles, M.A. Assistant in the Department of Oriental Printed Books and MSS, in the British Museum, 1910. http://classics.mit.edu/Tzu/artwar.html

Bingfa, as "The Art of War." For Sun Tzu, war was neither art nor beautiful. His mission was to tell that war was cruel and undesirable and that one should be prepared so well for wars that they could be avoided. In Europe, we should have studied Sun Tzu long before 1910. Today, we still need a deeper study of Sun Tzu. In China, classical Chinese works have been studied and commented on for 2500 years. In Europe and the U.S., knowledge of China's cultural heritage is small and brief.

With China's growing international influence, it's important to know what the Chinese themselves are thinking. It is important for us Europeans – for our own good – to learn how 18 percent of the world's population understands the world. In the future, in the West, we shall meet more and more Chinese who talk about their understanding of history, values, culture, and international cooperation. The challenge from China is formidable, not because of any particular Chinese ideology, religion, policy, or secret strategy but because of China's volume and cultural history. When China invites for dialogue and cooperation with the West, the West should welcome that.

China and the United States

The cooperation that the U.S. and China started 50 years ago barely exists today. Talking to Chinese scholars, businesspeople, and government officials during visits to China over the last few years, I heard disappointment that decades of understanding between China and the United States now seem to be over. Some said: "The sky is falling, and the earth is cracking." They are concerned because globalization, trade, and international cooperation also are necessary for China's continued economic development. Blockades and sanctions lead to an economic decline for everyone.

Confrontation and trade

Despite an increased confrontation between the U.S. and China and the attempt of the U.S. to hinder China's economic and technological development, trade between the U.S. and China has nevertheless continued to increase since Trump became president in 2017. U.S. exports to China create 1.2 million U.S. jobs, and U.S. investment in Chinese industry has reached new records. Despite American restrictions on Chinese IT technology and IT companies, the exchange of employees and the cooperation between Chinese and American tech giants such as Alibaba, Baidu, Tencent, Apple, Microsoft, and Tesla are extensive. In 2019, before the Covid-19 pandemic, 370,000 Chinese were studying at American universities, corresponding to 1/3 of all international students in the United States. The recent U.S. legislation in the Congress aims to narrow this cooperation.

Europe between the U.S. and China

The primary international focus of the U.S. today is not Europe but China and East Asia. The explanation is partly economic: World Bank's figures on the GDP of the U.S., China, and the EU show that the GDP of the U.S. from 2008 to 2020 grew by 1.4 times, China's GDP grew by 3.2 times, while the GDP of the EU grew by 0.9 times. In 2008, the GDP of the EU was almost four times larger than China's. In 2020, the EU's GDP was roughly the same as China's. Correspondingly, the GDP of the U.S. in 2008 was 3.2 times larger than China's. In 2020, that figure was 1.4.

The balance of power between the U.S., China, and the EU is this: 1) The U.S. has a soft power that dominates world opinion. The U.S. dollar serves as the world's reserve currency, and the U.S. control over the world's financial institutions is huge. In 2020, the U.S. accounted for 40 percent of the world's total military expenditure, to which should be added the U.S. defense industry's arms sale to other countries. 2) China has political and social cohesion, leadership with decision-making power, and sustained economic and technological development momentum. China has rearmed militarily in the last 25 years by keeping China's total military expenditure at around 1.7 percent of China's GDP. In this period, China's GDP increased by 18 times. Consequently, China's military spending has increased , too. For reference, at the NATO Summit in 2014 in Wales, member countries decided to reach 2 percent of GDP in military expenditure before 2024.[118] 3) The EU, an economy the size of China's, has a single market across 27 Member States. The EU's military strength is smaller, but the EU's position in the conflict between the U.S. and China can be decisive for the further course of the conflict.

The U.S. value-based campaign against China has impacted the European press and several European parliaments. At the same time, China is an important trading partner for the EU, and for some EU countries, like Germany, China is even the most important trading partner. A choice between the U.S. and China does not serve the EU's interests. In 2019, the EU Commission updated its view on China[119]: China is a cooperation partner, competitor, and systemic rival. China replied that cooperation and competition were fine and natural, but dialogue and association should be based on mutual respect for each other's societies and cultures.

How will the EU-China relations develop? Should the EU follow an American value-based policy and seek a showdown with China? Should the EU follow the changing U.S. attitudes toward rule-based international order? In 2003, the U.S. ignored UN regulations and invaded Iraq.

Today, I hear that some Chinese believe that the West's attitude towards China has not changed much since the Opium Wars 160 years ago. Then and

---

[118] "Allies whose current proportion of GDP spent on defence is below this level (2 per cent) will: 1) halt any decline in defence expenditure; 2) aim to increase defence expenditure in real terms as GDP grows; 3) aim to move towards the 2% guideline within a decade with a view to meeting their NATO Capability Targets and filling NATO's capability shortfalls."
https://www.nato.int/cps/en/natohq/official_texts_112964.htm

[119] https://commission.europa.eu/publications/eu-china-strategic-outlook-commission-and-hrvp-contribution-european-council-21-22-march-2019_en

now, three questions have been important for the West in relation to China: 1) How to do business and make money in China? 2) How to make the Chinese Christian, be civilized, have the right values, and respect the authority of the West? 3) Do we need to be afraid of China?

The challenge today is that China will no longer subordinate itself to the West but wishes to cooperate on an equal footing. This is the major change.

From the beginning, two different ways of thinking

Today, I think the wishes of the young Shanghai official in 2006 were visionary and, in many ways, close to what has happened in China. On the question of democracy and civilization, I believe there is no simple answer, and there has never been a simple answer. When I meet the young Shanghai official again someday, I shall give him this explanation:

Three thousand years ago, two different cultural perceptions developed. In the Middle East, the belief in only one God who ruled the world from beyond became known. God was almighty, righteous, and the only True God in the world. God commanded people to proclaim His presence across the globe. Only one God, one belief. Faithfulness to God was not rewarded here and now but elsewhere, as a redeemed human being in a paradise. Judaism, later Christianity, and Islam each worshiped in their own way the same God: one truth, one way, one God.

In East Asia, the thinking of *yin-yang* emerged and emphasized harmony, pragmatism, and inclusiveness. Confucius (551-479 BC) said, harmony is the sum of diversity. Harmony is like a musical chord. Without different, distinct and individual tones, no chords, no harmony. Diversity is the precondition and foundation for harmony.

If asked, people in the East would probably see the concept of "one God" as contrary to nature, which is based on diversity and inclusiveness. Sustainability is based on respect for diversity. There is no one truth. One tone gives no musical harmony. Just like biodiversity makes nature sustainable, cultural diversity nurtures inspiration, rejuvenation, and the continuation of civilizations.

In 1947, the Danish scientist and Nobel Prize winner Niels Bohr received the Danish Order of the Elephant and chose the *yin-yang* symbol for his coat of arms and the words "Opposites are complementary" (*Contraria Sunt Complementa*).[120] These words were close to Niels Bohr's own theory of complementarity.

In 2000, the European Union chose a logo: *In Varietate Concordia*, which means united in diversity.[121] It looks like a copy of the saying of Confucius, but it is not. The EU logo says that we strive for unity despite our differences. The EU logo wishes to reconcile different views but does not encourage diverse opinions. The consensus is a compromise and an average.

Musical harmony and biodiversity have no average. The precondition for both is uniqueness and diversity. Without robust individuality, we have no building blocks to achieve the goal of harmony and coexistence.

---

[120] https://www.researchgate.net/publication/343472590_Contraria_sunt_Complementa

[121] https://european-union.europa.eu/principles-countries-history/symbols/eu-motto_en

Syed Hasan Javed

Served as Pakistan's Ambassador in Germany, Singapore, and Mauritius, he has also worked as a diplomat in Zimbabwe, Tajikistan, and Belgium. Syed Hasan Javed served in the People's Republic of China in two diplomatic assignments for nearly a decade. After retirement from the diplomatic service, he served as Director of Chinese Studies Centre of Excellence, National University of Science and Technology (NUST) for six years. He is the author of several books on China, including *Chinese Soft Power Code*, *Rise of China and the Asian Century*, *Nation Building Paradoxes in India and Pakistan*, *China's Development Model — Lessons for Pakistan*, and *China, West and the Islamic World — Romance of the Three Civilizations*. His latest book, published recently and available in the market, is *China As Number One*.

China's Belt and Road Initiative: The Power of Thought

Abstract

China's list of successful stories and achievements during the last forty years (1980-2020) and the decade from 2010 to 2020 is long. Some of the successes during the previous decade include targeted poverty alleviation strategy leading to zero poverty, the successful landing of China's first Mars exploration, the response to the Covid-19 Pandemic crisis, the boom in foreign trade, etc. These are indeed great achievements. But what touched me as a professional diplomat who had served in China for a decade and visited nearly sixty countries is President Xi Jinping's idea of the Belt and Road Initiative (BRI). It was proposed in September 2013, followed by his announcement on the 21st Century Maritime Silk Road in October 2013 during his visit to Indonesia. The BRI is widely seen in the world now as the second phase of globalization endorsed by 1291 nations and entities, which covers more than two-thirds of the world community. President Xi Jinping announced the launch of the Global Development Initiative (GDI) at the 76th Session of the United Nations General Assembly in September 2021, which holds great promise for the world. The GDI's wholehearted reception by more than a hundred countries reflects China's growing influence and credibility. China contributes to one-third of global economic growth, helping narrow the gap between the haves and have-nots by making affordable goods and services to

---

[1] The data is originated from the year of 2017.

one-third of the poor global population. The BRI will open up the interior of the Eurasia Continent, help stabilize West Asia and the Middle East, reduce tension in South Asia, and build a "community of a shared future" by winning hearts and minds. The BRI appears as a "winning coalition" of states because only peace, prosperity, justice, and harmony have stood the test of time. It is in this context that President Xi Jinping's launch of the Global Development Initiative, which opens up new opportunities for partnerships, becomes enormously significant. The 21st century is fast developing into a China-led Asian century. The world is witnessing a recent history being made in Asia "as the biggest numbers of people begin rising into the middle class." The West's economic and technological excellence is being replayed in Asia but with the strength of Asian value systems. Asians are now engaged in a non-stop process of innovation, technological assimilation, upgradation of skills and knowledge, improving quality, adding value, multiple tasking, and cost cutting, making their products unbeatable. Unlike the Western technological paradigm, Asian economic and technological progress is not inspired by conflict or threat perception models. The Asian development paradigm is instead based on achieving a higher standard of life, social and scientific level to catch up with the world's most advanced nations. It is, in fact, a win-win situation for all. Asians like neither being preached nor being dished out moralizing lessons. Asians, who are inheritors of a rich heritage of diverse civilizations, are rediscovering themselves. The West confronts, however, a big dilemma in dealing with China due to a history of mistrust, biases, prejudices, jealousies, and outright conflicts. They know that among the non-Western societies, China is a relatively homogenous country with potential geography, economy, political, military, technological strengths, etc., of a great strategic competitor. In comparison, India is becoming an more and more important partner to the U.S. in the Asia-Pacific strategy. The smaller neighbors of India see it as too big to be feared rather than respected.

Introduction

Different civilizations, empires, and nation states have risen in history because of the power of an "idea" or a "dream." It is generally observed that no power, or a coalition of powers, can stop an idea that their time has come. American strategist and diplomat Dr. Henry Kissinger observes, "When an idea strikes an opportunity, it becomes a policy." Dr. Zbigniew Brzezinski's book *Out of Control: Global Turmoil on the Eve of the 21st Century* observes: "Without an instinctive, organic national aspiration (which need not even be forcefully articulated) nations do not emerge great powers. Only those who, in some indefinable manner, produce a culturally spontaneous outburst of assertive, competitive, and driving desire to explore and conquer transform themselves into an entity that becomes demonstrably more dominant than others.... That desire reflects a mysterious sense of mission expressed through the wholehearted dedication of countless individuals who share a shared commitment to the glory and destiny of national greatness. The emergence of great powers is also the consequence of special responsibility combined with inherent physical capability. The moment or the historical trend must be congenial to the flowering of a dominant, catalytic state that has something of importance to say to the world, be it through a civilization mission, a doctrinal revelation, or a compelling social example". [2]

Theoretically and conceptually speaking, an idea provides a concept, an ideology, or a framework to galvanize, mobilize or inspire a change in the status quo. That is how most revolutions have taken place in the world. But every idea, like power itself, has a "shelf life" too. The only constant in human existence is "change". A change is necessitated by the flow of time, political upheaval, economic expansion, demographic bulges, technological breakthroughs, climatic factors, health care, cultural revival, sociological transformation, etc.

---

[2] Brzezinski, Z. (1993), The faceless Rivals [pp. 116-118], in *Out of Control: Global Turmoil on the Eve of the 21st Century*, Canada, Maxwell Macmillan International.

Societies that avoid changes stay away from progress! However, the combined direct and indirect colonial onslaught of the Western powers over Asia, Africa, Latin America, and the Caribbean lasted for five hundred centuries. Seen through this perspective, the world is currently going through the ending times of the Western domination model, expected to last two or three decades more. The real change will be apparent from 2050 onwards, when China's Gross Domestic Product alone will be more than the combined GDP of the U.S. and the European Union. As credible forecasts, the combined GDP of the European Union is expected to come down to 10 percent in 2030 from 17 percent in 2020. The gap between the Trans-Atlantic Community and Asia is bound to grow over time as the Asian economies grow to achieve their full potential. The other Asian states closely follow China's lead. The Americans are not reconciled to China's rise, as is reflected in the annual opinion surveys conducted by Pew Research Center, Washington.

The great powers' fall is not discernible to ordinary eyes, although their rise is more easily felt. It is also because the fall of great powers is only visible over a longer time scale. The ordinary folks continue to chant National/ Imperial Anthems, beat drums, and salute the National Flag. These constitute a part of the orchestrated faith in national/imperial power projection, confidence building, and elevated egos to prevent any erosion in belief in national identity and "manifest destiny." Only historians, future watchers, and visionaries can see and feel the Teutonic shift or the slow demise of certain nations, empires, and civilizations in the chessboard of time and space. The greater powers face an inevitable decline, the greater their propensity to use "military" force as a means of power projection will become. The great power narrative has always been to promote the myth of "invincibility" as an act of faith and any breach of it as an act of taboo. The real factors contributing to the current economic predicament in the U.S., Euro-zone states, and Japan are, however, demographic decline, absence of social capital, environmental stresses, the dominance of narrow interest groups in policy making, skewed income distribution, absence of economic growth and lack of competitive advantages in a fast transforming world. In 2012, the European Union spent 47 percent of its annual budget on agricultural subsidies to its farmers. The U.S. spending on defense is more than the combined total defense expenditure of its first 19 competitors. A 1000 percent tariff protects the Japanese rice market. The public policy and institutional responses to these challenges have been a "mode of denial," initially followed by patch-up and short-term "smart solutions" that were not always so smart, as acknowledged by the financial wizard Alan Greenspan in his congressional hearings. There is also a growing tendency to look elsewhere or "blame others" for one's problems. In the Western world, there has been "systemic conditioning" of ordinary people's minds and those who believe that we are "too big and perfect" to fail. It does not solve any problem but adds to xenophobic, protectionist, and narrow interest groups who do not wish these challenges to be met by internal scrutiny, review, reorganization, and revival. These will be discussed in subsequent paragraphs.

Interesting times are ahead

The 21st century is fast turning out to be an era of interesting times, also described as an era of new normal, or by some as an era of new abnormal. It is not only emerging as the traditional East-West story but also the West against the rest of the world. It, however, appears to be an era of geo-economics, with the epicenter moving to the East. During the global financial crisis in 2008-2009, the Arab countries suffered a loss of US$2.5 trillion in Western investments, in addition to more than US$ 600 billion in the domestic market, worsened by oil price slumps and financial recession. China regards its relations with developing countries as the "cornerstone of its diplomacy," which is reflected in its intention to strengthen and develop its relations with Arab countries, one of the largest groups of developing nations. The global economic meltdown in 2007-2008 was still in its earlier stage, and its impact on the geostrategic balance was only evolving. An 87-page U.S. Congress Research Service (CRS) had nonetheless termed it a "national security threat" to the country, observing that the real impact would be visible in 5 to 10 years.

The U.S. political and economic model became discredited, with deeper implications for global stability, such as the rise of protectionism, nationalism, and regionalism and calls for decoupling. The greatest single impact of the crisis was the loss of American leadership. A new co-relation of powers is set in motion. The U.S. remained the most influential power for a while, but encountered a repeat of the financial crisis in 2011 and climatic disasters such as Katrina, Andrews, California fire, Midwest drought, etc. These came in addition to geostrategic follies/blunders in Afghanistan, the Middle East, and North Africa from 2010-2020, which confirmed the U.S. decline manifested in many forms and areas. The overwhelming majority of the population in Asia, Africa, and Latin America support China's proposal of the BRI and GDI as win-win frameworks against the model of the U.S.-led Cold war-II, containment, and zero-sum game.

Broadly, the 21st century appears to be an era of surprises and shocks, disruptions and eruptions, connecting and disconnecting, mega myths and mega transformation. The meltdown of the U.S. and European economies is having a sobering effect on the power projection potential of the U.S. and NATO to undertake kinetic adventures and missions in global "hot spots" or perceived "hot spots." On the other hand, China has risen as a global force and a "stabilizer" par excellence with goodwill, credibility, and influence in Korean Peninsula, the South China Sea, ASEAN, South Asia, the Afghan situation, Arab Israel Conflict, the conflict in the Caucasus, Arab-Iranian relations as well as Myanmar-Bangladesh relations on the Rohingya Issue. Rallying behind China, a revived Russia holds the strategic balance on the global chessboard. The weakening of the U.S. and the Western world is also leading to the rise of medium-sized powers to pursue their regional ambitions, such as Brazil, Iran, Turkey, Pakistan, Bangladesh, Indonesia, Egypt, and Nigeria. Only India stands aloof, showing its cards both ways with one leg in Quad and U.S. Indo-Pacific arrangements and the other leg of the BRICs and SCO. India will not let BRICs or SCO achieve their true potential. Truth tends to reveal itself. The future of India is the "wild card" of the 21st century. However, Western print and electronic media networks like BBC, CNN, Bloomberg, Fox TV, Discovery, and others would like the world to believe differently. The Indian hatred for the Chinese is only equaled by their hate of Muslims, Russians, Africans, and Latinos.

The power of ideas and dreams

Pakistan's poet Muhammad Iqbal (1877-1938) observed, "If you have to build tomorrow, you need to dream first." He had also foreseen the rise of China around the years of the Long March (1934-1936), "The Himalayan springs have begun to rumble; the Chinese are waking up from deep slumber." President Xi Jinping observed that "Life must have dreams. Without dreams, there is nothing to fight for in life and no direction to travel. There is a big picture and little pictures within the Chinese dream. To every Chinese person, his small undertakings will only flourish if the greater cause prospers." When a noble "idea drives power," it creates fortune, glory, respect, and influence. The law of nature demands the human beings be ready to make continuous adjustments, compromises, innovations, and reforms to ensure their existence. When change is averted, the human society begins being subverted. Societies that innovate do not stagnate, which is the other name for "decline", as others are moving forward in a relative time scale. Change is the only constant in life. Ancient Chinese philosopher Confucius (551BC-479BC) said, "Those who wish to remain constant in happiness must change." The Chinese centuries-old cultural heritage is strong and resilient enough to co-exist with all other cultures' foreign values and elements since the Chinese cultural paradigm is based on "positivism". The rise of China is a unique event of the 21st century, for it has come under difficult historical circumstances. For two hundred years, this mighty civilization was subject to severe suffering at the hands of the marauding Western colonial powers, who preyed on its wealth. Even after its liberation in 1949, China lived under sanctions and was denied its rightful place in the United Nations by the Western nations until 1971.

China follows its proposal of "win-win" diplomacy. The "Chinese phenomenon" is unique in many respects. Not only Sinologists but many other states have lived with myths, biases, and misunderstandings about the Chinese thought. The Chinese cannot do anything about that. With all their honesty and humility, they try their best to bridge the "cultural gap." But to be fair to them and everybody else, it is just not possible. A balanced assessment or judgment is not possible without knowledge. As it is said, ignorance is our worst enemy. The purity of knowledge and wisdom gives birth to "ideas" that signal the need for reforms, failing which revolutions occur. Sometimes the reforms are too late and too trivial to avert revolutions, while at other times, they become both the precursor and the outcome of revolutions. But the history books are full of episodes in which human societies have erred and tumbled badly, repeating the same mistakes as their predecessors, competitors, or enemies. The law of nature is, however, equal for everyone. Nature is the biggest equalizer! It does not discriminate too. The power of an idea is stronger than the power itself.

Among the greatest tragedies befalling the Western world in the 21st century has been their loss in the arena of ideas. The American establishment, mainstream media, and liberals have delivered "more of the same" as part of the change to the American people. The Americans are not an informed society. They need to know that all the superpowers throughout history started with their own exceptionalism, manifest destiny, and missionary zeal. But that alone was never enough to sustain any superpower in history. Many scholars, such as Arnold Toynbee, Paul Kennedy, Henry Kissinger, Zbigniew Brzezinski, Samuel Huntington, and Francis Fujiyama, have discussed this hard fact in their books. The Romans thought they had a "perfect solution" to their empire's problems, just as was believed by the Greeks before them and the Byzantines that followed. The Arabs started with missionary zeal to spread Islam but ran out of steam. The Mongols commanded a vast empire through missionary zeal but soon disintegrated. The British controlled "an empire where the sun never set." But soon, they had to recede to their island. The Soviet Union controlled the largest territory for a nation-state in history, yet disintegrated. It is difficult for

Americans, in particular, and the West, in general, to accept or acknowledge its decline.

US INTERVENTIONS SINCE WWII
BOMB ATTACKS, SABOTAGE, ATTEMPTED REGIME CHANGE

CHINA, 1945-46	LAOS, 1964-73	LIBYA, 1989
SYRIA, 1949	DOMINICAN	PHILIPPINES, 1989
KOREA, 1950-53	REPUBLIC, 1965-66	PANAMA, 1989-90
CHINA, 1950-53	PERU, 1965	IRAQ, 1991
IRAN, 1953	GREECE, 1967	KUWAIT, 1991
GUATEMALA, 1954	GUATEMALA, 1967-69	SOMALIA, 1992-94
TIBET, 1955-70s	CAMBODIA, 1969-70	IRAQ, 1992-1996
INDONESIA, 1958	CHILE, 1970-73	BOSNIA, 1995
CUBA, 1959	ARGENTINA, 1976	IRAQ, 1998
DEMOCRATIC	ANGOLA, 1976-92	SUDAN, 1998
REPUBLIC OF	TURKEY, 1980	AFGHANISTAN, 1998
CONGO, 1960-65	POLAND, 1980-81	YUGOSLAVIA, 1999
DOMINICAN	EL SALVADOR, 1981-92	AFGHANISTAN, 2001
REPUBLIC, 1961	NICARAGUA, 1981-90	IRAQ, 2002-03
VIETNAM, 1961-73	CAMBODIA, 1980-95	SOMALIA, 2006-07
BRAZIL, 1964	LEBANON, 1982-84	IRAN, 2005-PRESENT
REPUBLIC OF	GRENADA, 1983-84	LIBYA, 2011
CONGO, 1964	LIBYA, 1986	VENEZUELA, 2019
GUATEMALA, 1964	IRAN, 1987-88	

redfish
@redfishstream

Evolution of many global ideas

Historically, the rise of the Greek city-states was led by the idea of "people's representation or democracy." The Romans cherished the "Republic" as an end itself. At the same time, the Islamic empire was powered by the idea of "brotherhood"; the Chinese dynasties, by the idea of "heavenly balance and harmony" (*tianxia datong, renren weigong*)[3]; the European Empires, by the idea of "colonization"; and the American century, by the idea of what President Woodrow Wilson termed "making the world safe for democracy." The Soviet Socialist Revolution was powered by the idea of "equality," whereas Nazi Germany was driven by the idea of "Aryan racial superiority." During the medieval age, the European societies powered by the Renaissance, Political Reformation (Treaty of Westphalia 1648), Industrial Revolution, and expansion in naval power adopted "colonization" as an idea and a policy for

---

[3] 天下大同，人人为公

400 years (1500-1900) reversing the Moorish rule in Spain (Andalusia) and Ottoman Turk conquests in the Balkans and Central Europe.

European idea of colonialism

The idea of colonialism was driven by the search for raw materials, gold, slaves, and markets for merchandise. The Portuguese, who began it, were the first to learn about global shipping routes of the spice trade and to break away from the Arab Muslim Andalusia (Spain). The merchants of the Italian city-states of Venice and Genoa also built a formidable navy, learning the same lessons as the Portuguese from the Arabs about their knowledge, science, and domination of the Mediterranean islands from the 9th to 14th centuries. The Portuguese were followed by the Spaniards, Italians, Dutch, Germans, French, British, Belgians, Russians, and Americans. The power of ideas of "colonization", respectively, lasted for a century or two centuries. The U.S. was a product of a vision and a dream, and so was the lead of the Western world, a product of the historical circumstances prevailing in the world from the 15th to the 20th century. The American phenomenon also extended European ideas, dreams, knowledge, culture, and intelligence. The continuation of mutual wars, greed, and imperial goals for extending their empires weakened these European powers at the turn of the 20th century. "Roughly nearly all the 70 empires during the last four thousand years, including the Greek, Roman, Chinese, Ottoman, Hapsburg, imperial German, imperial Japanese, British, French, Dutch, Portuguese, and Soviet empires, collapsed in the same orgy of military folly. The Roman Republic, at its height, only lasted two centuries. We are set to disintegrate in roughly the same time".[4]

---

[4] Hedges, C. (2021). The Collective Suicide Machine, retrieved from https://www.sheerpost.com

China's story – The power of the idea of liberation

The neglect of the naval power by the Qing Dynasty also cost China two centuries of exploitation and a "century of humiliation" when the European colonial powers backed by "Canon and Cross" engaged in the "gunboat" diplomacy to extract maximum concessions from a weak Qing Dynasty. The imposition of two Opium Wars by the British and French in 1840 and 1856 decimated the Qing Dynasty's navy. It led to an era of looting and plundering and the imposition of hundreds of unfair treaties, penalties, and concessions with growing "do more" mantras, impoverishing the Chinese masses. The fall of the Qing Dynasty in 1911 made little difference as the elite refused to reform and stop Western interference. China's example from 1911 was no different from what has happened or continues to happen in the rest of the Afro-Asian-Latino and Caribbean world. One does not need to subscribe to Marxist Leninist ideology to understand how the law of nature operates. The Chinese people found themselves helpless when in 1921, a group of intellectuals, workers, and patriots established the Communist Party in Shanghai. The central idea, which subsequently became the ideology of the Communist Party of China, was "liberation". It sowed the seed of the people's revolution, which materialized in 1949 after decades of struggle against the Japanese aggression and the Civil war with the Nationalist Party (Kuomintang) backed by the imperialist powers.

The rise of China, drawing on the Soviet Socialist, Marxist, and Leninist thought of the political organization, mass mobilization, and armed struggle, was a unique event in Asian history. Chairman Mao Zedong, at the podium of Tian'anmen Square, declared that "the Chinese masses have finally stood up." As a result of this paradigm shift in ideological orientation, governance structures, systemic organization, social relationships, and worldview, China made tremendous progress in the first phase (1949-1979) since the founding of the People's Republic of China in economy, infrastructure, education, healthcare, and national defense. This era was dominated by centrally planned economic administration. The Western powers led by the U.S. remained hostile to the People's Republic of China throughout this era. China was denied its rightful place in the United Nations until 1971. The U.S. was compelled by the former Soviet Union's growing power, the high intensity of its conflict in Vietnam, the deteriorating condition of its economy, and strong support for the restoration of China's U.N. membership in the developing and the Islamic world to open up channels of communication with China and support restoration of China's rightful place in the United Nations. It was made possible by the secret visit of U.S. Secretary of State Dr. Henry Kissinger to Beijing via Pakistan in July 1971. It was obvious that the Western powers normalized relations with China, only to gain the upper hand in global power politics and seek markets for their products. Their imperialistic mindset had hardly changed.

Islamic world and China – two poles with one dream

The Muslim and Western worlds differ in their approaches to dealing with China in many critical ways. The Muslims ended their quarrel with the Chinese at their battle at Talas in 751 AD with the Tang Dynasty. The Arabs, Persian, and Turks became the defenders of the Chinese state henceforth, serving in the different Chinese dynasties. The enormous contribution of the local and foreign Muslim community to technology, trade, and commerce during the medieval age in China are well documented. For nine centuries, from 800 to 1700 AD, while China remained the largest economy, with one-third of global wealth, more than 50 percent of global GDP was contributed by the Islamic world's twelve dynasties/empires, including the Ummayads/Abbasids in the Middle East; Almoharids/Moors in Spain; Ottomans in Western Asia/ Southern Europe; Fatimids/Mamluks in Egypt and Levant; Fulani/Malian in the North and West Africa, Sultanate/Mughals in South Asia, Malay Majapahit in Southeast Asia; Timurids and Tartars in Central Asia. Europe's share was 13 percent, while the Europeans did not yet colonize the Americans.

The rising Western powers dealt heavy blows to Qing-era China and the

Islamic Empires in Asia and Africa. The two Opium Wars in 1840 and 1856, the Eight-Power Allied Forces' invasion of the capital of the Qing Dynasty in 1901, and the destruction of the Yuanmingyuan are stains in history. The West continues to treat China as if it were still in the "Qing Dynasty era." The Qing and Muslim dynasties had shown little interest in developing maritime capabilities. This strategic neglect cost both "nearly two centuries loss of sovereignty," unprecedented costs to their population, economy, culture, and dignity. Since the Ming Dynasty Muslim Admiral Zheng He's seven voyages from 1405 to 1433, China remained essentially a "continental power". Chinese naval strategists know well now that it has happened before and can happen in the future too. The Western powers failed to repent of past actions. Instead, their support to the Nationalist Party during the Civil War (1945-1949) with the Red Army added two million additional Chinese civilian casualties.

Since the dawn of the founding of the People's Republic of China in 1949, the Western powers maintained their boycott of China and denied it its rightful place in the United Nations until 1971. Even after the normalization of diplomatic relations between China and the U.S. in 1979, the Western powers were not truly reconciled to the choice of the Chinese masses, their ideology, and the system of government under the leadership of the Communist Party of China. Soon the Western powers started to interfere in Tibet, Xinjiang, and Hong Kong, China, with the U.S. restoring military ties with Taiwan, China and declaring its policy to contain China. In contrast to the permanent hostile attitude of the Western powers over the past two hundred years, the newly independent Muslim States were the most steadfast supporters of China and its rightful place in the United Nations and the World Trade Organization. The Islamic countries sided with China's position on Xinjiang and refuted the Western propaganda on human rights forcefully. The Islamic world is a growing pillar and pole of support for a powerful emerging China.

Fast forward to 2022. "Washington has declared war on China. The administration and its allies hope the war will be 'cold' but have no strategy for keeping it. For decades, the West has ignored the significance of China's rise – but we must recognize that it will be instrumental in all our futures. In the summer of 2021, the Communist Party of China (CPC) is marking its centenary. It has much to celebrate. The most powerful communist party and by far the most powerful political organization in the world, it has presided over the largest surge of economic growth ever witnessed".[5]

The power of the idea of perpetual reforms

Since 1979, the last more than forty years have witnessed China implementing the reform and opening-up policy in every sector of life with a concentrated focus on the economy with the objective of common wealth and poverty alleviation. China's statesman Deng Xiaoping undertook what is known as the Four Modernizations, which refer to modernization of agriculture, industry, national defence and science and technology (in that order). His able successors have successfully carried out the rejuvenation of the Chinese nation. For four decades, China provided American and European companies with a profitable market for their products, a thriving destination for investment, and a low-cost producer of their goods, giving them a competitive edge globally. China's cheap consumer and electronic goods and services also supported a large underclass in both America and Europe, blurring the income divide in those societies between the haves and have-nots. Further, China's more than US$ one trillion reserves supported the American profligate consumption by keeping the interest rates low. The Americans also loved the feeling and the glare of comfort of remaining the superpower for an extended period. For China, precious time was available to catch up with global knowledge, science, technology, and market conditions. It was, in fact, a win-win arrangement for both powers. But the Americans soon realized that the tables had been turned because of the inbuilt advantages of China. "China seeks no 'allies' and has no political satrapies or military dependencies. Crucially, China is not the Soviet

---

[5] Tooze, A. (2021), Why there is no solution to our age of crisis without China, New Statesman, International Edition, retrieved from www.newstatesman.com

Union. China has no messianic ideology to export. Its appeal derives from its performance, not its ideas. It is happy to be emulated but justly charged with callous indifference to how foreign societies govern themselves. China is not engaged in regime change operations to create an ideological sphere of influence".[6]

China learned a lot from Western management techniques, advanced technology, education facilities, market access, etc. China's own Special Economic Zones (SEZs) became global factory workshops for American and European merchandise goods for their own markets and the world at large. During these four decades, China spent its newly acquired wealth on improving its population's living standards, upgrading infrastructure, and investing in higher education, research, and scientific and technological projects. Simultaneously, the United States squandered its wealth on fighting right and left in bizarre wars in weird places with strange objectives. The result is that the American influence has touched its lowest ebb, now remaining in the company of a few, such as Japan, India, and Israel, the most isolated states in the world, struggling with strong challenges. "We have missed a great opportunity, but more importantly, we have damaged our position in the world very grievously. We're neither as liked as before, nor as feared as before, nor as respected as before.... Never in its history has America been so prone to fear and so subjected to such intensive brainwashing that we are going to get hit at any moment. And the fear of the unknown is the worst of all."[7]

Ground realities are important

Throughout history, no country or a coalition of countries has ever succeeded in fighting the world. Nazi Germany could not have fought the world with Japan, Vichy France, and Italy on its side. The Soviet Union could

---

[6] Chas Freeman (2020), "The Struggle with China is not a Replay of the Cold War", *New Statesman*, retrieved from www.newstatesman.com

[7] Shaw, J. (2008), "People of World Influence: Zbigniew Brzezinski", *The Washington Diplomat*, retrieved from www.washingtondiplomat.com

not have fought the world with India or Eastern Europe on its side. Similarly, if the lessons from history provide any wisdom, the Americans cannot battle the world with Japan and India on their side. A divided West confronts the rest of the world as China's statesman Deng Xiaoping once proposed "seeking truth from facts" (*shishi qiushi*)[8]. The Western (or so-called global) Financial Crisis was the breaking point of the Western domination of the World, which had continued for the past 500 years. The specter of another "Big Bang" Global Financial Crisis is haunting even the best minds and institutions. It is not a question of if, but when, with the "debt bombs" fast accumulating in the United States and the European Union. While the EU is imploding, the U.S., which has been used to leading the world, is beset with self-inflicted injuries. The U.S. finds itself flat-footed regarding human rights, immigration, religious freedom, multicultural values, plurality, trade, and climate change. The world has lost trust in the U.S. leadership, but more importantly, the U.S. has lost confidence in itself despite the presence of some best minds and institutions. The United Nations is fast becoming another "league of nations," having experienced the weakening of leadership, the loss of trust and credibility, and the absence of precious social capital in the global institutions. They include all the progress towards creating a new UN-led world order: inter-faith understanding, respect for the principles of sovereign equality, non-interference, non-intervention, human rights, humanitarian laws, protection of biodiversity, environment, climate, development agendas, and social and labor standards. The Western powers, in general, and the United States, now realize their loss of world domination but are not ready to amend their actions. Their mainstream media continues to repeat "make-believe" stories again and again, which does not help at all. Instead of reflecting on their intentions, actions, and devastating consequences, mainstream media goes the extra mile to create ghosts of others. For example, they see the rise of China as a threat to their neatly arranged global order of the post-Second World War era.

---

[8] 实事求是

The idea of the Atlantic Charter

The Atlantic Charter and the Breton Woods system comprising the World Bank, International Monetary Fund, and International Finance Corporation helped perpetuate the Western capitalist domination of the world. The United Nations, which was established "to rid the world of the scourge of all wars," ushered it into a new phase of the Cold war, which turned hot in the Korean Peninsula, Vietnam, the Middle East, and Africa. The Western world remains committed to its desire for global domination in perpetuity. The roles of the Soviet Union and the People's Republic of China as the major contributors to the Allied Nations' victory against the German Nazi, Italian fascist, and Japanese militarism in the Western (European) and Eastern (Asian) theatres were not fully either recognized or accepted. During the last three quarters of a century, from 1945-2020, the Western powers engaged in dozens of wars, proxy conflicts, insurgencies, violence, and sabotage against states with the potential to challenge their global writ. With the beautiful ideas of electoral democracy, market capitalism, and individual freedom, they ensured the achievement of their strategic objective of keeping the newly decolonized states perpetually politically unstable, economically weak, socially chaotic, and psychologically depressed for promoting brain drain and flight of capital. This model worked somewhat well for three quarters of a century. But as all political models, ideas, and power have a shelf life, so was the Western domination of the world. In more and more countries, liberal democracy has begun to be identified with majoritarianism and fascism, such as in India. By engaging directly and indirectly in scores of conflicts, the Americans, with their propensity to make waging wars a permanent tool of their foreign policy, have weakened themselves and invited hatred from the world. The U.S. has had conflicts with nearly 174 member states of the United Nations on one ground or another.

The idea of global hegemony

In their ultimate wisdom, the Western powers crafted a world order after the devastations of two world wars. They codified it in the so-called "Atlantic Charter" in 1945, which would perpetuate their global hold forever. They called it the so-called "rules-based order", saying little about who made these rules and for what duration. Every rule-based system or institution has a shelf life, a fact of human evolution. But no superpower willingly ever accepted oblivion. At the same time, history is also a witness to the reality that no power or coalition of powers has ever succeeded in fighting the world. One can see how the nationalists in Russia feel about the collapse of the Soviet Union to understand what the Americans may be going through. The Americans thought they had found a "nirvana society" for themselves and the rest of the world through the Breton Woods system, the UN system, and the goddess of electoral democracy. All the other countries were supposed to do was make America great, and they could remain sovereign to the extent that the American interests dictated. The dawn of hard realities of the global power equation and the rising resentment of rapid demographic transition at home make the task of any U.S. administration ever more challenging. The fact that the American electorate is equally dissatisfied with George Bush, Barrack Obama, Donald Trump, or Joe Biden shows that American society's problems have become deeper and more complex. Sadly enough, President Joe Biden also failed to make a difference, although, with long years of experience, even though he was best placed to reverse America's decline. The Indian high-caste Hindus and Jews now take America hostage. The American superpower was briefly referred to, in the last quarter of the 20th century following the Soviet Union's dissolution in 1991, as the "Hyper Power". It is now in an irreversible decline, despite the brave words of its legislators and its "make-believe world" propagandist media. More than anyone else, Americans themselves are responsible for this.

China leads Asian renaissance and reforms

With its huge population, Asia is better endowed. It could bring out "quality out of quantity" to establish its leadership in the next hundred years and become a repository of achievements of the Western societies over the past 500 years for the benefit of future generations of the global family, irrespective of civilization identity. One should not forget that the revival of Asia has been the courtesy of the Western knowledge, education, scholarship, research, and technology institutions that have enabled Asians to recognize and revive their centuries-old cultural and civilizational values. Southeast Asian societies, particularly with an overseas Chinese population, are utilizing their newly found development space to achieve wealth and prosperity through education and technology. The West finds China an enigma. It is baffled, bruised, and biased and shows a lack of respect and understanding. The phenomenal Chinese success with their unique homegrown model for the market economy by combining institutional, structural, and policy reforms with the utilization of social capital and soft power values, has completely put Western minds off balance. The Western intellectual elite had long believed in their own neatly constructed "make-believe" narrative of racial superiority, liberal values, free enterprise, the rule of law, freedom, and pluralist democracy. No wonder China's rise has created serious discomfort and disquiet in the ranks of those Western Nobel laureates who could not see it coming or preferred not to see it. China's success in developing its economic model cannot long be kept away from the notice, view, and attention of a world craving knowledge of the global best practices, irrespective of their source. The truth will be known eventually. The earlier, the better. The International Financial Institutions (IFIs) had long theorized to the developing countries that large populations were a "liability" and the main reason for their backwardness. China's success demonstrates that its huge supply of skilled, disciplined, and cheap workforce had much to do with it. China's spectacular success cannot be dismissed by flimsy grounds of negative and baseless propaganda based on racist bigotry, ideological foundations, a system of government, or economic policies or practices.

Scholars and right-wing strategists in the Western world feel that China has defeated the West in their game and on their turf. China's greatest success, among many, has been in the domain of ideas, dreams, and narratives, which the Western world cannot match. They are left crying hoarsely, seeking allies for the "containment of China" as part of discredited Cold War II narrative. The Western bankruptcy in political thought is evident from the many aspects of recent global developments. For example, bankruptcy is the idea of treating China as if it were the Soviet Union and using discredited "containment" and Cold War II narratives to subvert the rise of the People's Republic of China. China is not the post-1945 Soviet Union, nor is the U.S. the largest creditor nation with 50 percent of the global GDP. In 2022, while the U.S. debt is bulging, the U.S. GDP is 140 percent less than China's GDP (on purchasing power parity basis). China's lead continues to grow. The Western powers, in general, and the Americans, in particular, must know that China is no Soviet Union, which had its own reasons for its fall. On the other hand, China is still in the first phase of its rise, with its great prosperity arriving around 2050, when its GDP will be twice as the U.S. GDP.

"In the half century since 1950, Asia has been the fastest growing part of the world economy, outperforming all other regions. This was in stark contrast with past experience. In the four and a half centuries from 1500 to 1950, Asia stagnated whilst all other regions progressed. In 1500 Asia accounted for 65 per cent of world GDP, and only 18.5 per cent in 1950. Since 1950, the Asian share has doubled. In 1950–1973, Japan had super growth, with per capita income rising over 8 per cent a year compared with the 2.6 per cent for resurgent Asia. In 1973–99 as a whole, per capita growth in resurgent Asia was twice as fast as in Japan. In the 1990s it was four times as fast. Resurgent Asia consists of the 15 countries".[9]

---

[9] Maddison, A. (2001), *The World Economy: A Millennial Perspective*, Paris: OECD. p. 143.

West against the rest

No great power in history ever relinquished its influence and domination willingly, more so if it was a superpower. It was always prepared to give a fight, as it happens daily in the jungle kingdom. Every existing power becomes, however, a "status quo" power and, subsequently, a declining power. All superpowers, though, pass through a period of young adolescence, towards the zenith of power and influence into a plateau phase and eventually into a declining trajectory to become history. Nature ensures rotation, with or without conflict, to ensure the sustainability of human civilization. The old gives in to the new. The weak makes a place for the strength of the "human family" to continue its generational sustainability. Nature brings it about in so many ways that even the strongest of empires, powers, and individuals in world history, had to bow down in front of it. The fall of the European colonial empires and the break-up of the Soviet Union are just a few recent examples in contemporary times. The Western geo-strategists, scholars, or opportunists continue to perpetuate the myth of invincibility, driven by self-interests, short-sighted understanding, and egoistic compulsions. By perpetuating an unjust and unequal world economic order for decades, the Western powers benefited enormously from the "brain drain" and the "capital flight" from the other societies. The Trans-Atlantic powers used the model of "coalition building" and so-called "humanitarian missions" to wage wars and promote conflicts through proxies and direct intervention to maintain their global domination for as long as possible. This strategy is now rendered irrelevant by the fast turn of the worldwide situation. Great powers on the way to dissolution suffer from certain "symptoms": wars, civil disorders, violence, conflicts, xenophobia, riots, arrogance, and, above all, a "delusion" that could all mean a cause or effect: the beginning of the end or the end of the beginning. This natural paradox of power games of stability or disorder does not follow each other neatly.

As a state of civilization, China enjoys overwhelming competitive advantages such as the historical heritage of remaining the world's No.1

economic global power for nine centuries. China's comeback and the current lead are due to visionary and practical leadership, formidable social capital, cultural wealth, systemic organizations, economic strengths, political structures, technological edge, demographic profile, global solidarity, positive worldview, and soft power. There may be several reasons for the Western powers to adopt a self-defeatist and self-destructive approach in international politics concerning the rise of China. One of them could be the decline in intellectual capital of the so-called American Ivy League universities and renowned think tanks. Secondly, Americans do not like to read history. Thirdly, the geographical ignorance because of being shielded by the Antarctic and Pacific Oceans. Forthly, the psychologically depressed mind state, failing to understand foreign people and societies. Fifthly, mainstream media have taught ordinary Americans to be obsessed with themselves and how much the rest of the world loves them and their way of life. Sixthly, the narrative is that those foreigners who dislike the Americans must be either jealous or losers. Such was the simplistic reasoning of former American President George W. Bush. Seventhly, a delusionary belief in the U.S. power to turn other societies to stone ages, without understanding that other aspiring powers have developed the same capabilities now, too. "The much bigger challenge to America's global standing is domestic: American society is deeply polarized and has found it difficult to find consensus on virtually anything. This polarization started over conventional policy issues like taxes and abortion, but since then has metastasized into a bitter fight over cultural identity".[10]

The West has no counter-narrative to BRI

The Western powers led by the U.S. have no real counter-narrative to China's BRI or GDI narratives. President Donald Trump, who raised the slogan

---

[10] Fukuyama, F. (2021), "The end of American hegemony", *The Economist*, London.

"Make America Great Again," ended up losing his re-election bid and leaving behind a chaotic, divided, and depressed America. Democrat President Joe Biden, who has been part of the deep American state since the Vietnam War, was expected to lead his country out of the deep morass in which it landed. Unfortunately, that expectation did not happen. His ratings, as a result, have fallen to the lowest level. There is hardly any consensus among the major stakeholders of the deep American establishment. President Joe Biden, against common sense wisdom, has also preferred to maintain the discredited American policies with respect to China in particular. He has also sought to open a new front with Russia on the Ukraine issue. The American mainstream media are frustrated with the U.S. losing its strategic influence, power, and position. Therefore, they have taken to a propaganda blitz of various forms against China, the Islamic world, the Slavic world (Russia), the Latino world (Mexico), and the African world (Africa), holding them responsible for American fall from global grace and leadership. It is surely a recipe faced with a disaster for the Western world in general and the U.S. in particular. The fact of the matter is that the United States and a few European allies are suffering from a lack of ideas, visions, and strategic thinking and have relegated themselves to a "reaction mode". The Europeans are just following the Americans, who have lost their global position. In a somewhat bizarre move, President Joe Biden touts now "Build Back Better world (B3W) as the Western world's new narrative to compete with China's BRI." Firstly, nobody understands what BBBW means. Secondly, phonetically it sounds clumsy. Thirdly, there was no better world in the first place in the 20th century.

The Western domination of the world from 1500-2000AD in general, the American Century (1920-2020) in particular, was an era of colonial/ imperial exploitation, exterminations, wars, conflicts, genocides, crimes against humanity, environmental destruction, social decay, hate, injustice, and economic inequality. The result of all these were casualties many times more than the combined casualties of the two World Wars, with 90 percent of those being peaceful non-White European communities. The question is whether the Western world intends to recreate the world of the 20th century in the

21st century. If yes, the rest of the world sees BBBW as a non-starter. "The U.S. will not be at the heart of a new world order after this election. The Western world order was built on U.S. military, economic and ideological power. The U.S. was the essential member and de facto leader, not just of Nato but of multilateral institutions such as the World Bank, the International Monetary Fund, and the World Trade Organization. And this free world seemed to be dramatically expanding. After the fall of the Berlin Wall, it even looked like a world, stretching as it did around the planet. In the American crisis that Trump embodies, the whole concept of US-centred world order has imploded."[11]

Belt and Road Initiative and Global Development Initiative – Whose time has arrived

So, as it has been throughout human history, the law of nature is beginning to take its course. The time for a new idea, ideology, framework, or global governance model has arrived. Whether or not anyone likes it, the existing international economic governance order has outlived its utility and is beyond reforms. It has merely perpetuated inequality, injustice, social chaos, environmental destruction, hate, violence, and conflicts. As it is said, "Wherever and whenever there will be Goliath, David will rise." The rise of China and the dawn of an Asian century offer such hope. China, with its formidable cultural heritage, historical experience, social capital, economic prosperity, and positive worldview, can bring together humanity and restore harmony, peace, security, stability, balance, justice, and development. China's geo-economic proposal of the Belt and Road Initiative offers the best hope for building a new global governance order. It is against this background that President Xi Jinping proposed the Belt and Road Initiative (BRI) to revive the ancient land based on the Silk Road in September 2013 during his visit to Kazakhstan. During his

---

[11] *The Guardian newspaper*, November 13, 2016.

visit to Indonesia, in October 2013, he reiterated his plan for building the 21st Century Maritime Silk Route. These were crystallized in his vision to create a "community of a shared future for mankind". The BRI worth US$1.3 trillion investment in connectivity projects, power plants, ports, and infrastructure facilities comprising six corridors connecting China with 65 countries are meant to add US$4 trillion to regional economies and build a prosperous extended neighborhood. It is not only a strategic and timely move, but also more than 129 countries are on board with what is being termed the next phase of globalization. The post-Second World War Western global governance model, authored by the United States, lies badly exposed worldwide during the past three quarters of a century. "The United States has torn itself apart in its counterinsurgent efforts because of its inability to define attainable goals and link them in a way sustainable by the American political process. The military objectives have been too absolute and unattainable and the political ones too abstract and elusive." [12]

The isolation of the U.S. and its few allies and supporters in voting patterns over the past decade on global issues in the United Nations General Assembly is more than evident. "Even the rats leave a sinking ship," goes a South Asian proverb. The decline of the Western powers now comes as an opportunity for the overwhelming majority of the world's population to stand up in solidarity with China to build a shared future. The political and military orders in the world throughout history have always been guided by the strength of the "economic and productive" forces. Rising powers have always left an impact on history. The rise of brands of Chinese merchandise will follow the symbols of Chinese soft power in a gradual but sure way. The clock of history cannot be reversed. The Chinese will increasingly write the new rules of the game in Asia. Because China was never under colonial rule except the coastal cities occupied under unequal treaties with a declining Qing Dynasty, it does not share many values with the West.

---

[12] Kissinger, H. (2021). "The future of American Power", The Economist, London.

China shows the way in sustainable development – Global Development Initiative

Now let's discuss the themes of GDI and China's position and its contribution to international development cooperation. "China achieved astounding success in achieving zero absolute poverty level by lifting nearly 800 million people out of absolute poverty (measured at 2010 constant values, or 2.3 U.S. dollars in terms of purchasing power parity per person a day. This standard is higher than the World Bank's benchmark of 1.9 U.S. dollars per person per day). World Bank data says China contributed 70 percent of worldwide poverty reduction in the last 40 years by Dec 2020.[13]" The IPRCC(International Poverty Reduction Centre in China) is an platform for knowledge sharing, information exchange and international collaboration in poverty reduction and development. In 2021, 480 people participated in its exchange events, of which 44 were vice-ministerial-level officials or above. On October 19, 2021, 106 case studies collected during the second call of the Global Solicitation on Best Poverty Reduction Practices were recognized for their excellence at the 2021 International Seminar on Global Poverty Reduction Partnerships in Beijing.

The IPRCC is actively promoting intellectual exchanges and knowledge sharing as seen only from the cases of some major events in 2021, including: Seminar on Global Poverty Reduction Partnerships and Rural Development in Post-COVID-19 Era; Release of the best poverty reduction and development practices from China's Gansu Province; International Seminar on Best Poverty Reduction Case Studies; Forum to share poverty expertise between China, Latin America, and the Caribbean; China's VNR Report on Implementation of the 2030 Agenda for Sustainable Development. In the year 2020, some of the major international events organized by IPRCC included the Poverty Reduction and Development Forum, the 8th ASEAN+3 Village

---

[13] Poverty Alleviation: China's Experience and Contribution [White Paper], State Council Information Office of the People's Republic of China, April 6, 2021, retrieved from http://english.scio.gov.cn

Leaders Exchange Program, the Workshop on China-Japan-South Korea Rural Vitalization Experiences, the 13th ASEAN-China Forum on Social Development and Poverty, the 2019 FOCAC Africa-China Poverty Reduction and Development, and the Conference on China-Africa Partnership for Poverty Reduction held in Uganda. China promotes ecological civilization, environmental bio-diversity, curb on pollution, and mitigation of climate change. China is a major contributor to global agricultural development and food security initiatives. China's engagement with the global community developed bilaterally as well as under the auspices of the UN's Food and Agriculture Organization's South-South Cooperation established in 1996. Since then, China has sent more than 1000 experts to 37 countries and has received experts from more than 100 countries. China has signed 150 agriculture cooperation agreements with 60 countries and international organizations, including 50 African states. The main forms of Chinese foreign aid include complete projects; goods and materials; technical cooperation and human resources development cooperation; medical teams and volunteers; emergency humanitarian aid; and debt relief (for interest-free loans). China's economic and development cooperation accelerated considerably since the "Going-out" policy was introduced in 2000. "China is now one of the world's ten largest providers of development assistance, but China's development assistance is dwarfed by the much larger policy bank lending to developing countries. Official Chinese statistics state that between 2010 and 2012, China appropriated a total of USD 14.41 billion for foreign assistance commitments: 56 percent in concessional loans, 36 percent in grants, and 8 percent in interest-free loans (State Council, 2014). The China Africa Research Initiative at the Johns Hopkins School of Advanced International Studies finds that the Chinese government, banks, and contractors extended USD 94.4 billion worth of commercial and concessional loans from 2000 to 2015 to African governments and state-owned enterprises."[14]

---

[14] Carter, B. (2017), China's aid to developing countries, retrieved from www.gsdrc.org

China has merely taken only forty years to reverse the engineering progress the Western world took four hundred years to build through the wars of extermination, looting, plunder, gunboat diplomacy, imposition of canon, and cross. The Chinese have instead achieved this miracle, their ancient civilization's "soft power" heritage, without recourse to any conflict, wars, looting, and plunder. The Chinese revival proves that Asians are far smarter, and given good leadership and systemic reforms, they can revive their societies even under difficult conditions. China has faced extreme sanctions, boycotts, tariffs, strict conditions, outright discrimination, stringent rules for entry into the World Trade Organization, anti-dumping duties, protracted Western media hostility, and propaganda. Over the centuries, the Chinese have borne the indignities with patience and fortitude without being distracted from their mission of rejuvenating their state of civilization. The rise of China and the advent of an Asian century will ensure that these actions will never be repeated. The Asians can surely forgive but not forget their history of humiliation.

Conclusions

Human history shows that a power with ideas is larger, stronger, and long-lasting than the power itself. But all powers, like the ideas they stem from, have a shelf life too, because of the dynamic heavenly construct of life itself, in which the only constant element is "change". The power of ideas once made Athens, Rome, Baghdad, Xi'an, Istanbul, Paris, London, Berlin, Moscow, and New York recognized. According to the British economist and historian Angus Maddison, China remained the number one power for more than nine centuries in history. China's lead has been rooted in the strength of its centuries-old value system tested. The Communist Party of China has effectively exploited the advantages of "Chinese characteristics". It is the same power of ideas that has put Beijing and Shanghai among the front-line cities of the future. The overwhelming majority of the global population in Asia, Europe, Africa, Latin America, and the Caribbean welcome China's rise. The developing world is thrilled by China's masterstroke diplomacy initiative for building a "community of a shared future". It is indeed a once-in-a-century move at a time when history is taking a turn.

The Western world is divided, and the United States has lost the global leadership it had enjoyed since the end of the First World War and the Treaty of Versailles signed in 1919, particularly since the end of the Second World war and the signing of the Atlantic Charter in 1941. The 20th century undoubtedly belonged to the Americans, who made history in wars, conflicts, politics, economics, education, science, technology, environment research, exploration, innovation, defense, and diplomacy. That American era, for all practical purposes, is over now! For several reasons, the advent of the 21st century marks the end of the American-led 20th Century. They include stagnating economy, bulging debt, divided polity, chaotic society, disturbing demographics, reluctant allies, declining influence, fading social capital, weakening governance, rising inequality, lagging research, and lost technological edge. However, the greatest deficit of the current U.S. paradox is in the domain of ideas. The U.S. has no option but to repeat old discredited "containment and cold war narratives," building so-called "Quad"[15] and "AUKUS" coalitions for the global realities of the 21st century. Unfortunately, some states have joined the U.S. instead of standing up to such strategic follies. The power of an idea, such as the BRI and GDI, to shape and build human destiny has only just begun. No propaganda against China can stop the BRI or GDI. The world had enough troubles, tribulations, hate, conflicts, violence, and wars over the past century. It was a nightmare for the world community. The Chinese are adored globally for their hard work, humility, discipline, family values, mild manners, rational mindset, moderate outlook, pragmatic style, low profile, cautious optimism, resilience, diligence, teamwork, community spirit, networking, patience, solidarity, passion, and determination. China has no colonial power's historical burden. It has always remained within its centuries' old boundaries.

---

[15] The abbreviation of Quadrilateral Security Dialogue.

Trust in China far exceeds trust in any Western influence among the masses of the developing nations. The world needs a break! Fortunately, nature provides such an opportunity every century or two centuries. Indeed, the 21st century will be shaped by the BRI and GDI. Both initiatives are based on a positive worldview promoting cooperation, collaboration, and connectivity for win-win cooperations for a world with shared dreams, prosperity, and future destiny.

Kim Jin Ho

A professor and journalist, Ph.D. at the School of International Relations, Peking University. According to his research, East Asian society is characterized by a mixture of tradition and modernity and is moving toward the international community. It plays an important role economically and culturally. In particular, China's history of change and development is a part of world history that deserves attention. He wrote *Xi Jinping New Era* (Korean version, co-authored) and more than 30 papers, including *Research on Chinese Traditional Political Thought and Political Culture in the Age of Xi Jinping*. Currently, he writes a column on current affairs in Asian Weekly from Hong Kong, China.

Traditions and Present Situation of the Chinese Society and Culture in the Era of Xi Jinping

Leader of China and His Political Philosophy

The Chinese society and culture in the era of Xi Jinping are being developed within the framework of the state administration system, laws, and social norms organized or formulated under the leadership of the Communist Party of China (CPC). It means that the basic policies for leading national and social development also need adjustments in accordance with the socialist political system to promote the development of socialism with Chinese characteristics under the leadership of the CPC. In the era of Xi Jinping, the society and culture will be developed under the guidance of the CPC and centering on the theme of "developing a socialist culture with Chinese characteristics in the new era." This also means that a stable society and culture will be built by strengthening the government's capability to govern.

Generally speaking, the "Chinese Dream" represents a process in which China realizes its territorial integrity, the Chinese people unite as one, the comprehensive national strength of China is enhanced, and China ultimately wins the respect of the international community. In this process, the overall plan for fulfilling the "Chinese Dream" is to transform China from a socialist developing country into a moderately developed country and realize the great rejuvenation of the Chinese nation through the transition from building a moderately prosperous society to finally becoming a society of great harmony under the current political system of China. Such an overall plan of national development has been implemented more comprehensively since the second term of office of Xi Jinping. However, many problems need urgent resolution for China, including maintaining sustained economic development, preserving social stability, avoiding environmental pollution deterioration, and narrowing the gap between the rich and the poor. On the other hand, it is also important for China to maintain good relationships with other major countries and its neighboring countries. In this process, inevitably, things would not go off smoothly. Despite so many difficulties and challenges, it is clear that the efforts made to eliminate poverty and its results during the terms of office of Xi Jinping can be regarded as important political achievements and great contributions in the era of Xi Jinping.

In the era of Xi Jinping, sticking to the values of building a global community with a shared future, China hopes all members of the international community can achieve mutual respect and pursue common development. From this perspective, China's view of international politics is in fact based on Chinese thinking. With such a political view, China must maintain its influence while integrating itself into the international community. Being aware of this, China has often stressed its hope of achieving mutual respect through multilateral cooperation. Although China's efforts fail to be responded to extensively in the international community within a short time, China will inevitably progress in its multilateral cooperation as long as the Chinese government continues to work hard.

Regarding China's current development, the socialist system with Chinese characteristics conforms to current conditions in China. Under such a characteristic system that serves as the guiding philosophy of the CPC, the nation and the society have made further development in the new era. The domestic political goals set may not necessarily be closely linked with the problems of the international community at any time. However, the Chinese government still hopes to steadily pursue common development with other countries based on social stability and global communication. In other words, Chinese politics emphasizes fulfilling domestic political goals when carrying out the strategy of handling diplomatic relations. Such a choice is made based on the fact that China is a vast and populous country and owns the political experience garnered from its long history.

Prior to the era guided by the CPC, China underwent revolutions and turbulence in modern times when it was vulnerable to attacks because of long-term backwardness and invasion. Since the founding of the People's Republic of China under the leadership of the CPC, China has gradually developed and grown stronger. With notable achievements obtained since the implementation of the reform and opening-up policy, China has seen the growth of its national strength. In the era of Xi Jinping, with the integration of the past political elements with economic elements featuring socialism with Chinese characteristics, a new model of sustainable development conforming better to the domestic and international political situation has taken shape in China. Among what has been done in this era, formulating policies to handle corresponding domestic and international affairs while developing the society and culture is in line with the political philosophy of Xi Jinping. Simply put, the Chinese government stresses that a system of social development and cultural inheritance guided by the government should be put in place.

Beginning from the legend about "Three Emperors and Five Sovereigns", the successive dynasties ruling the Central Plains in China and the nomadic tribes from the north of China had been confronted or merged with each other. China constantly expanded its territory and cultural influence in such a process. From the perspective of historical evolution, the Chinese nation is still inheriting the traditional culture, and the Chinese civilization is still thriving. Currently, China still works hard to prove the existence of the Xia Dynasty before the Shang Dynasty (the earliest dynasty of China supported by archaeological evidence). Such a spirit of attaching importance to passing on history, culture, and traditions of its own ethnic groups confirms the close link between Chinese history and the current efforts of the Chinese people to develop its own culture, which is a cultural trait inherent in the Chinese nation. In other words, China regards historical inheritance as the basis of national orthodoxy. China is intended to build socialism with Chinese characteristics instead of the so-called socialism as preached by Western countries. On the one hand, China is required to complete the reunification of its territory; on the other, China made effort to demonstrate to the world how to create advanced cultural achievements that integrate long historical traditions with current national conditions in China. Historically, China began to accept modern civilization at the end of the feudal society and founded the Republic of China through revolution. And Chinese people made concerted efforts in the founding of the People's Republic of China. Although China had experienced long feudal dynasties, numerous leaders put forward their views and propositions after a modern China was established. In the evolution of modern China, the Chinese government and its leaders held the view that the dream of China and the Chinese nation should follow the tide of the times despite the long-existing clash of power. The present Chinese government adheres to and promotes such a view.

The feudal rule that had lasted for thousands of years was overthrown by the 1911 Revolution, and the founding of the Republic of China followed the collapse of the Qing Dynasty. It means that China got rid of the straitjacket of feudal dynasties and attempted to evolve into an entirely new Western-style country. However, the compatriots involved in overthrowing the feudal dynasties and founding the Republic of China with Dr. Sun Yat-sen (1866–1925) as the central leader of the revolution failed to break free of the constraints of Chinese "traditions" thoroughly. Yuan Shikai (1859–1916) was to blame because he attempted to restore the hereditary monarchy after becoming the president of the Republic of China following the abdication of the last emperor of the Qing Dynasty. It can be seen that the then leaders of the Chinese nation wanted to break away from the conventions of history and establish a new society in a new country by launching a Western-style capitalist revolution. However, they were overburdened with Chinese history, traditions, and culture under the circumstances at that time. When speaking of the political issues in China, leaders in modern times and today invariably mention the traditional Chinese culture. Obviously, it is hard for Chinese society to accept the sweeping change in traditional social life, habits, and customs, it is hard for Chinese society to accept the sweeping change in traditional social life, habits, and customs at once, although socialism has become as the framework and tool of the Chinese revolution.

China today is called "G2" in the field of economy. In the era of Xi Jinping, the ruling legitimacy of the CPC in the historical context is further affirmed. The problems needing urgent resolution in China today are also listed. To a certain degree, the appearance of the term "Chinese Dream" is aimed to stress that Xi Jinping may probably become the special leader who will resolve the major questions left by Chinese history.

However, will China be able to become a developed country in the era of Xi Jinping? Will China restore its past prosperity that profoundly influenced the world economy and culture? The answers are yet to be known. At any rate, China needs Xi Jinping's leadership in all respects, including politics, economy, society, and culture. The CPC will continue to lead the development of China. But it remains to be observed whether the Chinese people and society will adapt to and continue to support the present policies. The Chinese society and culture, seen from many aspects, can become the barometer reflecting the social phenomena, including Chinese politics, law, and governance. In other words, the strength of the government can be enhanced, and China's external influences will be extended if the government can continue to be supported by the Chinese people and bring about changes favorable to the society. Suppose there appear the phenomena of going against the policies of the Chinese government, and unexpected problems arise in implementing the government-set policies concerning socialist cultural development. In that case, the political power led by Xi Jinping may be faced with severe challenges, and the government's influence will be seriously undermined both at home and abroad.

The social and cultural phenomena created by ordinary people are closely linked with the economy in the long history of China, which has had a far-reaching influence on China's leadership. Currently, Xi Jinping prioritizes various problems arising among the Chinese people and in all spheres of Chinese society. In addition, given that the external issues will ultimately influence China's domestic environment and further impact the Chinese people and the Chinese society, Chinese politics, for most of its parts, can be regarded as being tightly linked with the Chinese people and the Chinese society. Proceeding from its realities, China has finally selecte the socialist market economy system whereby it centers on the policy of encouraging agricultural and commercial development and giving impetus to economic growth.

When it comes to personal standing, the ordinary people under the feudal rule would never become country leaders even though ensuring the country's prosperity and people's peaceful life was also the core task of running the country in Chinese feudal dynasties. After the founding of the PRC, however, those who have fought heroically for the country and worked hard in its construction are entitled to ascend to the high positions once held by rulers of the feudal dynasties. Moreover, those who have long served as national civil servants (the CPC members) and obtained political achievements are also qualified to become members of the leadership team. This is similar to the traditional way of selecting talents in Chinese history. The current CPC leadership also adopts a way to choose and train talents identical to the traditional personnel system. The leaders of China today still shoulder heavy responsibilities for the whole Chinese nation. In other words, the Chinese leaders should work hard to meet people's expectations for a happy life and build a country characterized by economic affluence, powerful military force, and cultural prosperity.

As the current paramount leader of China, Xi Jinping should take responsibility for the present and future of the Chinese nation. Chinese politics and culture today will inevitably become an important part of history tomorrow. To build a country with a stable society and a flourishing culture, it is necessary to observe the present social situation reflected in various phenomena that also test whether the country's leaders correctly rule the country. China's political philosophy, domestic governance, and international strategy cannot be isolated from the Chinese people and society. Chinese leaders prioritize national security and people's safety. It is on this point that there is no essential difference between the past and present ruling practices. In line with the Chinese political philosophy, more attention should be given to overseas Chinese and foreign citizens of Chinese origin in addition to focusing on the Chinese people. The significance at a higher level for the country should be considered when issues are considered; in particular, history should not be ignored when policies are carried out. Such a political outlook seems to have been universally recognized by the Chinese.

The socialist system continues to be maintained in China today, and it is being constantly improved to benefit people and make the country rich and powerful. It not only signifies the success of the socialist system but also testifies that the Chinese leaders can fulfill the dream of the Chinese people through such a state system. The Republic of China is founded on the concept of building a socialist country, and it does not deny the achievements of the founders of the PRC and their successive national leaders. The national leaders of the PRC at different periods have taken as their historical mission and responsibility to build a more developed country and society and meet people's needs. So does Xi Jinping, who is embarking on the path of putting into practice the historical mission of the Chinese nation. In this sense, creating a culture with Chinese characteristics should also be regarded as an important task for Chinese leaders in addition to considering issues of politics, economy, safety, and military affairs. The formation of such a society and such kind of culture can be said to provide an inexhaustible source for uniting people and enhancing national strength. In Xi Jinping's era, China faces a more complex and volatile situation than in any other period after the founding of the PRC and has opened to the outside world at a higher level. Therefore, the formation of a social atmosphere and prosperous cultural development is endowed with important historical significance.

From the overall global perspective, the degree of Chinese society's openness differs from that of the Western democratic society in terms of law and order. Therefore, the Chinese government urgently needs to stress the legitimacy and correctness of establishing Chinese-style law and order conforming to China's national conditions through building "socialism with Chinese characteristics." A general survey of China's feudal period and the Republic of China demonstrates that China's society is by no means backward against the historical background of China despite that it is different from the Western democratic society in terms of development and social systems. In particular, Chinese people's "life quality" has improved greatly due to the changes in the economic environment and the increasing degree of opening to the outside world. In the era of Xi Jinping, the attempts to change China through carrying out deep reform account for why the role of the government is stressed in ruling the country and administering the society.

The 1911 Revolution directly led to the downfall of the Qing Dynasty and the onset of the Republic of China. The CPC waged the War of Liberation and conducted a socialist revolution, and domestic political struggles took place. Isn't it that the orthodox view of "leaders and the world under heaven" as upheld by the Chinese people is put into practice by "leaders and people"? It can be regarded as the basic view of Chinese leaders about people and nation. It can be seen from this that the "Chinese Dream" proposed by Xi Jinping not only represents the integrity of China's territory and the harmony of all ethnic groups in China, but also symbolizes China's national tradition and demonstrates China's determination to stand on its own at the top of the world, which has always been the firm belief of the Communist Party of China in the country and the world.

In other words, the dream of the Chinese leaders lies in working hard to build China with a long historical tradition into a better country to enhance the Chinese nation's self-esteem and make China stand at the top of the world. The Chinese dream can be regarded as the product of combining the ideals of Chinese leaders about developing the country and the dream of the Chinese people. From this perspective, like the previous successful leaders of the Chinese nation, the present leader Xi Jinping also takes as his historical tasks to make China stronger, improve the economic prosperity, and enhance the national confidence. However, China sometimes comes into conflict with some members of the international community. Therefore, whether China can integrate into the world with its own values or change itself to adapt to the world order remains to be seen. For example, East Asia has been deeply influenced by Chinese culture since ancient times. In today's world, China's changes will have a great impact on East Asia. We don't know whether this impact will be positive or negative? In any case, this will affect the development of China's relations with relevant countries and the development of the world order.

Life Experience of Xi Jinping and His Governance Philosophy

Development of Xi Jinping's political philosophy is closely related to his life experience. Based on his historical view on China, Xi Jinping has a strong will to achieve sustainable development in China. Some scholars believe that Xi Jinping has turned his experience into his political philosophy about national development by putting forward the "Chinese Dream". In his speeches and work reports, Xi has often mentioned rule of law, deepening reforms, the Chinese Dream, and building a community with a shared future. Xi also stresses the importance of "Further consolidate national strength by developing economic strength and maintain national security and its diplomatic strength by building a stable government leadership." What he emphasizes is consistent with the proposition building "a community with a shared future for mankind," which has become the basic values China promotes in its communication with other countries. Such values stress the interdependence among members of the international community and the consistency of China's development, and the development of the world as a whole.

People generally acknowledge that it is necessary to learn about life experience of Xi Jinping before understanding his political philosophy. Xi Jinping was one of those urban school graduates sent to the countryside for resettlement during the "cultural revolution". In those days, he overcame difficulties and obstacles, became a CPC member, received a college education, and learned how to become a leader by giving on-site direction at the primary-level government organizations. With such life experiences, Xi Jinping gained a full understanding of the society and the country by observing political and economic phenomena based on traditional Chinese thinking, guided by the thought of socialism with Chinese characteristics. He gradually formed his political values about national development and people's wellbeing.

In the following brief introduction, we can learn how Xi Jinping developed his career by overcoming difficulties and building up his political philosophy about the CPC and the nation.

It should be pointed out first that a key point in the thoughts of Xi Jinping is to achieve peaceful development along with other countries in the world with the happiness of Chinese people as the basis. Before becoming a leader of the Central Committee of the CPC, Xi Jinping had accumulated a large amount of work experience in Fujian, Zhejiang, Shanghai, and other places. He had a thorough understanding of China's economic development and society. He had worked for alomost 18 years in Fujian, a province separated from Taiwan by a strip of water, where he obtained a fuller understanding of the situation of Taiwan. He has made resolving the Taiwan Question to realize national reunification an important goal of his governance. Fujian is inhabited by many people from Taiwan who are active in all fields of society. Fujian is also geographically linked and culturally and economically bonded with Taiwan through water and air transportation. It was probably in Fujian that Xi started to form his political thoughts of realizing China's economic and social development, increasing national strength, and realizing the reunification of the country. In other words, Xi Jinping was sent to live and work at Liangjiahe in Sha'anxi Province at a young age. Such experiences shaped Xi's character and views about the country, the CPC, and its organization. Later, his work experiences in Fujian, an economically developed province neighboring Taiwan, helped him form his policies about China's economic and social development and national reunification.

Xi Jinping's work experiences at primary-level organizations provide valuable wealth to him when he puts into practice his strategic concepts about national development. It can be seen Xi Jinping is a leader who has both political ideals and the ability to live up to his ideals. While strengthening diplomatic ties between China and the international community, Xi Jinping is also devoted to putting into practice the Chinese-style worldview as mentioned in the Chinese Dream.

In the era of Xi Jinping, the development of Chinese society and culture focuses on forming a stable environment where Xi Jinping Thoughts and political philosophy of Xi Jinping can be implemented to build socialism with Chinese characteristics vigorously. To this purpose, first of all, it is necessary to change the present situation of China from the cultural aspect, promote cultural dissemination with the vision described in the blueprint for the future, and effectively narrow the rich-poor gap between urban and rural areas through eliminating the gap between the rich and poor, constructing modernized cities and advancing urbanization development. It means the Chinese government will further impose policy-based interferences with cultural development and social order and advocate creating an advanced culture compatible with economic and social development.

Like previous leaders, Xi Jinping often quotes ancient Chinese texts reflecting traditional Chinese thinking. It demonstrates that Xi Jinping takes a strong interest in, loves, and feels proud of traditional Chinese culture and history. It also shows Xi Jinping is given appropriate support from his political think tank. The notion of rule of law, as stressed by Xi Jinping, combines the thoughts of the Legalist School in ancient China and part of the Western philosophy of law and expresses the importance of China following the correct path of development. If China goes the wrong way in its development, it will "head in the direction opposite to its intention," and its efforts will never amount to anything. The path of "socialism with Chinese characteristics" that China adheres to in the era of Xi Jinping can be said to represent the fundamental principle of rule of law. Such a path emphasizes the following points: "First, upholding the leadership of the CPC; second, ensuring that the people are the masters of the country; third, ensuring that everyone is equal before the law; fourth, promoting a combination of the rule of law and rule of virtue; and fifth, proceeding from the actual conditions of China in all endeavors." The path further clearly points out that upholding the "deepening reforms" and "rule of law" is the basic guideline of the socialist construction in China. In other words, traditional Chinese political thoughts are rapidly merged with socialist political thoughts; the changes in law and order take place in Chinese society under the leadership of the CPC.

In retrospect, Xi Jinping returned to the school campus after the institutes of higher learning recruited students again. Probably he envisaged from then on what would be necessary for the future development of the society and the country. In the relevant speeches of Xi Jinping, the socialist system with Chinese characteristics has been fully integrated with traditional Chinese thoughts. It means that changes and development will take place in China by blending traditional Chinese beliefs, socialism with Chinese characteristics, and a socialist market economy. From such a perspective, building a socialist culture with Chinese characteristics will undoubtedly become the basic condition of creating the atmosphere of Chinese society.

| Social and Cultural Characteristics in the Era of Xi Jinping

The present Chinese society and culture can be said to have the following distinctive characteristics:

First, the present Chinese society and culture have slowly taken shape following the founding of a socialist country, the strengthening of the ideological commitment to socialism, and the initiation of reform and opening-up policy. It demonstrates distinctive Chinese characteristics. Politically, the present Chinese society and culture are based on the thoughts of socialism with Chinese characteristics; in the final analysis, it is not cut off from the traditional Chinese society and culture. Part of the society and culture is undergoing constant development and changes. It becomes an important motive that can promote China's continuous growth and the unity of people under the guidance of the CPC.

Second, the socialist culture with Chinese characteristics plays the role of a cohesive force for the compatriots in Taiwan, Hong Kong, Macao, and overseas Chinese who live in an environment different from the Chinese mainland. Objectively speaking, positive affirmation should be given to the constant development of China, and positive comments should be made about Chinese society and culture through media publicity. The Chinese government always forges a bond with the overseas Chinese by integrating the traditional Chinese culture with the contemporary socialist culture. In their efforts to closely link Chinese society and culture with overseas Chinese, foreigners of Chinese descent, and other countries worldwide, the organizations and societies established by China also encourage relevant activities. In particular, in the era of Xi Jinping, the Chinese government is implementing a targeted strategy for rendering effective overseas publicity by adjusting the media outlets in charge of international publicity. These efforts demonstrate the positive side of Chinese society and culture and elicit positive changes in the perspective of looking at China on the part of the external world.

Third, more comprehensive social and cultural administration is being exercised in the era of Xi Jinping than in the reform and opening-up period when high-speed development was achieved. We believe the reinforced administration aims to eliminate the negative elements accumulated in rapid economic growth and social changes. From the perspective of political analysis, such administration represents the government's means to strengthen the power of control. It also demonstrates the leader's sense of mission toward the changes and development of China. The opinions appear that it is a political retreat when "the Chinese government makes the political influences more felt than before in the relevant fields of society and culture." Seen from the present government's stance, however, strengthening the administration is a political choice made for the long-term development of China. It is also a policy formulated by the government for social and cultural development in China today.

Fourth, the Chinese government has become aware that the inequitable, irregular, and unreasonable phenomena run rampant daily with the continued development of the market economy in China. Some analysis points out that many phenomena deviating from the fundamental concepts of socialism appeared along with the rapid economic development in governance and social administration. Some other analysts believe China will not be able to continue to develop stably unless these problems are resolved in the era of Xi Jinping. In other words, many existing issues in Chinese society have been exposed despite the continued economic growth since the beginning of the 21st Century. To address these problems, the government led by Xi Jinping believes that the government must tighten the regulation of society and culture while pursuing the economic progress to deal with the present low growth registered under the "New Normal".

Fifth, creating a socialist culture with Chinese characteristics is a policy based on the spirit of building China into a "role model" of socialism in the era of Mao Zedong for anti-corruption campaign to achieve sustainable development in China. In the age of Xi Jinping, efforts are always made to invigorate the market economy and to turn a society laying excessive stress on material progress into a healthy and sound one. In this process, the government attaches importance to developing and improving the socialist system through films, radio programs, publications, and other forms of publicity. The analysis points out that in the eyes of the Chinese government, if capitalist elements are blindly accepted, the government will lose its capability to control society. Such a loss may lead to social division and chaos that may be taken advantage of by foreign forces.

Generally speaking, many basic works have been done and represent the necessary changes for promoting further development based on China's present times and environment.

Economic Development and Social Stability in the Era of Xi Jinping

Chinese society has undergone tremendous changes since Xi Jinping started his governance at the end of 2012. Some scholars believe that China builds a strong social foundation by implementing an anti-corruption policy, improves governance efficiency through paying attention to people's needs, and therefore provides incentives for stably developing the Chinese society and overcoming difficulties. From securing a victory in the fight against poverty to achieving phased results in preventing and controlling COVID-19, the Chinese government has made considerable efforts and contributions to eliminating the negative elements arising in the past. What is worth mentioning is that China successfully held the 2022 Winter Olympics in Beijing against adverse circumstances and under the unprecedented pressure of fighting against COVID-19. Such a feat is of special significance.

As to the characteristics of economic policies and necessary improvements in the era of Xi Jinping, I summarize my opinions into the following points:

First, one of the achievements in the economic policies in the era of Xi Jinping is making appropriate and stable adjustments to China's economy, which was characterized by extensive development. The government builds a relatively stable economic structure based on reform and law-based governance despite many problems in the real estate and finance sectors. China's economic and industrial structures need improvements in many aspects, however. Adopting legal means, the market and policies should be considered more to promote reform further.

Second, the problems with China's labor force are not confined to rural areas and farmers but pose severe challenges to China at large. Developing rural areas and agriculture and lifting the population living under the poverty line out of poverty is always important for the sustainable development of China's economy. Objectively speaking, great efforts have been made to address these problems in the era of Xi Jinping. China hopes to realize balanced development across the country by attaching importance to rural areas and agriculture. It will lay a sound foundation for the stable development of not only China but also the whole international community.

Third, financial reform lays the foundation for the steady implementation of economic policies in China. The financial system constitutes one of the basic elements for trade and industries' sustainable and healthy development. Only when financial reform can be further advanced will China have the motive to continue to grow in strength. In this sense, great achievements have been scored in the real economy in the era of Xi Jinping when reforms targeting agriculture, the manufacturing industry, and the service industry have been steadily implemented. In the long run, steady adjustment of the macroeconomy must be coordinated with the development of the real economy that has direct bearing on the people. At the same time, ensuring the connection with the international economy may also help China's long-term development.

Fourth, the achievements in urban development and balancing urban and rural development have been obtained by relying on the high-speed development of transportation and logistics. Because of this, the Chinese government needs to devise a long-term plan for the urbanized development of backward areas and the distribution and adjustment of population and industries. In particular, the Chinese government needs to continue to make macroscopic adjustments as to the well-being of the elders and children, education and employment.

Fifth, China has achieved impressive achievements in developing science and technology and relevant fields of economy. Based on these achievements, the smart urbanization organically connected with science parks and related investments will provide considerable impetus for China's long-term development. From this perspective, investments should be increased in training talents, and the reform should be intensified to make scientific and technological innovations.

Sixth, excessive consumption became a common phenomenon along with the growing wealth accumulation in Chinese society. Finding a solution to excessive consumption and low efficiency will provide another incentive for the sustained development of China's economy. The Chinese government should continue to adopt relevant reform measures to promote social development.

Seventh, an adage says, "the will of the people can be regarded as the will of Heaven." The relevant reforms conducted during the era of Xi Jinping have significantly contributed to the formation of a sound social system and good social atmosphere that are favorable for national development. To build a developed country at a higher level, however, it is necessary to create a more stable and positive social space for the people. Because of this, I believe that the social atmosphere of achieving sustainable development should be further created, and efforts should be strengthened to raise national awareness and educational level.

A review of China's development process shows that China has made changes and progress on an unprecedented scale in the world since the 1980s. China has developed from a backward agricultural country into an economic power. It is attributed to the joint efforts of successive Chinese leaders and all Chinese people. However, excessive consumption, the gap between the rich and the poor, and other social problems run rampant behind the rapid economic development. The development in the era of Xi Jinping is characterized by "uprooting corruption in the society, achieving stable development, and depicting the blueprint for the future development of the country and society." Historically, extravagance and excessive consumption spread from urban areas to rural areas, from schools to workplaces. Active actions have been taken to address these problems, creating a new social atmosphere for healthy national development. The wide gap between the rich and the poor has been constantly narrowed with the improvement of the well-being of both farmers and urban laborers. All the people, entrepreneurs included, are working unremittingly for common prosperity. It is undoubtedly a great accomplishment for the future development.

In the past, some people in China blindly pursued and went for things imported or introduced from abroad. In comparison, however, now products and commodities with the Chinese cultural features are increasingly popular with the Chinese people. It shows the improvement in the quality of the products made in China and proves the increasing confidence the Chinese people place in domestically manufactured products. It also means great changes have occurred in people's mindsets and behaviors over the past ten years with the social progress and economic development. More importantly, however, the government guiding the people has exerted profound influences on society with their political philosophy.

As the world is still undergoing complicated changes, the economic cooperation among different members of the international community does not run smoothly. To make matters worse, wars break out from time to time.

However, the case of China demonstrates that so long as the government, the national leader, and the people are united to make joint efforts, they may create a joint force to promote the further development of the society and the country, no matter how hard the situation may be. Although China is faced with many problems, and the Chinese government and society need to be changed in many respects, having a powerful leader and government means that China enjoys more sustainable development opportunities under the present circumstances.

As far as I see, there is no right answer regarding the confrontation between China and the US. The continuation of such a confrontation is unfavorable to both countries. China and the US vary in the degree of their cooperation and conflict. Over a long period to come, China and the US may enter a vicious circle of alternation between cooperation and confrontation. I believe that both China and the US will enjoy increasing cooperation opportunities so long as China can maintain its development speed and social stability. In this sense, multilateralism, mutual benefit, equality, and mutual respect are important in international politics. Therefore, strengthening the cooperation between China and its neighboring countries and other countries in the world and integrating global values with Chinese values will play an increasingly significant role in helping China's development.

I believe a stable foundation for economic development has been laid through implementing the standard rules and social regulation. Under such circumstances, the US and other major countries will increasingly seek opportunities to cooperate with China if China can maintain domestic and international economic progress and a social and national order despite global changes. China has suffered from natural disasters and external invasions for a long time. Since the founding of the People's Republic of China, China has sought to develop in a way that suits China politically and economically. And since the implementation of the reform and opening policy, China has steadily developed economically and culturally. This time-saving development has entered a stage where China's political economy and social culture must be reorganized once again. And with the changes in the international environment,

China has also entered a stage where it must prepare foreign policies that fit the new environment.

Maintain a positive relationship between China and South Korea

While China and South Korea have long maintained a positive cooperation, there are structurally negative elements within such relationship. In their long history of mutual communication, China and South Korea sometimes become mutually cooperative partners and sometimes contain each other due to geopolitical and historical reasons. From a future perspective, both countries within the Asian cultural circle should maintain their respective cultural characteristics and coordinate with each other for innovation and joint development.

When Northeast Asia was plunged into the imperialist colonist war, China and South Korea joined to fight against invaders. However, both countries confronted each other during the Cold War following the end of the Second World War. It can be said that great changes took place in the relation between the two countries because of the evolution of the international situation. History shows that South Korea has made remarkable achievements known as the "Miracle of the Han River" and hosted the 1988 Summer Olympics. At that time, neoliberalism in the world created an opportunity for South Korea and China to establish diplomatic relations. At that time South Korea implemented "Northern Policy" to establish diplomatic relations with socialist countries. The establishment of diplomatic relations between South Korea and China was achieved through the interaction of China's reform and opening-up policies and South Korea's Northern Policy. The experience drawn from South Korea played the "channeling water" role in China's economic development when it launched the reform and opening-up policies. It proves that mutual complementation is favorable to the joint development of both countries. It was a decision of historical significance for South Korea to establish diplomatic relations with China during the term of President Roh Tae-woo, symbolizing the new beginning of the relation between both countries. South Korea is a capitalist country practicing a market economy under the Western political system. At the same time, China is a socialist country confronted with South Korea during the "Cold War". Establishing diplomatic relations is a significant decision favorable for the development of both China and South Korea. Both countries' leaders improved the relation between their countries with visions by getting out of the ideological straightjacket under the hard circumstances then. For this reason, both countries should be grateful for those who fought to make the present possible. With success in implementing the reform and opening-up policy and increasing national strength, China also makes unremitting efforts to realize peace and stability in the Korean Peninsula and the world.

Economic and cultural communication has increased following the establishment of diplomatic relations between both countries, which greatly promotes the further development of bilateral ties. It is positive. However, further development of the bilateral relation is hindered by the accumulated contradictions, although both countries can examine their relation with the changes in the international social environment. The hindrance is mainly manifested in the national defense issue centering on the Korean Peninsula.

In terms of China, the Chinese government was interested in learning the industrial technologies and economic development experience of South Korea after both countries established diplomatic relations. The young Chinese people know a lot about the popular culture and way of life in South Korea. In each of the three decades leading to the upcoming 30th anniversary of the establishment of diplomatic relations between both countries, the impression left by South Korea on the then-Chinese people has been greatly different from that of the young Chinese people. As China has become the second largest economy in the world with its influences gradually felt in the international community, the Chinese people born in this period hope they will win recognition from all members of the international community, with South Korea included. They also hope that China will no longer be looked down upon as it was before and during the early days of the reform and opening-up period. Such hope is more or less enlightening to South Korea.

In the communication between the two countries, both governments should provide their citizens with more communication opportunities based on a social atmosphere characterized by mutual respect and acceptance. Only in this way can the cultural communication between both countries prosper, and only when the people-to-people communication becomes active can the media outlets further help improve the bilateral relations. The cultural communication conducted through the media can give the green light to the dynamic development of bilateral relations if the decisions and efforts of both sides are regarded as the basis for promoting such ties. Otherwise, the media may serve the role of a catalyst for the worsening bilateral relations.

For instance, most young South Koreans who live in an open media environment are inclined to have a negative impression of China when frictions and confrontations arise in its culture and economy. They are the two main fields in the relationship between China and South Korea, and the negative relationship recurs due to the unchecked spreading of the conflicts. It would be impossible for both countries to develop a mutual-beneficial neighboring relationship through cultural communication if such confrontations appear again and again. In addition, fishing disputes, trade frictions, rumor spreading, and hateful online comments also exercise severe negative influences. It is also hard for the Chinese people to face events that inflict damage to their self-esteem or to accept criticism of China. It proves the necessity of respecting the culture and national system of other countries and peoples. In view of this, the lack of mutual respect would make it impossible for China and South Korea to become friends even though they share close economic links and geopolitical proximity. As the Chinese say goes, "Virtue is not left to stand alone. He who practices it will have neighbors." Only when both countries are sympathetic to each other's feelings can their relationship be developed positively. Culture and economy are closely related to people's daily life, so they should be simultaneously considered because they are sometimes more important than policies.

As to the role of media, sometimes the reporting inclination of the media determines whether the report can give positive guidance or produce a negative effect. But It is not easy to understand this in the same way across different media environments. From this perspective, media outlets not only pursue the sunlight of social justice, but also have the artistic attribute of enabling the society to become better. In other words, in shaping public opinions, the media should not only keep in the correct direction regarding the government, the society, the nation, and the international community, but they should also well observe the mid-to-long-term development trend of the relations among countries. The media should play an important role in shaping the public opinions in society and politics. In this sense, it is important for China and South Korea to cooperate in areas where they can understand each other more deeply and cooperate. However, government policy should also be taken into consideration. We should objectively report the present situation if we can look at the bilateral relations from a long-term point of view. The media has become increasingly developed, and the political situation also changes rapidly. All these prove the important roles of the policy, culture, and public opinions in dealing with bilateral relations. When shaping public opinions, the media in both China and South Korea should look at the bilateral relations from an international perspective, base themselves on mutual respect, and enable citizens of both countries to enjoy cultural feasts and the tangible benefits of economic development.

The government leaders also care about the public opinions on the present situation of bilateral relations based on the media. It is obvious that public opinions exert quite significant influences on the policies on bilateral relations. It is therefore highly important for either country to publicize from a correct point of view. Any media that can express public opinions from a valid point of view can play an exemplary role in handling bilateral relations, like a barometer or locomotive. In the efforts to encourage the media to play positive roles, economic and cultural communication, which serves as the core of people-to-people communication, is of incomparable importance in addition to government policies that are also important. People of both countries may enhance their mutual understanding and tolerance through cultural communication. The economic benefits generated from such mutual communication can further deepen bilateral relations. People of both countries must understand that only when mutually recognizing each other's culture, coordinating their economic benefits, accepting each other's government policies can they live harmoniously, which has been unseen in the past 30 years since the establishment of the diplomatic relations.

We often say that economic problems lead to conflicts in a family in daily life. However, the lack of mutual care is more likely to lead to friction among family members. It is very important to fully understand and respect the ideas and habits of each other. Likewise, we should observe the rule of "putting ourselves in the shoes of others" when handling relationships with neighbors, even with other countries. An old saying goes, "Do unto others as you would be done." China and South Korea should continue to work hard to become good neighbors.

To wind up the paper, I believe that when any problems arise in handling bilateral relations, we should face up to them instead of evading them or brushing them aside. Only when we can jointly discuss how to embark on the path to becoming culturally and economically developed countries can we conduct further cooperation in culture and economy. I hope that the governments, people, and public opinions on the media in both countries can reflect the will of "jointly tiding over difficulties", give up the thought of "looking on each other's trouble with indifference", and work hard jointly toward a still better future!

Semenov Alexander Vladimirovich

Associate professor, head of the Department of Oriental Languages, Diplomatic Academy of Ministry for Foreign Affairs of Russia. His study fields include Chinese history, China's foreign policies, linguistics, translation, translation research, and Chinese language teaching. He published academic reports and articles such as *Language Support to the "Belt and Road" Initiative, Peace and Development: The Theme of China's Foreign Policies in the Era of Reform and Opening-up, Well-being Issues in Modern China*. He also translated and edited such works as *Narrating China's Governance Stories in Xi Jinping's Speeches*, *Narrating China's Governance Stories in Xi Jinping's Speeches (teenagers' edition)*, and *How Does the Communist Party of China Fight Against Corruption?* In 2019, the Ministry for Foreign Affairs of Russia granted Semenov Alexander Vladimirovich a medal of "Honor Professor of Diplomatic Academy of the Ministry for Foreign Affairs of Russia."

Aspiration for Happiness:
The Development of Contemporary China

Since joining the WTO in 2001, China's rapid development has led to tremendous economic and social changes. Many cities in China have transformed into modern international metropolises with modern infrastructure. For the Chinese people, their living standards have improved, their pursuits have become more diverse, their vision has been broadened, and their mentality has also changed.

Issues such as quality of life were then put on the agenda. In the past, Chinese people used to greet each other by asking: "Have you eaten?" But from the first decade of this century, the question has turned into: "Are you happy?"

In *Are You Happy?*, published by Changjiang Literary and Art Press in 2010, the author Bai Yansong, a famous Chinese TV host, raised the topic of happiness in contemporary Chinese society. The book reflects the author's own thoughts and feelings about a series of changes China has gone through since 2000.

The topic of "happiness" first appeared on television right before the 18th National Congress of the Communist Party of China. During the National Day holiday in October 2012, China Central Television broadcasted a new program called "Going to the Grassroots: Voice of the People," which, for the first time, interviewed ordinary people on questions such as "Are you happy?" "What is happiness?" The program showed the views of ordinary Chinese people on their lives. Overall, the show reflected the importance of "happiness" in contemporary China.

The 18th National Congress of the Communist Party of China announced that socialism with Chinese characteristics had entered a new era. So, what is the essential difference between this new stage of socialism with Chinese characteristics and the previous stage? The answer lies in the document of the 18th National Congress. The document declares that as the ruling Party, the Communist Party of China regards the realization of the people's yearning for a better life as its goal. Chinese media interprets the "better life" here as "happiness" and emphasizes that it is important to pay attention to the hopes and concerns of ordinary people. In this way, "better life" has become an important topic in the new era, and "happiness" has become a keyword of the new era and a synonym of "better life."[1]

In 2012, when the topic of "happiness" was widely discussed in China, the United Nations raised the concept of the "Happy Planet Index" and designated March 20 as the "International Day of Happiness."

With the rapid development of developing and emerging countries, Western developed countries are no longer at the top of the table in terms of macroeconomic indicators such as gross domestic product (GDP) and purchasing power parity (PPP) in particular. In 2011, China's GDP ranked second in the world; in 2014, China's PPP surpassed that of the United States, ranking first in the world.

In order to maintain a conceptual economic advantage, Western countries have begun to introduce new composite indexes, including objective indicators such as ecological status, which is significantly better in Western countries than in developing countries due to the transfer of production to Asia, as well as subjective indicators based on Western values.

One of them is the "Happy Planet Index" proposed by the New Economics Foundation of the United Kingdom in 2006. The index reflects people's livelihood and ecological environment in different countries. At the same time, the "Quality-of-life Index" proposed by the Economist Intelligence Unit under the British Economist Group in 2013 also serves this goal. The research

[1] Cao Dongbo, "Why Did Xi Jinping Talk about 'Happiness' Three Times in Three Months?" *Shanghai Observer*, March 29, 2018.

and surveys conducted each year based on the above indicators provide a bellwether for academic publications and the media to publish information on the living standards and well-being of people around the world.

The indicators are also used by Western journalists who have actively participated in discussions on happiness in China.

Canadian *Globe and Mail* reporter Nathan Vander Klippe raised this question: Why didn't China's rapidly developing economy give the Chinese people a greater sense of happiness? As an argument, he pointed out that from 2013 to 2022, China's GDP increased by nearly 50%, while in 2013, China's happiness index only ranked 93rd in the world, and in 2020 it was even lower, ranking 94th.

On March 3, 2019, the news website of Deutsche Welle published an article titled "Chinese Are Getting Unhappy?" The article lists the data and changes in the happiness index of Chinese people from 2017 to 2019. During this period, China's happiness index ranked 79th, 86th, and 93rd, respectively. Accordingly, the article concludes that the living standards of Chinese people have fallen and that reforms have brought about a series of problems.

Ke Long, an observer of the Chinese website of *Nihon Keizai Shimbun*, also published an article entitled "Chinese, Are You Happy?" The author believes that the premise of happiness is a normal and peaceful life, but the reforms brought about imbalances in life, which eventually became the cause of people's dissatisfaction with life. When asked, "Do you feel happy (after winning the Nobel Prize)?" Chinese writer Mo Yan answered: "I don't know, I never thought about this question." In this regard, Ke Long thinks happiness should be a feeling that can be intuitively expressed, not a matter of cognition.[2] However, Mo Yan's answer reflects a mixed attitude of the Chinese people toward "happiness."

As a complex and multidimensional concept, "happiness" is regarded as the leading factor of social and cultural development.

---

[2] KE Long. Do Chinese People Feel Happy? [J]. Nikkei - Japan Economic News China Online, April 13, 2017

The concept of "happiness" includes objectivity and subjectivity. In a specific historical period, it provides an objective model of an ideal life reflected in people's subjective understanding and encourages people to realize these apparently utopian ideals in real life.

As a way of existence, happiness is realized through the interaction of contingency and necessity. In the Western tradition, happiness, with the root "hap" (Old English), means "luck" or "opportunity." In French, "bonheur" means "good time," referring to temporary and accidental happiness or good luck. In German, the word "gluck" still means "happiness and luck" today.

The concept of "happiness" can be reflected in spiritual and material life. Western scholars regard "happiness" as a psychological phenomenon (feeling happiness and spiritual satisfaction in life) and an economic phenomenon (according to Anglo Saxon's way of expression, it can be called well-being, that is, blessing, welfare, and wealth).

When considering the concept of "happiness" from the perspective of social and cultural dynamics, the society and individual experience show an inward orientation (i.e., inward-looking) and an outward orientation (i.e., outward-looking).

We can find a way to define "happiness" from ancient Greek philosophers.

The word "happiness" can be expressed in several terms with similar meanings.

The first is "εὐτυχία" (eftychía), which can be translated as "good destiny" and "lucky opportunity." In other words, "happiness" in Greek not only expresses accidental factors but also means destiny.

The second is "ὄλβος" (ólvos), meaning well-being and material wealth.

The third is "μακαριότης" (makariótis), indicating the highest degree of happiness. The word is used to refer to gods and souls in the afterlife.

The fourth is "εὐδαιμονία" (evdaimonía), usually interpreted as happiness and joy, referring to a person's destiny under the protection of the gods.[3]

---

[3] L.A. Petrova The theme of happiness and joy in ancient culture and Christian tradition. 09.00.13 – Philosophical anthropology, philosophy of culture. Doctoral thesis of philosophy. St. Petersburg, 2016, p14

The etymology of the Greek word "happiness" shows that people's lives and goals at that time depended on the external environment, namely, opportunities and destiny, as well as the sacred forces that might affect the external environment.

In life, the protection from gods alleviated the impact of inevitable fate on individual psychology and, to some extent, revealed the possibility that individuals can gain happiness through hard work.

How can one live happily when he cannot control his destiny? Ancient Greek philosophers gave their answers.

Aristippus (about 435 BC–355 BC) is the founder of the hedonism school. He believed that the purpose of life is to enjoy and the goodness of human beings lies in happiness. Happiness can be achieved through conscious and reasonable behavior toward this goal.

Epicurus (342 or 341 BC–271 or 270 BC) is the founder of Epicureanism. He believed that happiness is the pursuit of joy and the elimination of pain. In this sense, happiness is the standard to measure good. Epicurus believed that a happy life is a good, moral, and just life. Happiness can give people peace of mind and the health of the body. If Aristippus agreed that happiness existed in motion, Epicurus acknowledged that happiness existed in a static state.

Even amid happiness, it is necessary to maintain moderation and modesty so as not to anger the gods.

Antisthenes (between 455 and 445 BC–about 366 BC) and his disciple Diogenes of Sinope (about 412 BC–323 BC) are representatives of cynicism (the word means "cynic" in Latin). They lived by their passions and instincts without scruples. They opposed tradition and convention and believed that the most important thing is to follow their own nature, which is the only way to happiness. They are convinced that unrestricted freedom is a virtue and a prerequisite for a happy life.

Democritus (about 460 BC–370 BC) is one of the founders of atomic materialism. He did not recognize happiness on the material level but believed that happiness was a special state of mind: happy, harmonious, and balanced. He thought that the value of happiness lay in wisdom, not money, unbridled passion, and extravagance.

Socrates (about 469 BC–399 BC) is the first philosopher in Athens. He also believed that happiness did not come from the body and external things but from the spirit. It is not the enjoyment of the outer material world but the satisfaction of the heart. When one's spiritual world is in order and has good morality, he will feel happy.

Aristotle (384 BC–322 BC), the greatest philosopher in ancient Greece, was the teacher of Alexander the Great. He also believed that "happiness was the practice of the soul in line with morality," [4] which could bring people supreme happiness and moral satisfaction. The road to true happiness is not entertainment and meaningless recreation but activities that benefit society.

However, ancient Greek writers were in the position of philosophical dualism. They believed that, on the one hand, happy people referred to successful people, who did not suffer hardship, lived modestly and fairly, and showed civil and military virtues. On the other hand, even with these virtues, nobody could guarantee that he would not be affected by irrational forces because nobody could predict his destiny.

In the Middle Ages, the concept of "happiness" was related to the incarnate God. Although it is a term, the word "happiness" hardly appears in the *Old Testament* and the *New Testament*.[5] "Joy," close to the meaning of "happiness," is widely used in medieval works.

"Joy" refers to worldly pleasure, a reaction to the events that bring happiness. It is close to the ancient Greek word "satisfaction." Writers also used the word "joy" in religious incarnations believed to originate from God. At this time, "joy" expressed the meaning of "happiness," which was associated with the gods in ancient Greece.

In the Middle Ages, a happy life first meant a pious life. God was in a person's soul, a humble and gentle existence. The ancient Greeks were divided into the spiritual holy and material evil sides, and the former was the key.

---

[4] *Aristotle: Collection of Works*, Vol. 4, T.4.M. , Thoughts, 1983, p613.

[5] L.A.Petrova, ibid, p67

"Happiness" was declared the supreme good, which only God could have, and the way to happiness was to approach God.

In the Middle Ages, the contingency of happiness was solved by transforming it into a necessity, that was, by declaring its sacred intention.

The Renaissance (14-16th century) marks the lifting of the religious veil and the beginning of the humanization of life. People's attitudes toward happiness had also changed, and the road to happiness was open in people's secular lives. The opportunity to obtain happiness through one's own efforts in secular life was a powerful driving force for the development of personal and social life.

In modern times, the transition to capitalism was completed. The religious reform movement gave a heavy blow to Catholicism, and religious factors no longer played an important role in social life. A new class, the bourgeoisie, joined in the struggle for political rights to remove the feudal obstacles on the road to developing productive forces. The concept of "happiness" "fell from the sky" and has become a reality in material consumption. Happiness in the process of consumption has become the dominant factor in life for a long time.

In the Russian tradition, the concept of "happiness" has two interpretations. One is the "good part" (luck, destiny). Another is "joint participation." The word "Eucharist" is also its cognate, representing the main sacraments of the Eastern Orthodox Church.

In Vladimir Ivanovich Dal's famous *Russian Dictionary*, the first explanation of the word "happiness" is "accident, surprise, luck, success..." In other words, luck is a coincidence, and success is not achieved through calculation.

The second explanation is "happiness, well-being, peace, and contentment." In fact, this refers to material abundance.[6]

In the dictionary, there is also an explanation similar to its etymology "fate, luck." But in modern Russian, "happiness" has no such meaning.

---

[6] Vladimir Ivanovich Dal, *Russian Dictionary*, URL: https://slovardalja.net/word.php?wordid=39717 (Search time: 2022.08.25).

At the social-cultural level, the word "happiness" in Russian has greater religious significance than its counterpart in Western languages. The religious element constitutes the basis of this word and is a "reminder" of the sacred nature of happiness. Real happiness can only be obtained in heaven.

In Russia, happiness is an accidental and unexpected event that requires great efforts to control in one's own hands. Therefore, happiness becomes sacred and secret. Happiness is not shared with the outside world so as not to cause jealousy and lose it.

The attitude of Russians toward happiness is also influenced by their personality, especially the binary opposition. It is a rational description of the world, emphasizing two opposite concepts, one of which affirms a certain quality, and the other denies it. The Russian language contains many binary opposites: "victory or death," "win or lose," "truth or lie," and "happiness or misfortune." According to the Russian tradition, evaluating any situation is usually positive or negative. All intermediate options will lead to inaccurate evaluation and vague meaning, which is not in line with the Russian character. A typical example is "Russian Roulette,"[7] which is reflected in literary works and widely popular among Russian officers in the 19th century. The bet is not life but death.

Although the traditional Russian attitude toward "happiness" is very personal, the public's pursuit of a better and happy life is still influenced by advanced European ideas.

In the history of Russia, due to its territory, geographical location, and socio-economic and political characteristics, public-owned agriculture developed, and rural communes owned land. In order to use land fairly, communes redistributed land every year. In addition, members of the commune would help each other in an emergency. The representatives of revolutionary democracy in the 19th century (Nikola Gavrilovich Chernishevski, Nikolay

---

[7] "Russian Roulette" is a game played by Russian officers. According to the rules of the game, put one or more bullets into empty cartridge slots of a revolver, and leave empty cartridge slots. Spin the revolver several times, so that players do not know which cartridge slot has the bullet and which is empty. Then the players take turns to aim the barrel at their head and pull the trigger.

Aleksandrovich Dobrolyusv, and others) linked their utopian plans — to achieve national happiness — with rural communes.

Although the commune system laid the foundation for the "lower class" to form a sense of collectivism, the "upper class" still had its own way of coordinating different interests. In Russia, this collaboration is called "collectivism." Important religious and organizational issues needed to be resolved at the local meeting of the Orthodox Church. Since the 16th century, the Zemsky Sobor had been held, with the engagement of senior classes representing nobles and clergy as well as public representatives. In the czarist monarchy of Russia, this hierarchical representation mechanism expressed the concept of "collectivism," that was, "unity in pluralism."

The interests of the "upper class" and the "lower class" continued to contradict each other, and their understanding and realization of a happy life were different, which eventually led to a crisis state incompatible with the continuous development of Tsar Russia.

The change in social paradigm and the establishment of the Soviet Union led to the complete transformation of social consciousness. After losing its pluralism and diversity, the concept of "collectivism" became a pure "unity." Commune collectivism was the main social psychological environment of the country, indicating that collective interests were higher than individual interests.

The social-cultural project "happiness" was first positioned as "global happiness" in the world dimension, then narrowed down to the Soviet Union, and was updated as "universal happiness." However, the feasibility of implementing the project was not fully explored.

In 1991, Russia's command bureaucracy was broken, which seemed to open up a broad road for the country's prosperity. However, the Western countries took advantage of Russia's temporary weakness and only promoted the development of industries necessary for their own "global economy" projects. The West opposed all attempts to pursue an independent policy.

The concept of "happiness" has dropped from "universal happiness" to the "individual" level, which varies from person to person. At this time, the possibility of achieving happiness has expanded. However, under the influence of Western consumerism, some spiritual features in the Russian world vision have been lost. Finding the balance between the material and the spiritual in public and individual consciousness should be the future direction of the new Russia.

The image of "happiness" is also reflected in Chinese culture. The hieroglyph of the Chinese character "福 (good fortune)" expresses the meaning of "happiness." It was related to a religious ceremony in ancient times: witches offered good wine to gods to pray for mercy and protection.

In modern Chinese, the word " 幸 福 (happiness)" can be traced back to the period of oracle bone inscriptions (14–11th century BC). Even at that time, "happiness" also expressed good wishes for ancestors. In addition, the hieroglyph "幸 (luck)" reflects the kindness of the emperor: amnesty for prisoners under sentence of death, while " 福 " implies heavenly grace: health and prosperity due to God's blessing. Therefore, in modern Chinese, two characters of the word "happiness" have already expressed luck and good destiny.

Unlike the dualism in ancient Greece, the ancient Chinese believed that deities predetermined happiness, but individuals (citizens) could experience happiness in their personal or social life. In ancient China, happy life was more of a game of chance on earth or in heaven, in other words, the favor of God or the emperor. The interweaving of secular and religious life made people dare to fight with fate and try to change it.

In the article "*Hongfan*" from the Book of History, written between the 10th century and 9th century BC, the concept of "happiness" was elaborated. Happiness contains five aspects: longevity, wealth and nobleness, health and peace, virtue, and natural death due to old age.

In ancient times, the Chinese understood family happiness as a natural and continuous noble moral life. Death at the end of life is the natural end of good deeds. The continuity of life lies in future generations, which will keep in touch with the spirit of their ancestors through appropriate rituals.

It is interesting to compare it with the concept of perfect happiness in ancient Greece. Herodotus, an ancient Greek historian (484 BC–425 BC), recorded a story about Solon (7–6th century BC) meeting with King Croesus of Lydia (famous for his wealth). Solon was an Athenian politician and one of the "seven sages" of ancient Greece. Croesus asked Solon, who was the happiest person in the world? The King wanted to hear the answer was his name. But Solon, the ancient Greek sage, replied that the happiest man was Thales, an Athenian, for these reasons: Thales lived in the era of prosperity of his city state; his sons were excellent and noble; when he was alive, he saw that all his children had their own children, and they had grown up; he lived on his own and was rich; he died in the battle of Eleusis for defending his motherland; Athenians held a state funeral for him and awarded him honor. Based on Thales' life, Solon concluded: the overall happiness of ancient Greek citizens was to have good luck and virtue.[8]

The dualism of overall happiness combines the views of ancient China and ancient Greece, that is, a person must live a good life, and only after death can we judge whether he is happy in his life.

In addition to the similarities in subjective psychological factors with the Western view of happiness, the Chinese concept of happiness demonstrates distinctive cultural and philosophical features:

1) The foundation of the Chinese worldview is "*tai chi*," which advocates the interpenetration of opposite sides. The great Chinese philosopher Lao Zi said: "Misfortune might be a blessing in disguise, and vice versa. One cannot predict the outcome, so nothing is certain until the end." It is a typical view of happiness in China.

According to Chinese philosophy, happiness cannot exist without the concept of "misfortune." The two opposing aspects are interdependent and interpenetrating, and both are constantly developing.

In the article "*Hong fan*" from *the Book of History*, the "six misfortunes" concept was raised corresponding to the "five feelings of happiness." The "six misfortunes" are early death, disease, sorrow, poverty, evil, and cowardice.

---

[8] L.A.Petrova, "Happiness and Joy in Ancient Greek culture and Christian tradition", 09.00.13 — philosophical anthropology, philosophy of culture. Doctoral thesis of philosophy. St. Petersburg, 2016, p19.

Westerners also encounter misfortune in their lives, but they consider it an accidental or external phenomenon. They must pray to God for forgiveness. In Chinese tradition, "misfortune" is the opposite of "happiness," which directly depends on how individuals maintain an appropriate balance between the two. Teachers or wise people can point out the right direction, but individuals must complete moral efforts.

Auspicious signs and mascots are hints of people's pursuit of happiness. They can protect people from the blow of fate and help people to control happiness in their own hands.

2) The prevalent philosophical systems of Confucianism, Buddhism, and Taoism in ancient China established a cultural code of happiness different from that of the West.

Western philosophers, from the ancient Greeks to medieval scholastics to the positivists of the new age, are concerned with the individual and the individual's emotional satisfaction, cognitive satisfaction, or spiritual longing for God. Western individualists are positive, outgoing, obsessed with their own goals, and willing to make all humanity happy.

Eastern philosophy advocates harmony between the individual and society (Confucianism), harmony between the individual and nature (Taoism), and harmony between the individual and himself (Buddhism). In Chinese culture, people are socially oriented, introverted, obsessed with self-improvement, and spiritually they tend to let things take their own course. For Chinese people, happiness always means adapting to the impermanence of life. In this process, people realize a good life in a small society of their own family through hard work and self-cultivation.

3) Chinese people's worldview is holistic, and the difference lies in their attitude toward the overall situation. For Chinese people, the opinions of people around them are very important. Because of this, when asked, "Are you happy?" The writer Mo Yan replied: "I don't know." He also explained: "Happiness is to think about nothing, to let go of everything, to have good health, and to be free from any stress. I'm under a lot of pressure now, and I'm worried. Can I be happy? But if I tell you I'm not happy, you'll say I am being

pretentious. I just won the Nobel Prize, and I am supposed to be a person of happiness."[9] These words of Mo Yan contain the Chinese concept of happiness. His view is contradictory. On the one hand, winning the Nobel Prize means obtaining happiness because he has achieved his goal and is recognized by the world. On the other hand, inner pressure and emotions make him unable to feel happiness fully.

The traditional concept of happiness reflects ancient China's complex social and cultural landscape. In China, happiness is not as much a personal psychological concept as a social psychological concept because it is considered and realized at the family level. A happy life is a kind of natural existence, which means one understands his position in the family, abides by family rules, and bears children. The moral life of a gentleman is a model for society to honor. In addition to family happiness, there is also luck in life (passing official examinations and getting a promotion), which is not only luck but also the result of personal efforts. The happiness model of the Chinese people is to work hard to achieve goals and make full preparations and overall plans to avoid accidents.

If the traditional concept of happiness of Chinese people only involved individuals, in the 1980s and 1990s, Chinese leaders raised the issue of a happy life at the national level.

Since the reform and opening up, China's economy has developed rapidly. The Chinese people have experienced profound changes in economic and social life from pre-industrialization to industrialization and then informatization ages in one generation. The extensive economic growth model of large-scale production, big consumption, and high emissions has begun to transform into a high-quality development model focusing on efficiency, balance, and sustainability.

The field of social life has also undergone fundamental changes. The people's livelihood issues have been addressed efficiently, which is what the

---

[9] Lu Guocheng, "Mo Yan, Are You Happy?", *Ebao Monthly*, February 15, 2013.

great Chinese revolutionary Sun Yat-sen once hoped to achieve. Chinese leaders solved the problem of food and clothing for the people and ensured the supply of necessities of life in a relatively short period. In the next stage, the people's living standards were raised to moderate prosperity. Subsequently, the goal was set to realize a happy and beautiful life for the people. If the first two stages have solved the quantitative problem of economic development, happiness becomes a comprehensive problem related to the quality of life in the third stage. It includes politics, economy, society, culture, and ecology. The Chinese cultural code originated in ancient times and is embodied in Chinese hieroglyphs, and Chinese national mentality constitutes the historical basis for the issue of happiness.

The earliest views on how to study and measure happiness were formed in the first several years of the 21st century, during the presidency of Hu Jintao. The concept of happiness put forward during his administration is mainly expressed as a "harmonious society" and "people-oriented," advocating further integration with the world, pursuing convergence toward a "harmonious world," and paying attention to the interests of individuals. Rather than deviating from the traditional Chinese cultural code, the issue of happiness is raised to seek and study Western ideas that can be used for reference and adapted to the country's cultural model.

During the same period when President Hu Jintao was in power, Chinese experts and scholars conducted in-depth research on the Western concept of happiness to formulate quantitative indicators of happiness and the happiness index by learning from Western scholars.

In February 2005, the Beijing Municipal Bureau of Statistics released the "Beijing Harmonious Society Survey," which set up seven basic indicators to measure the happiness of residents in the capital, including health status, family harmony, and job satisfaction.[10]

---

[10] Le Zheng, "The Composition and Influencing Factors of Happiness Index", *Nanfang Daily*, June 22, 2006.

In 2006, the Shenzhen Academy of Social Sciences carried out the "Harmonious Shenzhen" sociological research and conducted two surveys on citizens in terms of "social harmony" and "personal happiness." This sociological survey on happiness includes cognitive, psychological, and interpersonal indicators.[11]

In 2008, Ye Nanke and Chen Ru, president and vice president of the Nanjing Academy of Social Sciences, formulated and announced a complex happiness index system for Nanjing citizens. The system consists of three levels.

The first level consists of social life and individual life.

On the second level, social life is divided into four elements: economy, politics, society, and culture, whereas individual life falls into three components: economy, interpersonal communication, and individuality.

The third level lists 19 indicators related to social life and individual life.[12]

The system aims to comprehensively reflect life satisfaction and views on the happiness of ordinary citizens in Nanjing.

In 2007, *Oriental Outlook Weekly* of Xinhua News Agency organized an event to select "China's Happiest City." They applied the happiness evaluation system of Christopher K. Hsee, a professor at the Booth Business School of the University of Chicago. The system consists of 12 evaluation indicators, including the natural environment, traffic conditions, development speed, civilization level, moneymaking opportunities, medical services and healthcare, education, housing price, interpersonal relationship (friendliness), public security, employment, and comfort level of living.[13] This system has become the only set of indicators for evaluating the happiness of urban residents that has been officially recognized and is still in use today. In 2021, Chengdu, Ningbo, Wuhan, Qingdao, Xining, Hangzhou, Changsha, Nanjing, Guiyang,

---

[11] Ye Nanke, Chen Ru, et al., "The Main Motive Force, Ultimate Goal and Deep Strategy of Harmonious Society — the Evaluation and Promotion of Modern Urban Residents' Happiness", *Social Science in Nanjing*, Issue 1, 2008.

[12] Ye Nanke, Chen Ru, et al., "The Main Motive Force, Ultimate Goal and Deep Strategy of Harmonious Society — the Evaluation and Promotion of Modern Urban Residents' Happiness", *Social Science in Nanjing*, Issue 1, 2008.

[13] Report on the Happiest City in China, December 30, 2008 http://www.lwdf.cn/oriental/cover-story/20081230161419147.htm

and Harbin were selected as the "happiest" cities in China.[14]

In the first decade of this century, due to China's rapid economic growth, economic indicators were given a heavier weight. At that time, it seemed that the higher the GDP (including per capita GDP), the higher the happiness index. Over a certain period of development and when a certain income level is reached, there is a direct correlation between GDP and happiness.

It is what Richard A. Easterlin's "Easterlin Paradox" (the happiness-income paradox) says. The happiness of the poor increases along with increases in their income. However, for the middle class and the wealthy, any new increases in their income no longer bring them satisfaction after their income reaches a certain level.

Easterlin first proposed this theory in 1974, whose validity was proved in 2010. Peng Kaiping, head of the Department of Psychology at Tsinghua University, also believes that happiness does not necessarily depend on economic development. A study showed that neither of the two biggest cities, Beijing and Shanghai, made it into the "50 happiest cities in China" list. Peng Kaiping thinks that in poor areas and cities, the happiness index will increase along with the development of the economy, but there is a critical point of US$3,000 per capita GDP. That is, when the per capita GDP exceeds US$3,000, economic growth will not further impact the happiness index. At this point, other factors will contribute to people's sense of happiness.[15]

Since President Xi Jinping came to power in 2012, China's political, economic and social development model has changed. China has jumped to the second place in the world in terms of GDP, entering a period of direct competition with the United States. China is more active and determined to fight for its rightful place in global governance, expand its influence in the International Monetary Fund and consolidate its position in the World

---

[14] "Cities such as Chengdu, Hangzhou and Ningbo Selected as the Happiest Cities in China for 2021", ThePaper.cn, December 30, 2021

[15] Jin Haotian, "Chinese People Are Happiest on Saturday, According to the Tsinghua University Research", *Guangming Daily*, March 24, 2014.

Trade Organization. As a global power, China has proposed a series of major international initiatives, such as the "Belt and Road Initiative" in economics and the joint construction of a "community with a shared future for mankind" in politics. In the face of China's rising international status, the United States and other Western countries first imposed economic and political sanctions to contain China. Then they launched the trade war during the Trump administration.

On the one hand, the international situation has become increasingly complex, and China's economic growth has slowed down. On the other hand, the need to rectify political life, such as anti-corruption, completes the strategic task of building a moderately prosperous society in all respects. China has eventually achieved comprehensive poverty alleviation, starting to adjust a range of living quality indicators, including the happiness index.

The 19th CPC National Congress proposed to "remain true to the Party's original aspiration." It aims at the Party members who take the Party Constitution as the norm of moral behavior and all the Chinese people so that they will not forget their cultural codes in the context of globalization. The happiness index has changed from "people-oriented" to "people-centered". The slogan "serve the people" put forward by China's first generation of leaders has been raised again, becoming an important terminology in the political discourse emphasized by the new generation of leaders and the main theme of President Xi Jinping's social and economic policies. To benefit the people is to get rid of poverty in an all-round way and achieve moderate prosperity for all.

The research on happiness is also different from the past. It has shifted from quantitative research on happiness, such as formulating indexes and indicators, to thinking at the philosophical and ethical levels. As Wan Junren, a professor at the Department of Philosophy of Tsinghua University, said: "In a sense, economists always stand beside the wealthy, and ethicists always stand behind the poor."[16] Economists study wealth, while ethicists study fairness.

---

[16] "Wan Junren: What is Happiness and How to Create, Pursue and Share Happiness", *Tianjin Daily*, August 8, 2011.

Therefore, the country's poverty alleviation has pushed China to examine the issue of "happiness" from an ethical perspective.

In January 2017, *Guangming Daily* launched a discussion on the theme of "What concept of happiness do modern people need." Famous Chinese philosophers and ethicists, including Jiang Chang, a professor at the School of Philosophy of Hubei University, participated in the discussion. Li Yitian, a professor at the Moral Education Research Center of Tsinghua University, Zhan Shiyou, a professor at the School of Humanities of Nanchang University. Wan Junren, a professor at Tsinghua University and president of the China Association for Ethical Studies, presided over this discussion.

The core question they discussed was: should and could Chinese society reach a consensus on happiness? The purpose of the discussion is to find the answer to this question: what should the concept of happiness in the new era be like?

As Jiang Chang pointed out, before the reform and opening up, the Chinese avoided discussing happiness. With the "Chinese Dream" proposed by President Xi Jinping in November 2012, the people's happiness was written on the banner of the Party and the country. People have widely talked about happiness in recent years and boldly pursued it, and "happiness" has become one of the most fashionable keywords in contemporary China. However, many people still have a relatively narrow understanding of happiness and only regard it as a personal feeling. It seems that only one's own feeling of happiness is true happiness.[17]

Zhan Shiyou agreed with him. In his view, people intuitively believe that happiness is a person's continued satisfaction with his life. Therefore, an individual's happiness has strong subjectivity and obvious differences from one person to another.[18]

Li Yitian said that everyone wants to live a happy life. In an age of constant change like today, individuals' self-actualization and their universal connections

---

[17] Jiang Chang, "What Concept of Happiness Do We Need?" *Guangming Daily*, January 23, 2017.

[18] Zhan Shiyou, "An Examination on the Objective Dimensions of Happiness", *Guangming Daily*, January 23, 2017.

are intricately intertwined. People differ in their views on happiness. Some think happiness lies in "possessing more social resources and wealth". Some believe that happiness lies in "satisfying more desires", while others argue that happiness lies in "finding a place for one's heart, or even pure meditation."[19]

Experts participating in the discussion agreed that people's understanding of happiness in China is becoming more individualized and diversified.

In response to the increasingly prevalent consumerism in China, other scholars who participated in the discussion put forward more views on life and happiness.

They objected to being too subjective and understanding happiness purely from a material perspective. They came up with their solutions on the premise that the entire society should reach a consensus on understanding happiness.

So, in their view, what should a common concept of happiness be like? Maybe it is made up of many individualized views of happiness, or perhaps there is a comprehensive system of ideas that applies to everyone!

They share the view that people should have a holistic approach to happiness. In other words, we need to consider objective and subjective factors, external and internal factors, and idealized and practical conditions.

During the discussion, they raised various existing views on happiness to a full concept of happiness from different perspectives.

Li Yitian emphasized that we must correctly understand the subjectivity of happiness. He agreed with the famous ancient Greek thinker Aristotle that "happiness is the highest good." And the highest good is a virtue. As the highest moral quality, virtue is the inner condition for people to obtain happiness.[20]

Li Yitian said that as a subjective factor, virtue first refers to such ethical virtues as courage, moderation, generosity, and honesty. These virtues are psychological constraints on desires and demands. In addition, the actor should restrain his desires to a moderate state when dealing with practical affairs.[21]

---

[19] Li Yitian, "Realization of Happiness: the Significance and Priority of Virtue", *Guangming Daily*, January 23, 2017.

[20] Li Yitian, "Realization of Happiness: the Significance and Priority of Virtue", *Guangming Daily*, January 23, 2017.

[21] Li Yitian, "Realization of Happiness: the Significance and Priority of Virtue", *Guangming Daily*, January 23, 2017.

Li Yitian thought that virtue is an important intrinsic motivation to pursue happiness, and external factors are also significant. Good habits, institutions, and luck are all necessary conditions for happiness.[22]

Different from Li Yitian's point of view, Jiang Chang and Zhan Shiyou thought that a correct understanding of the characteristics of external objective factors helps to find the common measure of happiness.

Zhan Shiyou thought that although happiness is subjective to a great extent and demonstrates individual differences, the first and foremost thing we need to consider is its objective dimension, given the definition of happiness as the complete good life of a person.[23]

Zhan Shiyou said that the precondition of happiness is material wealth. Food, clothing, housing, and transportation are the basic elements that bring people happiness. As the demand increases, people are eager to enable themselves and future generations to receive a better education and develop their endowments and cultural quality. The threshold for the necessary conditions for happiness is getting higher and higher, as are the requirements for the country.[24]

He thought that Chinese leaders had made great achievements in satisfying the people's sense of happiness and fulfillment. By 2021, China will build a moderately prosperous society in all respects, laying the material foundation for universal happiness for all.[25]

Jiang Chang said neither possessing social resources nor satisfying material desires could bring true happiness. He had his definition of happiness. He applied Marxist theory and believed that happiness is human beings' free and all-round development. The goals of a socialist society meet exactly the requirements of this definition. To realize the freed and all-round development of human beings is to have a "complete good life," which includes all aspects of

[22] Li Yitian, "Realization of Happiness: the Significance and Priority of Virtue", *Guangming Daily*, January 23, 2017.

[23] Zhan Shiyou, "An Examination on the Objective Dimensions of Happiness", *Guangming Daily*, January 23, 2017.

[24] Zhan Shiyou, "An Examination on the Objective Dimensions of Happiness", *Guangming Daily*, January 23, 2017.

[25] Zhan Shiyou, "An Examination on the Objective Dimensions of Happiness", *Guangming Daily*, January 23, 2017.

life such as family, professional, individual, and network life.[26]

In his view, society should take the general well-being of its members as the goal of value pursuit and create all possible conditions for realizing this goal.[27]

At present, to realize the people's general happiness, the most important and urgent task is to make our country strong and prosperous and realize national rejuvenation. It is also the objective prerequisite for implementing the concept of happiness and bringing happiness to people.

For the core question of the discussion: Can China reach a consensus on the issue of happiness? The three scholars all gave positive answers.

Scholars believe that to reach a social consensus, happiness must be regarded as a complex, multi-dimensional phenomenon, which integrates various internal and external, subjective and objective factors, and is in continuous dynamic development.

Scholars' views on this issue were different. Jiang Chang regarded the concept of happiness as a continuum composed of many aspects. He believed that happiness is, to a greater extent, a dynamic development process and an all-round development achieved by people pursuing a better life. Zhan Shiyou focused on the objective conditions of the concept of happiness, in which social factors play a decisive role while luck is also very important. But it depends a lot on the social relations of individuals. Li Yitian also regarded happiness as dynamic, but he believed happiness depends largely on an individual's internal subjectivity, including virtue. Virtue and a degree of moderation help to restrain the growth of one's desires. External conditions also depend on subjective factors: the higher the morality, the better and more effectively one can make social achievements.

Chinese scholars' discussion on "happiness" in the new era shows a deep understanding of the subject and trend of Western research.

---

[26] Jiang Chang, "What Concept of Happiness Do We Need?" *Guangming Daily*, January 23, 2017.

[27] Jiang Chang, "What Concept of Happiness Do We Need?" *Guangming Daily*, January 23, 2017.

Chinese scholars either emphasized the objectivity of happiness, namely, the material living conditions, or the subjectivity of happiness – short-term psychological and emotional responses to changes in the outside world. In addition, they also paid attention to moral life from the perspective of benefiting society.

Chinese scholars thought about happiness in the Western thought paradigm, but they did not give answers to the national characteristics of China in solving the issue of happiness.

In modern times, Western countries have stepped into capitalism, characterized by the constant emergence of a consumer society. In the middle of the 20th century, the modernist culture and philosophy trend with rational and progressive thoughts were replaced by postmodernism. Postmodernism is the crisis philosophy of Western thoughts, which involves the fundamental questions – the death of God (Nietzsche), the death of the author (Barthes), and the death of man (Foucault). Francis Fukuyama's theory of the end of history marks the end of development. The time and space continuum of this age focuses only on the present. The collapse of social consciousness and the escape from the unsolvable contradictions in life have led to unrestrained happiness, excessive consumption, and cultural degradation. It is the philosophical basis of Western writers' concept of happiness.

Chinese society has reached the level of a consumer society in a very short time and has learned from the world's experience in seeking further development. Therefore, both individuals and society have more or less accepted the outdated stereotypes of the post-modern West. Chinese scholars are also committed to studying advanced scientific ideas – many subjective psychology theories about happiness. However, the research of this scientific frontier is too superficial, and the research often focuses on atypical personal cases. The results are only quantitative records, and no qualitative breakthrough has been made in studying "what is happiness in the new era."

China already has wise leaders with a vision of the overall situation, an economically developed society, and well-educated people. Contemporary Chinese society must integrate traditional and modern experiences to find its own way to happiness.

The dominant social culture factors are nature, God, and man, which develop along the time track, representing the past, the future, and the present. In the ancient past (nature), in the medieval future (God), and in modern times (people), they are absolutized.[28] It is the Western view of individual happiness.

China has an unlimited opportunity to become the first country in history to propose and realize the happiness of the whole people. Everyone here will feel happy, not limited to the present, but also know the road to happiness in the future. It will be the best solution for China to achieve all-round happiness.

As China enters the information society, there is an increasingly urgent demand to define happiness properly. Integration with the world promotes rapid economic development, improving people's living standards and changes in the social and psychological environment.

The improvement of the living standards of most Chinese has brought about new social problems, one of which is related to the problem of happiness.

The traditional concept of happiness combines the views of important philosophical systems such as Confucianism, Buddhism, Taoism, and the ancient Chinese people's simple concept of happiness.

Contemporary Chinese people's concept of happiness not only reflects Western scientific concepts and stereotypes of Western life but also reflects the academic achievements of Chinese scholars and the country's educational activities in this regard. At the same time, it is also influenced by traditional Chinese culture.

On the issue of happiness, the policy adopted by Chinese leaders is to actively establish role models, commend their deeds, and work proactively for the benefit of the people under the guidance of socialist values.

---

[28] A.N.Zadvonov, "Origins of View on Happiness in Europe and Eurasian Philosophies", *Journal of Vyatka State Humanities University*, Science Journal, 2015, No.1, p26.

Bruno Guigue

Born in January 1962, a well-known French political scholar and expert on international politics. He once studied at the Ecole Normale Su-périeure (ENS) and École Nationale d'Administration (ENA) in Paris, then served as a senior official in the Ministry of Interior Affairs of France from 1990 to 2008. Studying China for many years, he often writes articles to refute the smears of China by Western media on issues of Hong Kong, Xinjiang, and human rights. He has written many works and articles on political philosophy, contemporary history, geopolitics, and other fields. In recent years, he published several articles on China's development, including "Hong Kong: The Intervention of the US Behind the Scenes," "Hong Kong Returning to Reality," "COVID-19 to Witness the Collapse of the Western System," as well as his latest monograph *Communism*.

What does the Poverty Alleviation Campaign by the PRC Teach Us?

Background

Improving the well-being of the people has been one of the most important goals of the Communist Party of China (CPC) since its founding in 1921. As early as the founding of the People's Republic of China (PRC) on October 1, 1949, the Chinese government adopted a series of major economic and social reform measures to lift the country out of backwardness. With these initiatives, the country achieved its intended purpose of increasing productivity and improving people's living standards. The CPC, under the leadership of Mao Zedong, led the Chinese people in successfully liberating and unifying the country, abolishing autocratic rule, allocating land to peasants for farming, developing the nuclear industry, starting the process of industrialization, eradicating illiteracy, and raising the average life expectancy of the Chinese from 36 to 64 years. Mao Zedong completed his historical mission as the head of the CPC and the state. His successors, also the leadership core of the CPC, have greatly increased the country's Gross Domestic Product (GDP), built a series of modern infrastructure projects, and significantly improved the living conditions of the entire people. So far, China's average life expectancy has jumped to 77.3 years, surpassing that of the United States in 2020. With almost 100 percent of Chinese children attending school today, it is no wonder that the Organization for Economic Cooperation and Development once rated China's education system as the best in the world. However, some remote and impoverished areas have not been lifted out of backwardness yet, and the gap in their development with the rest of the country remains to be narrowed. The fruits of the extraordinary growth achieved since implementing the reform and opening up policy have yet to be truly shared by all Chinese. Since the 1980s and 1990s, poverty alleviation policies formulated and implemented based on substantial GDP growth have somewhat shown their limitations.

To speed up the pace of the poorest areas and families in achieving a middle-class standard of living, it is necessary to enhance their help and technical support. Therefore, since 2012, China has implemented a pilot policy to lift impoverished areas and groups out of their plight. Obviously, implemented with great determination and force, this policy is essential for consolidating the social cohesion and territorial integrity of the entire Chinese nation. According to the overall goal of building socialism in the new era, the battle against poverty has become a continuation and an indispensable part of the strategy for building a moderately prosperous society in all respects. This special poverty alleviation policy focuses on helping the poorest areas and the most vulnerable groups out of poverty by promoting rural revitalization. This paper analyzes the objectives, results, and implementation methods of this policy in detail. While following relevant commentaries, we will also try to study the lessons we can learn from them.

President Xi Jinping's Speeches on Poverty Alleviation

On many occasions, Chinese President Xi Jinping has made remarks on China's efforts to end poverty. For example, in his special address at the World Economic Forum Virtual Event of the Davos Agenda in 2021, Mr. Xi said: "As a steadfast member of developing countries, China will further deepen South-South cooperation and contribute to the endeavor of developing countries to eradicate poverty, ease debt burden, and achieve more growth." Speaking at the 12th BRICS Summit in November 2020, which also gathered leaders from Russia, India, South Africa, and Brazil, Mr. Xi said: "We need to call on the international community to place the implementation of the 2030 Agenda for Sustainable Development at the heart of international development cooperation. Poverty eradication must be a primary goal, and more resources must be channeled to poverty reduction, education, health, and infrastructure development."

Addressing the 27th Asia-Pacific Economic Cooperation (APEC) Economic Leaders' Meeting in November 2020, Mr. Xi said: "The digital economy represents the future direction of global development, while innovation has fueled the economic takeoff of the Asia-Pacific." He pledged in the meeting that "next year, China will host a workshop on digital technology-enabled poverty alleviation in a bid to unleash the role of digital technologies in eradicating poverty in our region." At the 20th Meeting of the Council of Heads of State of the Shanghai Cooperation Organization (SCO) in November 2020, Mr. Xi said that true development is development for all and good development is sustainable. He said: "China supports setting up an SCO joint working group on poverty reduction and stands ready to share our good experience with other parties." At the general debate of the 75th session of the United Nations General Assembly in September 2020, Mr. Xi said, "China has every confidence to meet ten years ahead of schedule the poverty eradication target set out in the 2030 Agenda for Sustainable Development and lift out of poverty all rural residents living below the current poverty line within the set time frame."

"China now contributes over 30 percent of global growth and has lifted more than 700 million people out of poverty by the UN standard," Mr. Xi said in 2018 in a signed article titled "Open up a New Future Together for China-Philippine Relations" and published in three Philippine newspapers ahead of his state visit to the Southeast Asian country. In the past few decades, China has lifted more than 700 million people out of poverty and will completely eliminate poverty by 2020. The Chinese economy has been contributing over 30 percent of the global growth for many years. Xi delivered a speech titled "Harnessing Opportunities of Our Times to Jointly Pursue Prosperity in the Asia-Pacific" at the 26th APEC Economic Leaders' Meeting in 2018. "We should strengthen development cooperation and help developing countries eliminate poverty so that people in all countries will live better lives. This is what fairness is essentially about; it is also a moral responsibility of the international community," Xi said in 2018 at the APEC CEO Summit.

"Through the continued efforts of the whole Party and the entire nation, we have realized the first centenary goal of building a moderately prosperous society in all respects. This means that we have brought about a historic resolution to the problem of absolute poverty in China, and we are now marching in confident strides toward the second centenary goal of building China into a great modern socialist country in all respects." This statement by President Xi Jinping is a terse summary of the connotation of China's poverty alleviation policy. Chinese experts tell us that a moderately prosperous society is an ideal social state for which the Chinese have strived since ancient times. Since the very day of its founding, the CPC has made seeking happiness for the Chinese people and rejuvenation for the Chinese nation its aspiration and mission. In the early days of reform and opening-up, Deng Xiaoping, who was regarded as the "chief architect of China's reform and opening-up," used the term "*xiaokang* (moderately prosperous)" to indicate the only feasible path that could lead China to modernization, that is, "a moderately prosperous society," and clearly set the goal of building a moderately prosperous society in China by the end of the 20th century. With the joint efforts of the whole Party and the people of all ethnic groups in the country, this goal was achieved as scheduled. By the end of the last century, the Chinese people had indeed, on the whole, attained a moderately prosperous standard of living. "After entering the 21st century, our Party set a goal to be achieved by its centenary: to build a higher-level moderately prosperous society in an all-round way to the benefit of over one billion people. This was a solemn promise to the Chinese people." these are President Xi Jinping's important remarks in an explanatory speech on the CPC Central Committee's proposals for formulating the 14th Five-Year Plan (2021–2025) for National Economic and Social Development and the Long-Range Objectives Through the Year 2035.

Objectives of the Poverty Alleviation Policy

These poverty alleviation goals, formulated by the highest-level decision-making bodies of the Party and the state, are naturally published in the official documents of the Chinese government on poverty alleviation. In August 2021, China published a white paper on human rights protection, explaining why "China's realization of moderate prosperity represents comprehensive progress in ensuring universal human rights in China and a new contribution to the world's human rights cause." In the white paper entitled "Moderate Prosperity in All Respects: Another Milestone Achieved in China's Human Rights," it is pointed out that under the leadership of the CPC, the Chinese people "finally completed the historic transformation from poverty to secure access to food and clothing, to a decent life, and finally to moderate prosperity." Moderate prosperity in China, according to the document, is evident in all respects: "a buoyant economy, political democracy, a flourishing culture, social equity, and healthy ecosystems; balanced development between urban and rural areas to the benefit of all the people; and high respect for and comprehensive protection of human rights." (Excerpted from *People's Daily*, August 13, 2021)

The white paper covers the topics of "achieving moderate prosperity; advancing human rights; ending extreme poverty; securing the right to an adequate standard of living; boosting human rights with development; securing economic, social, and cultural rights; protecting civil and political rights with law and governance; promoting social equity; and protecting the rights of special groups." From this perspective, "China's population is about one-fifth of the world's total. China's success in realizing moderate prosperity is a milestone in global human rights history. Other countries can learn much from China's unique experience because 'China's approach and experience have provided a distinctive path forward for human progress.' Through China's poverty eradication practices, the country has embarked on a path of poverty alleviation and designed an approach with Chinese characteristics, which offers enlightenment to the international community in its battle to reduce poverty."

The white paper titled "Poverty Alleviation: China's Experience and Contribution" says: "The nation had long been plagued by poverty at a scale and a level of severity that has rarely been seen anywhere else in the world." Therefore, "the CPC has taken the people's happiness and the nation's rejuvenation as its aspiration since its founding." The Chinese Communists have fulfilled their promise after going through two historical stages. First, the founding of the People's Republic of China in 1949 and the establishment of the socialist system have provided basic institutional guarantees for addressing the root causes of poverty. Then, the reform and opening up, which started about four decades ago, accelerated the country's development and poverty alleviation. "Seeing that poor people and poor areas will enter the moderately prosperous society together with the rest of the country is a solemn promise made by our Party." It is the oath President Xi Jinping, the true advocate of poverty alleviation in the new phase, has emphasized since 2012.

The Main Indexes of China's Development

Under the leadership of the Communist Party of China, the development indexes of China since 1949 are impressive. Especially since the start of reform and opening up, China has lifted 770 million rural people out of poverty: the number accounts for more than 70 percent of the world's total over the same period. We have noticed that in terms of the number of people lifted out of poverty, China has achieved the goal set on the UN 2030 Agenda for Sustainable Development 10 years ahead of schedule. In addition, China established the world's largest social welfare system during its 13th Five-Year Plan period (2016–2020). By the end of 2020, 95 percent of Chinese had been covered by the country's basic medical insurance. In 2020, China's average life expectancy reached 77.3 years, while the average life expectancy at the time of the founding of the PRC was only 36 years! The special poverty alleviation policy currently implemented in China is more focused on lifting the most vulnerable people out of poverty, thus consolidating the fruits of development already achieved. This poverty alleviation policy is actually a powerful means of enhancing social cohesion. Its purpose is to help the poorest people improve their living standards and integrate into a moderately prosperous society.

China's current poverty alleviation policy entered a decisive implementation stage after the 18th National Congress of the Communist Party of China in 2012. After eight years of hard work, by the end of 2020, China declared that it had "achieved the goal of eliminating extreme poverty – a key goal for the new era of building socialism with Chinese characteristics." According to Chinese official data, "The 98.99 million people in rural areas living below the current poverty threshold all shook off poverty; all the 128,000 impoverished villages and 832 designated poor counties got rid of poverty. China has eliminated poverty over entire regions in 14 contiguous poor areas across the country." An important indicator of shaking off extreme poverty is a remarkable increase in the incomes of the relevant population. For example, in the past eight years of poverty alleviation, the incomes of poor families have increased significantly. The per capita disposable income of poverty-stricken areas increased from 6,079 yuan in 2013 to 12,588 yuan in 2020, up by 11.6 percent per annum on average. The improvement of the living conditions of the impoverished is not only reflected in the increase in income but also the accelerated development of poverty-stricken areas. For example, the once impoverished areas in China have now had access to transport, electricity, drinking water, and communications and have since got rid of the poverty and backwardness label.

China's achievements in poverty alleviation have also been recognized by the World Bank (The World Bank and the United Nations are major international organizations concerned with global poverty alleviation). According to the World Bank's data, 66.3 percent of Chinese people lived below the international poverty line in 1990. The number slumped to only 0.5 percent in 2016, as measured by the percentage of people living on the equivalent of US$1.90 per day in purchasing price parity terms, an international standard of the World Bank mainly applicable to comparisons between countries. In China, the poverty line was set at a per-capita annual income of 2,300 yuan. Since the per capita disposable income of rural residents in China reached 12,588 yuan in 2020, there is no doubt that people in poverty-stricken areas in China are living far above the poverty line. Some commentators noticed that the national poverty line set by China is lower than that specified by the World Bank, accounting for only 85 percent of the latter (See the article "China: The Great Battleground in the Fight Against Inequality" on *Les Echos*, March 4, 2021). That is well said, but it is proper for a country to adjust its national poverty line based on its actual consumption level. For example, the subway fare in Paris is ten times more expensive than that in Guangzhou. If a higher standard is adopted to assess the percentage of the poverty-stricken population, the results will naturally be different. If the World Bank had set China's poverty line at US$5.50, then the poverty-stricken population of the country would have been 225 million, or 16 percent of its total population, which is similar to the poverty rate of the developed country France (14 percent).

China's Measures for Poverty Alleviation

There is no denying that China has made solid progress in poverty alleviation. It created a national database of impoverished households in 2014 which has been updated annually since 2017. China's standards for deregistering those who have emerged from poverty are comprehensive, including all aspects of people's lives. "To help the poor, we must know who they are," said the designer of the poverty alleviation program. To take targeted measures to alleviate poverty, China has developed a set of standards and procedures to identify the poor and the causes of their poverty accurately. The individuals and villages confirmed as poor were then registered, and a national poverty alleviation information system was created. Through this registration system, China has identified every poor individual in every village for the first time in the history of poverty alleviation. Generally speaking, China's poverty alleviation efforts are focused on six areas: identify the poor accurately, arrange targeted programs, utilize capital efficiently, take household-based measures, dispatch first Party secretaries based on village conditions, and achieve the set goals.

China is successful in its poverty alleviation program because it has upheld the "people-centered" philosophy. "The problem of poverty, in essence, is how the people should be treated: the people-centered philosophy is the fundamental driving force behind this cause." What is the main cause of poverty? The white paper mentioned above states: "The root cause of poverty is inadequate development." It means that adequate development is the most effective way to eradicate poverty. During its fight against poverty, China has mainly adopted five measures to address the causes of poverty: boosting the economy to provide more job opportunities, relocating poor people from inhospitable areas, compensating for economic losses associated with reducing ecological damage, improving education in impoverished areas, and providing subsistence allowances for those unable to shake off poverty through their own efforts alone. It has been noted that the core of China's poverty alleviation policy is to create more sustainable employment opportunities, more specifically, to encourage the poor to choose their own modes of operation that suit their actual abilities. Chinese experts told us: "Employment is an important channel for income growth. Steady employment guarantees a stable income for those elevated from poverty."

Moreover, per capita net income is not the only criterion Chinese authorities use in their poverty alleviation efforts. They refer to the criteria other than net income as "Two Assurances and Three Guarantees," meaning assurances of adequate food and clothing and guarantees of access to compulsory education, basic medical services, and safe housing for impoverished rural residents. Although relatively general, the standard is higher than the World Bank's 2015 benchmark of US$1.90 per person per day and is also higher than the UN's Sustainable Development Goals standard. "In many countries, people would be classified as a part of the middle-income class if they were 'free from worries over food and clothing and had access to compulsory education, essential medical services, and safe housing,'" Chinese experts said. Income is the basic but not the only yardstick for measuring poverty in China. While boosting and sustaining the incomes of impoverished rural residents, China has moreover implemented a raft of supportive policies, such as relocating people to more habitable areas, to guarantee better living conditions and public services for low income families in rural areas. Even if China's national poverty line does not meet the World Bank's higher standard for middle-income countries, China's standards ensure that rural Chinese residents can enjoy a better life after they are lifted out of poverty.

The Role of Culture and Tourism in the Fight Against Poverty

Another feature of China's poverty alleviation policy is the promotion of poverty reduction through vigorous development of cultural and tourist undertakings, which gives the cultural and tourist industry a huge role in enriching the rural population. In some old revolutionary base areas, ethnic groups' areas, border areas, and impoverished areas, many measures have been introduced to transform cultural and natural resources into employment and income sources for the poverty-stricken population. Such efforts in tapping the advantages of tourism have greatly promoted the economic and social development of impoverished areas. The Chinese news media specifically cited the example of a village called Simola, surrounded by green mountains and clear waters in Yunnan Province on the southwestern border of China. It is the habitat of the Wa ethnic people. In the past few years, this village has become a national tourist attraction, and in 2020 alone, it received 210,000 visits. Li Shunfa, a villager once trapped in poverty, has embraced a well-off life thanks to the local tourism boom: he can sell more than 300 rice cakes to tourists daily.

In Xuanhan County, Dazhou City, Sichuan Province (located in Southwest China), there is a natural scenic spot called Bashan Grand Canyon. Thanks to the development of cultural tourism, the local residents have shaken off poverty, too. Apart from the 910,000 local residents of 102 villages, 500,000 people in 25 townships in Sichuan's adjacent province Shaanxi and municipality Chongqing also see an increase in their income. Chinese news media have noted that many impoverished areas in China abound in ecological resources, and "the development of rural tourism is turning green mountains and lucid waters into invaluable assets." Economic growth, environmental protection, and improvement of living standards in the relevant areas have shown good momentum due to the incorporation of farmland and scenic spots into the virtuous cycle of rural development. As some experts have said, this poverty alleviation policy "has effectively turned resources into assets, capital into equities, and villagers into shareholders. More and more residents are beginning to enjoy the dividends of tourism development after shaking off poverty."

This poverty alleviation policy has also boosted a large amount of capital investment. According to the Ministry of Culture and Tourism of China, the ministry and other relevant departments will invest 6.5 billion yuan in supporting 656 tourism infrastructure projects in "three regions" (Tibet Autonomous Region, the four prefectures of Hotan, Aksu, Kashgar, and Kizilsu in southern Xinjiang, and the ethnic Tibetan areas in Sichuan, Yunnan, Gansu, and Qinghai) and "three prefectures" (Liangshan Yi Autonomous Prefecture in Sichuan, Nujiang Lisu Autonomous Prefecture in Yunnan, and Linxia Hui Autonomous Prefecture in Gansu). In addition, the ministry will issue about 70 billion yuan in loans to continue improving the rural environment and advance rural tourism in impoverished areas.

Just as poverty alleviation actions have promoted other aspects, investment in culture and tourism has boosted the emergence of a large number of talents in impoverished areas and stimulated the enthusiasm of local people. The Ministry of Culture and Tourism of China has implemented a talent support plan in old revolutionary base areas, ethnic groups' areas, border areas, and impoverished areas, such as helping these areas to introduce scarce professionals, launching a program to nurture leaders of rural cultural and tourist enterprises, etc. It has offered more than 700 training sessions in poor and backward areas free of charge, thus effectively promoting the self-development capacity of these areas. For example, in the Xiangxi Tujia and

Miao Autonomous Prefecture in Hunan Province, traditional ethnic handicrafts have been revitalized. The local government has made great efforts to protect and integrate local intangible cultural heritage into economic development. Some institutions of higher learning, like Jiangnan University, offer training courses on bamboo weaving and brocading. The news media reported such a case: After attending two training sessions, a farmer named Luo Weiying successfully set up a handicraft cooperative in her village with 132 workers and an annual income of 580,000 yuan.

Western Criticism of China's Poverty Alleviation Policy

Some people can view China's poverty alleviation policy objectively and in good faith in the Western world, but some always criticize it. The BBC questioned it in an article titled "Has China lifted 100 million people out of poverty?". The first point of view is that China's achievements in poverty alleviation are not as impressive as publicized, for other countries have also achieved positive results in poverty alleviation. It is true that China is not the only country engaged in poverty alleviation, but according to the evaluation of relevant international institutions, the number of people benefiting from poverty alleviation in China alone accounts for 70 percent of the total number of people lifted out of poverty in the world. In the past eight years, about 10 million people have been lifted out of poverty in China every year, amounting to the total population of a medium-sized European country! In the face of this fact, it is indeed difficult to underestimate the great efforts and major achievements China has made in its fight against poverty.

The BBC's second point of view is that China, an upper-middle-income country categorized by the World Bank, should set its national poverty line at US$5.50 per day, which is among the highest standards for upper-middle-income countries. In response to this criticism, we would like to say that a country's income level is defined by its gross national income (GNI) per capita. As an average number, this indicator can be easily influenced by extreme outlying values and cannot provide a whole picture of the situation. In fact, the World Bank's poverty line is no more than a monetary threshold indicating the typical value of essentials needed to sustain one adult. However, China has developed a comprehensive, multi-dimensional standard comprising not only per capita income but also a series of other requirements, such as housing security, basic medical care, and compulsory education. China's standard is clearly more realistic than a simple monetary standard, which varies considerably from country to country.

Camille Boullenois, a French researcher specializing in contemporary Chinese issues, has put forth a series of criticisms on China's poverty alleviation policy. Her article "Poverty Alleviation in China: The Rise of State-Sponsored Corporate Paternalism" was published in *China Perspectives* in 2020. This expert on China acknowledges that "since taking office, President Xi Jinping's government has granted massive funding to what has become China's strongest poverty-reduction campaign ever." China's official statistics show that poverty reduction funds allocated by the central budget more than doubled between 2012 and 2018, with a particularly notable jump in 2016 and 2017. Camille also acknowledges that poverty alleviation has become a major task of the Chinese government and accounts for a large proportion of the national budget. For example, in Henan's X County, one of the counties studied in Camille's paper, special poverty alleviation funds amounted to 273 million yuan in 2018, slightly more than local government revenues from taxation (272 million yuan) and general non-taxation sources (97 million yuan). Camille believes that the way these funds are distributed has important consequences on social stratification locally.

Camille argues that China's poverty alleviation policy has shifted since the early 2000s. The rising inequality and social instability "led to another policy shift, towards more inclusive growth and more redistribution of wealth." At the same time, several nationwide social insurance schemes were rolled out and progressively included migrant workers and rural residents. The 2000s were also characterized by tax reforms benefiting the rural poor and increased poverty alleviation funds. It was during this time that *dibao* (minimum livelihood guarantee) became one of the major pillars of poverty reduction in China. But its conceptualization and implementation changed over time. Originally thought of as a way to support laid-off workers during the transition to the market economy, the program was then redirected towards prioritizing aid to the old, the sick, and people unable to work. This re-targeting of the *dibao* program has diminished the stigma associated with being taken care of by the state. But it has also limited the program's ability to reduce poverty significantly. Overall, the extant literature shows that the *dibao* significantly affects the poverty of its recipients but has a very small effect on overall poverty.

Camille's study points out that since coming to power in 2013, Xi Jinping's government has been credited by analysts with several innovations in poverty alleviation approaches. First, the "targeted poverty alleviation" approach targets poor households rather than whole villages and creates custom-made projects adapted to their needs to allocate funds more accurately. Second, in line with Xi's focus on eradicating corruption and the misallocation of funds, the government has sought to increase and better supervise the role of Party institutions in village-level poverty alleviation. Poverty alleviation criteria were established on which officials are evaluated, alongside established criteria such as GDP and social stability.

Based on the study of detailed budgets in eight rural counties and ethnographic and interview data in a ninth county, Camille argues that China's poverty alleviation program shapes the distribution of power and resources in its rural areas. She also believes that China's poverty alleviation predominately focuses on infrastructure investment and support to the local economy rather than on social insurance, education, and household subsidies. Support for local companies, she argues, entails co-opting established enterprises rather than supporting new entrepreneurship among poor households. In Camille's eyes, the Chinese approach to rural poverty alleviation highlights "the emergence of a state-sponsored corporate paternalism that strengthens local hierarchies of wealth and power."

If this study is not without interest, it can be noted that it often uses concepts that are not always adequate to explain China's poverty alleviation policy. For example, it says that "local governments allocate funds to infrastructure development and economic growth, rather than direct financial transfers and social insurance. It highlights a market-oriented approach to poverty alleviation that relies on trickle-down effects, reproducing patterns that China experimented with in the 1990s." But remember that the development of public infrastructure, which is an essential part of rural revitalization, has nothing to do with the liberal doctrine of "trickle-down," according to which the wealth of the rich will eventually overflow and benefit the poor. Infrastructure is an investment direction that directly benefits all people. Moreover, in terms of poverty alleviation, it is far more effective to create conditions for local economic development than to hand out subsistence allowances directly, even if a safety net (minimum livelihood guarantee) is naturally needed to deal with the most serious situations.

In her study, Camille has repeatedly criticized China's poverty alleviation policy for imposing some kind of corporate paternalism on poor households. "The frequent emphasis on poor households' willingness to work shows that, for local governments, at least part of the problem of poverty is the result of poor mental dispositions of poor households. As a result, the government must rely on 'ideological education' to encourage poor households to work in poverty alleviation workshops and increase their income. This argument hints at a paternalist approach to poverty alleviation, seeking to 'bring discipline to the lives of the poor so that they can become competent actors who recognize and act on their interests as freely choosing agents of the market.' Poor people are considered bad market actors who need incentives and coercion from the government to enforce rational and disciplined behavior." The problem with this argument is that it ignores the real driving force behind China's poverty alleviation drive. In fact, China is trying to create and sustain jobs and stabilize the material conditions of the poor through various factors. To achieve this goal, it is necessary to help and support the poor in all aspects, encouraging them to work. The best remedy for poverty is undoubtedly paid employment.

In fact, when studying China, Camille always seems to stick to a frame of reference more suitable for poverty alleviation in the West. The West does allow high unemployment, but to mitigate the impact of low employment on the economy, the Western governments have introduced numerous assistance schemes. She commented on China's poverty alleviation policy: "In contrast to infrastructure spending and subsidies to enterprises, the surveyed budgets are characterized by a striking absence of direct financial help, subsidies to poor households, and living allowances." Regarding poverty alleviation, China's logic differs from most Western countries' social-liberal logic. While providing work opportunities for the poor, the Chinese government strives to create conditions for the employed population to ensure they have access to education, housing, health care, and transportation. This multi-dimensional and non-monetary rural poverty alleviation policy is obviously more stringent and effective. The brilliant achievements of China's poverty alleviation in 2021 have been recognized by relevant international organizations, which is enough to prove that its efforts are successful. In stark contrast, in Western capitalist countries, the government is only satisfied with providing subsistence allowances for the poor without introducing any measures that will help the unemployed integrate into the world of work, even if they are young and still able to work. In order to understand the connotation of China's poverty alleviation policy and to correctly view its achievements in this regard, we must first understand the goals and methods of China's poverty alleviation.

Positive Comments from International Organizations and Foreign Experts

On March 16, 2021, Elliott Harris, Chief Economist of the United Nations, said, "This (China's success in ending extreme poverty) is a very valuable lesson for us all: the elimination of poverty is not something that can be achieved in one quick action or with one policy change. It needs a constant and strong commitment and a consistent approach." Noting that China's poverty alleviation achievements are reflected in all aspects, not just in economic growth, Mr. Harris believes that two aspects deserve special attention: rural development and digital transformation. "The first is that China's success in eliminating extreme poverty is at least partly a success of rural development, for that is where the majority of the remaining poverty was, and that is where many of those who first benefitted from poverty reduction were." As for the second aspect, Mr. Harris stressed "the role that digital technoogies, and more generally, digital transformation, have played in generating wealth and helping to lift the poor out of poverty."

Mr. Harris believes that China has long been committed to poverty alleviation. He said the country's success resulted from "the impressive achievements in poverty reduction in the second half of the MDG (Millennium Development Goals) era."

Talking about the relationship between development and poverty, Mr. Harris emphasized that China's achievements in poverty alleviation are solid. Harris said that "progress in development is often tenuous. One often hears of shocks causing people to slide back into poverty. But that seems not to have been the case in China." Therefore, resilience to shocks seems to have been one of the hallmarks of the anti-poverty effort. "That will also be a part of the valuable lessons that China's experience offers to other countries." "There are many characteristics of the Chinese society and economy that set it apart from other developing countries," he said. "The most evident of these, of course, is the sheer size of the population and the massive scale of the domestic market," he said, adding this offers China an option of "transition to growth driven by the domestic market, shifting away from the dependence on trade and investment."

According to Mohammad Saiyedul Islam, a Bangladeshi expert (a doctoral student from the School of International Trade and Economics at the Jiangxi University of Finance and Economics and an independent journalist in China), the achievements in poverty alleviation demonstrate China's "real strategic advantages." He also stressed that over the past 40 years since China implemented the reform and opening up policy in 1978, it has helped 770 million rural people escape poverty. The Asia Poverty Reduction Report 2020, published at the Boao Forum for Asia on December 15, pointed out that East Asian countries, particularly China, have played a decisive role in poverty elimination and reduction. After being elected as president in March 2013, Xi Jinping has put the fundamental task of eliminating poverty in an all-round way as an absolute political priority, for which generations of Chinese people have been striving. In November 2013, President Xi, who was on an inspection tour in the western region of Hunan Province (in central China), put forward the concept of "targeted poverty alleviation" for the first time. From then on, the strategy of targeted poverty alleviation has been one of the important guidelines for poverty relief. Under this guideline, Mr. Xi required the local governments to formulate policies and take measures to alleviate poverty for targeted households and individuals to ensure the effectiveness of policy implementation.

During the Thirteenth Five-year Plan (2016-2020) period, the goal of poverty alleviation was realized. Especially in terms of poverty reduction and resettlement of poor people in poverty-stricken areas, China completed the task of resettling the 9.6 million poor population with meager resources within eight years. It may be said that this is a great contribution to the poverty reduction campaign worldwide. While making tremendous achievements in poverty alleviation, China may support other countries in poverty reduction and promoting economic growth. At the Johannesburg Summit of the Forum on China-Africa Cooperation (FOCAC Summit), President Xi announced China would implement ten cooperation plans with Africa, including the China-Africa poverty reduction plan. In the future, China will overcome the difficulties brought about by the COVID-19 pandemic to reinvigorate its economy and make continuous efforts in poverty eradication. Mohammad Saiyedul Islam said some Westerners commented that in a country with a huge population of 1.4 billion, such a poverty eradication plan was overoptimistic. However, China has made it. He explained that this is because the goal of socialism is to build a moderately prosperous society in all respects. The representatives of the Communist Party of China (CPC) at different levels have made concerted efforts to eliminate poverty by systematically implementing the aid-to-the-poor policy. "Under the leadership of President Xi, millions of Chinese people have been lifted out of poverty and filled with contentment. Suppose leaders of other countries wish to get millions of their people out of extreme poverty and end the tragedies brought about by impoverishment. In that case, they should learn from China's poverty alleviation campaign and realize that China is ready to share its innovative poverty alleviation mode."

According to the standard formulated by the World Bank, one with a daily living expense of less than US$2 is deemed poor. With this standard, over 700 million people in the world are living below the absolute poverty line. The prospect is far from promising, as the pace of poverty elimination worldwide has been slowed due to the COVID-19 pandemic. Statistics from the World Bank show that by the end of 2021, the population living below the absolute poverty line in the world had been likely to amount to 150 million. Against this background, it is a magnificent feat for China, a country with a population of 1.4 billion, to win the battle against poverty and greatly contribute to the world's endeavor in poverty eradication. Figures explain the facts. Among 100 people worldwide who have shaken off poverty, 70 are Chinese. Such remarkable achievement naturally drew attention from the officials of the United Nations. For example, according to Niger Brett, director for the Asia Pacific Region at the International Fund for Agricultural Development (IFAD), China's success proves that poverty eradication is not a fantasy but feasible. So far, China's method works well in practice, and other countries may draw some inspiration from it.

Meanwhile, China has taken concrete measures to help other developing countries to implement the 2030 Agenda for Sustainable Development. Over the past 60 years, China sent more than 600,000 people to help 166 countries and international organizations and provided RMB 400 billion yuan as assistance funds worldwide. Moreover, China has unconditionally cancelled the mature interest-free government loans of the poor countries with heavy debts and the least-developed countries. The UN Secretary-General

António Guterres spoke highly of China's efforts in this regard, saying that China has made a remarkable contribution to worldwide poverty alleviation undertakings.

Inspiration from China's Poverty Alleviation Policy

Poverty is a major problem that all countries face, with developed countries no exception. Poverty alleviation is one of the top priorities of every country, and it has long been a difficult task for the international community. People in extreme poverty are often deprived of all the basic necessities for a decent life, such as food, drinking water, housing, education, health care, and transportation. It is for this reason that the Millennium Development Goals and the Sustainable Development Goals formulated by the United Nations have placed the eradication of poverty and hunger in an important position. In its modernization process, China has always prioritized poverty alleviation. It introduced and implemented a set of proactive poverty alleviation policies, and fruitful results were finally obtained. At the National Poverty Alleviation Summary and Commendation Conference held on February 25, 2021, President Xi Jinping solemnly announced that China had secured a "comprehensive victory" in the fight against poverty.

The accomplishment comes after President Xi promised in 2013 to end extreme rural poverty by 2020. Since the fight against poverty started, China has spent massive funds totaling 1.6 trillion yuan, equivalent to US$40 billion every year. This tough battle was deployed and carried out by a powerful country led by the Communist Party of China, which always keeps the people's well-being in mind. Thanks to the unremitting efforts of all the Chinese people, especially the more than 3 million officials and Party members, great achievements have finally been made. These efforts have contributed to enhancing social cohesion and improving the living conditions of people in need. In the years to come, such efforts may continue to accelerate the elimination of social inequalities. Facts have proved that poverty can be completely overcome as long as the strength of the entire country and society is mobilized.

Gustavo Alejandro Girado

An Argentine expert on China issues, the Councillor and Consul General of the Argentine Embassy in Beijing. He is a professor at the University of Buenos Aires, and director of the "Directed Research Project of Science and Technology" of the National University of Cordoba. He is also the founder and director of the Graduate Program of the Studies on Contemporary China at the National University of Lanús. He has taken part in the writing of several academic works and hundreds of academic papers, including *The Rising China and Future Relations between China and Latin America in the Aspects of Politics, Social Culture and Economy, A World Made in China, and China's Technological Independence and Innovation.*

The Essence of the Road of Technological Independence Taken by the People's Republic of China

Some time ago, I researched whether the People's Republic of China has a dependent economy. I always believed that China had, and still has, a dependent economy,[1] which, however, was immediately clarified by the Chinese side: China's economy is not what it used to be. Policies, people and things have all changed, and the dependent nature of China's economy is just the reason behind the country's determination to restructure its economy. China has made enormous efforts to reverse this situation politically and economically, so it is crucial to focus on the transitional process. Starting from a full understanding of its own situation, China embarked on a long road characterized by the transition from dependence to independence. China has initiated the world's largest infrastructure development project designed, promoted, and funded by itself, which I mean the New Silk Road, now known as the Belt and Road Initiative (BRI).

It is a brand-new model of development characterized by starting from the cooperation with neighboring countries, then with other countries, with the promise of benefiting all. On the other hand, however, it is a path of interdependence. This dependency relationship resulted from the exertion of influence from outside. As the early participant and beneficiary of production internationalization, China could not have developed as it is today without

---

[1] *How Did the Chinese Succeed? Reasons for the Asian Giant's Great Development*, ASTREA, 2017. *A World Made in China – Long March to Building the New Global Order*, Intellectual Capital, 2021. Both works were released in Buenos Aires, Argentina.

advanced knowledge imparting. In other words, the lack of knowledge will result in dependence. Without the mastery of knowledge, one cannot create anything and is subject to dependence. As we see, China is moving towards independence because it has witnessed how powerful countries set the standards, models, and norms we must use daily. Some powerful countries are standard setters and users (and so are we). If China does not participate in the formulation of these norms and standards, there is no way out of it. And it will have no choice but to follow other powers forever.

Therefore, by implementing the Belt and Road Initiative, China is trying to build its own new cooperation model to become independent and benefit all the partners eventually. In short, China is following its own rules on the new path to achieve its stated goal of building a "moderately prosperous" society (which China has explicitly expressed). In addition, we will be the witnesses of the times. Since there have been too many discussions about hegemonism in this era, I don't have to go into details here. I only want to summarize the hegemony in the production links of technology which affects daily life to a large extent. The precondition for establishing norms, standards, and processes in the information and telecommunication technology field is to acquire invention patents that must be transformed into innovative technologies. Next comes standardization, global modeling, and the eventual extension to all enterprises in powerful (not necessarily large) countries.

As we see in the media, the difference in the manufacturing industry model is the background of the trade war between China and the US. It is certainly true of the disputes over tariffs and trade quotas between the two economies. We believe that this is just the tip of the iceberg of conflicts, and it is inevitable that there will be problems between China and the US. At the moment, we don't know how this conflict will be resolved. How things will play out is often unexpected: the conflict between the leading power and the challenger usually ends up in the use of force.

Peaceful solutions are rare and usually achieved through the formulation of cooperative plans. I want to talk about how China initially relied on the technical knowledge created and standardized by the enterprises of the victorious nations in World War II to achieve its development. I also want to discuss how China succeeded in breaking away from such dependence through initiatives such as the Belt and Road Initiative, what path China intends to take, and what position China's decision-makers will occupy in the world to make the world take China's interests into account and help to realize mutual development. In short, efforts are made to let the whole world accept China. The world under the post-Bretton Woods System is in a difficult situation. China knows that the opportunity to participate in drafting new rules for the so-called "global governance" has arrived.

China and Standardization of Schemes, Models, and Norms

Before the beginning of the 21st century, China did not seek technology transfer from foreign countries. Instead, it tried independent innovation many times but found it difficult to make breakthroughs. In 1988, China's Torch Program enjoyed special attention and promotion. The heart of the program is creating the necessary infrastructure and ecosystem to support innovation and start-ups, including many business technology incubators and mass creator spaces (Damien Ma, 2019). It was not until the introduction of the *Outline of the National Program for Long- and Medium-Term Scientific and Technological Development (2006-2020)* that China's road to scientific and technological independence turned the corner. Finally, with regard to policy design, national resources were concentrated on "independent innovation" and "harmonious development." When China's political decision-makers realized it should reduce its dependency on foreign countries, standards became an important tool to reduce technological dependency and improve independent industrial innovation capability. It was closely related to export-oriented enterprises (the prevailing pattern of development in China since the establishment of exclusive economic zones) and a small number of state-owned enterprises engaged in export business. Based on this interest consideration, the policies of patent standards were successively rolled out in China. Previously, people were fully aware of the high cost paid by using foreign patents. Then, in 2009, the Standardization Administration of China (SAC) issued the "Rules for the Disposal of National Standards Involving Patents."

In the past, China regarded technical standards as a means of promoting foreign trade. But technical rules and standards were the first obstacles to its products entering the international market.[2] China's standardization system proved to be burdened by a planned economy. Since the reform and opening up, the standardization strategy and its system have significantly changed. In a very short time, China improved its ability to set and implement standards and began to participate in international organizations that can boost its development.

Since December 2001, when China became a full member of the WTO, the country has experienced a period of rapid growth. The policy proved extremely effective in promoting independent innovation through the extensive use of standards, which were only confined to the country itself. Ten years later, things changed drastically. According to Según Ziegler (2010), "China's standardization system is quite mature. Today, China has more standards than Europe, covering more areas of the economy than any other industrialized country." This situation has continued to this day.

Therefore, China's growth is bound to translate into development. The use of independent standards drives technological progress included in the industrial policy making, which, in turn, is incorporated into economic development plans. Through communication, Ernst (2011) identified a set of priorities from experts' studies and suggestions. The most prominent of these is that the state will continue to play an important role as a facilitator and coordinator of standards and innovation policies and fundamentally view

---

[2] In the planned economic system, ministries and commissions involved in industrial activities were responsible for standardization work of large state-owned enterprises under their governance. National and ministerial regulations were binding and enforced by the government.

standardization strategies as platforms for independent innovation. We think there are two prominent key points. Based on the above understanding, China formulated the "single national champion of manufacturing industry" policy to consolidate the progress and integration of large-scale enterprises. A large number of small companies, which had emerged and developed under the wing of big companies, subsequently became the suppliers of the latter. As a result, the technological level of the manufacturing industry as a whole was enhanced accordingly. The industry's contribution is so important that it now becomes the focus of the struggle for supremacy between China and the US.

First, Chinese companies have to pay for using foreign patents and licenses. Reducing such expenses is a top priority for China to set standards. To that end, China has developed a plan to incorporate foreign enterprises into its standard-setting organizations. In exchange, foreign businesses must make corresponding contributions, including, for example, the disclosure of necessary patents in the technology field. Second, companies are encouraged to become "major players in rule-making," as Wang Ping et al. mentioned in 2010. At the time, China had no experience setting out an institutional framework for standardization programs. After discussion, it was agreed that China should adopt a dual-track strategy by combining international standards with national independent innovation standards (within the newly-established institutional framework). In this way, China gained space in international standards organizations.

China's leaders firmly believe in the importance of the country's economic reform. Therefore, they are determined to improve scientific equipment and technology (Girado, 2017). The *Outline of the National Program for Long- and Medium-Term Scientific and Technological Development (2006-2020)* is the outcome of a series of actions taken over the years since the policy of reform and opening up was implemented, which has resulted in formulating sound policies for scientific and technological development. The outline has catalyzed China's standardization strategy. The exposition of the standardization development in the 11th Five-Year Plan (Standardization Administration of China, 2006) gives a detailed account of how institutions should implement independent innovation projects because previous innovation processes were neither satisfactory nor had institutional channels to be promoted.

The attempt to achieve economic development simply through technological integration will increase the degree of dependence on foreign countries. As Halty Carrere (1974) said, technological development policy should ensure decision-making power over technological progress. Otherwise, as Alejandro Nadal Egea (1973) pointed out, failure will be incurred. He regarded the weaknesses in the system of science and technology as a simple delay in developing economies' lagging independent development. The use of the concept "gap" makes it impossible for people (in a politically correct way) to use "technology dependency" as a tool for analyzing the structure of the state. There is no doubt that some people will talk about spiritual dependence ("cultural colonialism"), an idea that is helpful to the layering of dependence in a different sequence, and to change such dependence is just the kernel aspiration of the Communist Party of China.

This view forces us to analyze the interaction between development and technological needs. It is done not only to define the technological needs of a given sector (for example, industry) but also to ensure that the demand for certain technologies meets with a response so that the development process of domestic technologies is sustainable and the dependence on foreign technologies is reduced. China pursues innovation policies because it has no other choice. It has to tackle the difficulties head-on in unfamiliar fields because it cannot integrate into other economies. China needs steady growth to eliminate dependence, which means a big increase in per capita living standards. However, it depends on a significant improvement in the systematic competitiveness of its economy. Of course, competitiveness can also be boosted by expanding productivity. But the economy does not always determine a country's future automatically. As a result, China will succeed economically but risk losing the political sovereignty that determines its future direction.

Like other countries' plans for independent development, China's has the features of nationalism and autarky, reflecting policymakers' determination to reduce China's dependency on the intellectual property of transnational capital and their dissatisfaction with being forced to pay high fees for the utilization of unrelated patents.

China had planned to reduce its dependence on foreign technology to 30 percent or less by 2020 or 2021 (this article was written in March 2022). Some parts of the plan showed China's concern and China feared that relying on other countries (by implication, referring to the United States and Japan) would threaten China's national and economic security. Now the US is making the same argument, negotiating with China on several areas where it feels threatened. To get out of the dilemma, China holds that economic growth requires a proper balance between national innovation and the use of imported technology. The key to the plan's success is not purchasing core technologies in critical areas that affect the economy and national security (such as next-generation Internet technology, high-end CNC machine tools, and high-resolution land observation systems). In August 2006, Ernst wrote: Regarding semiconductors, China's Ministry of Information Industry said, "We should increase the self-sufficiency rate by a large margin. The self-sufficiency rate of the integrated circuits used in national defense information and security should reach more than 70 percent, and that of integrated circuits used in communications and digital home appliances should reach more than 30 percent... Basically, self-sufficiency in key products is to be realized."

Not long ago, China's focus on innovation and standardization constituted a small part of its international economic diplomacy. However, China's assessment of policy issues has changed markedly with its development. Today, China's innovation policy has been seen as a threat to US innovation and competitiveness and become the most concerned issue in the bilateral relationship (Girado, 2021). Moreover, the United States accuses China of using the policy to harm the global trade (a "discriminatory" WTO term) and challenge the dominant position of the US in the knowledge economy, which reflects not only the viewpoint of the American companies that have suffered loss due to the competition with China but also the attitudes of the research institutions they fund.

As Ernst (2011) pointed out, the American Chamber of Commerce believes that China's innovation policy "has restricted American enterprises' access to the Chinese and world markets and their competitiveness. China is creating an advantage for its state-owned enterprises. By supporting the enterprises to become a single manufacturing champion, China will severely undermine the innovation ability of the US economy in key areas, which will, in turn, impair the competitiveness and livelihoods of US businesses and their employees."[3]

China's entry into the global standard-setting system and coordination with independent innovation policies are impressive. Faced with its diminished leadership, the US has to respond to the new challenger. Standardization and intellectual property rights are at the heart of this conflict. In addition, standardization is the main regulatory tool to ensure product quality and safety in global value chains and international production networks. It must be combined with intellectual property rights and original standards. As a result, international standards, nationally uniform standards, and bilaterally recognized standards (bilateral agreements, regional agreements, free trade agreements, etc.) are unexceptionally under constant pressure from trade stakeholders. The above are typical alternative and normative responses to globalization and economic integration's political and economic demands. Each country or region must balance its own priorities with its own interests, whether regional or international.

That is why it is important to understand China's determination to become a technological superpower. Reducing the dependency on technology is a fundamental consideration in the decision-making of the Political Bureau of the Central Committee of the CPC. Compared with the American Dream, the Chinese Dream — not of individuals, but of the collective — aims to build a "moderately prosperous" society (improving the living standards of

---

[3] Ernst evidenced the testimony given by Jeremy Waterman, Senior Director of "Greater China" on June 15, 2010 during Investigation No. 332 by the US Trade Commission Hearing. The investigation alleged that China committed crimes in making intellectual property and independent innovation policies and may do harm to the US economy.

the Chinese people) by 2021, the 100th anniversary of the founding of the Communist Party of China. By 2049 (the centenary of the founding of the People's Republic of China), it will enter the stage of "all-round development" and realize "national rejuvenation."

The Influence of Policy

The latest professional literature reviews the next step in China-US relations. Perhaps the US will isolate China to prevent it from making technological advances, make it unable to establish its model in certain fields, and prevent it from making the kind of progress in the formulation of norms and standards as the US claims. On the other hand, China has accelerated its strategy of "independent innovation" unprecedentedly. China will continue to promote innovation construction in three (or even four) five-year plans, making innovation a basic national policy. China continues to subsidize, stimulate and promote innovation. While its industrial technology still lags behind the West in some areas, for example, chips, China could take further steps to prevent foreign products from getting in. It is better to let China become "independent at an early date" than to hold it back. I agree with Xulio Ríos (2020) that "Huawei is de-Americanizing by leaps and bounds." China is rapidly investing in state-of-the-art chips to reduce its dependence on American manufacturers. We try to describe the world-shaking events today. It is generally recognized that everything will change after the world goes through this subtle transformation.

Therefore, we might as well take a step back and choose more appropriate wording from other perspectives. We took inspiration from Martin Jacques[4], a British scholar. After the British government announced it would ban Chinese tech giant Huawei from its 5G sector, he said: "(...) the story has

---

[4] Senior research fellow, Department of Politics and International Studies, Cambridge University.

returned to its original point. In 1793, China's emperor Qianlong of the Qing Dynasty told the British king that China did not need goods made in Britain. It marked the beginning of the following 150 years of decline for China. In 2020, the UK told China that it did not need the latest Chinese technology. Any country with a glorious past will feel uncomfortable confronting an emerging power. Anyone familiar with the Qing Dynasty's history knows the policy of secluding the country from the outside world pursued by the Qing Dynasty during that period. When George Macartney, an Englishman, was ordered to show Emperor Qianlong of the Qing Dynasty models of telescopes, clocks, cannons, and warships, the emperor regarded them only as strange feats of art." The Chinese emperor refused to take the British inventions as a light of enlightenment because China at the time could not understand what was happening in Europe. In his letter to Britain's King George III in 1793, the Qing emperor insisted there was no need for the products of the industrial revolution, which the British took with them all over the world. For the subsequent 150 years, China grappled with this situation, trying to find its way into the real outside world, but that was not necessarily what the Qing emperor wanted. The transition is painful and unsustainable. The definition of standards is important because technology will dominate the future market, and whoever standardizes technology will reap huge dividends.

We have a hunch that it is extremely difficult (legally or practically) to challenge the established standards unless new technology triggers a complete replacement. At the same time, rolling it will not be easy for the United States to roll out policies to stop China's technological upgrading. China's policies affect the interests of the entire Western world by creating Chinese counterparts visible or partially visible to traditional Western standard-setting organizations. They can lead to unforeseen decoupling (although there is a certain economic cost), for example, the establishment of new international standard-setting organizations with Chinese characteristics. The protagonists of decoupling—the US and China—are both seeking greater control over different parts of the global technology value chain and trying to exert a greater influence on setting international standards. By building digital systems at the physical and basic technological levels, competing economies hope to gain a structural and long-term advantage over their competitors. As China's ability to define its own technology standards grows, it will increasingly set international standards in its own interests.

Up to now, it seems that the US containment policy has failed to produce the desired result because China is very different from the Soviet Union. Chinese companies have close ties with foreign companies, including those in the United States. There is a similarity between America's rivalry with Russia and China because Washington views both Moscow and Beijing as (geopolitical and ideological) rivals but views China as "more dangerous," for which the reason is that it prospered economically and undermined an important tenet of the American ideology: the US holds that the liberal political model of the democracies of the West must accompany economic prosperity. Therefore, the American government's anti-China measures should be understood as a sign of the new normal. Suppose the West chooses to build technological barriers. In that case, it is not surprising that the East will decide to set up various organizations to regulate the technical operation and standardization patterns, establish new management models, and carry out standardization construction in the Chinese style, mode, and norms.

On the other hand, beyond manufacturing, the financial sector is well aware of what it means to be Asian players. By contrast, they are very flexible and work energetically at full throttle. In fact, China is building a thoroughfare to these ideas and new models and, through powerful tools, stimulating and advancing its participation in the global governance. We agree with Martin Jacques that the Belt & Road Initiative reflects China's relations with developing countries. This relationship is rooted in China's semi-colonial history and status as a developing country. Like the "indigenous innovation" policy devised by the Political Bureau of the Central Committee of the CPC, the Belt and Road Initiative has become another tool. To understand the policy of formulating technical standards, one must analyze the specific political and economic dynamics of a country like China and its industrial structure and position in the global production network.

In the tide of change, it is necessary to understand what types of problems are emerging. China is a very typical example. We can see the shift from total dependence to independence through the strategic transformation. In a sense, this is an unprecedented stage of change. In the near future, people must learn to adapt to the world's changes. Learning to be adaptable is not just the preserve of the Western world but a required course for everyone.

References:

- Ernst, Dieter. (2011) "Indigenous Innovation and Globalization. The Challenge for China's Standardization Strategy", East-West Center, Honolulu.

- Girado, Gustavo Alejandro. (2017) "How Did the Chinese Succeed? Reasons for the Asian Giant's Great Development", Ed. Astrea, Buenos Aires.

- Girado, Gustavo Alejandro. (2021) "A World Made in China", Ed. Intellectual Capital, Buenos Aires.

- Girado, Gustavo Alejandro. (2021) "China's Technological Independence and Innovation," Ed. Prunus Press, EE.UU.

- Halty Carrère, Máximo. (1974) "Production, Transference, and Adaptation of Industrial Technology," *Studies on the Development of Science and Technology*, No.11, Program for Regional Development of Science and Technology, Department of Scientific Affairs, General Secretariat of Organization of American States.

- Ma, Damien. (2019) "Torchbearer: Igniting Innovation in China's Tech Clusters," the article published in MacroPolo.com on August 14.

- Nadal Egea, Alejandro. (1973) "Normative Planning and S&T Construction," Exterior Commerce, Mexico.

- Ríos, Xulio. (2020) "Huawei and the Mantra of Security," article on the *Observation of the Policy of China*, Pontevedra, Spain, July 20, 2020.

- Wang Ping, Wang Yiyi, and John Hill. (2010) "Standardization Strategy of China: Achievements and Challenges." *East-West Center Working Paper,*

Economics Series (No.107).

- Ziegler, Klaus. (2010) "Foreword to Talk Standards Online Forum 'Standards Policy in China'," June 24.

Chea Munyrith

Currently, a Project Consultant of the General Secretariat of the Senate, Director of the Planning and Projects Department of the Civil Society Alliance Forum, Office of the Council of the Ministers' Office, Member of the Directors' Board of Cambodian-Chinese Friendship Association, and President of the Cambodian-Chinese Evolution Research Association. He served as the Director of the Confucius Institute at the Royal Academy of Cambodia. He has devoted himself to studying Sino-Cambodian relations over the years and actively promoted the exchanges and cooperation between China and Cambodia. He completed the translation and proofreading of the Cambodian version of (*Xi Jinping: Governance of China*) (Volumes I and II). He has published books such as *Sino-Cambodian Relations in the Sihanouk Era* and *The Millennium Friendship – The Ancient Times of the History of Sino-Cambodian Exchanges.*

The Model of Poverty Alleviation by China: Towards a Community with a Shared Future for Mankind

When I first read *Xi Jinping: Governance of China* from Volume 1 to Volume 3, and translated Volume 1 and Volume 2 into Cambodian, I started to realize the greatness and wisdom of the great leader of China, and also felt the great power of China. Since I love reading books on poverty reduction and enjoy the social work contributing to the reduction of local Cambodian people's poverty, I have become more aware of the merits of China's reform and poverty reduction. Let me brief about some of my views. China began its reform and opening up in the late 1970s. For the past 40 years, it has addressed the food and clothing problems of the people and advanced towards a more prosperous society. In 2013, President Xi Jinping put forward the concept of "a community with a shared future for mankind." The priority is to solve the problem of poverty and improve people's life.

I have been participating in poverty alleviation projects in cooperation with China in recent years. Therefore, we pay close attention to the content of poverty alleviation in the government work report every year, and this year is no exception. China has completed the task of eliminating absolute poverty, but it is also a significant challenge to prevent these people from returning to poverty. I would like to know what China is doing. This year's government work report states that a five-year transition period will be established to help the people lifted out of poverty find jobs, provide skills training, develop poverty alleviation industries, and prevent them from returning to poverty. In the past ten years, as I have seen, the wealthy provinces in the eastern part of

China directly help the poor areas in the central and western regions. These developments reflect the thoughts of "letting those who become rich first help those who become rich later" and "realizing common prosperity for all." The ideas and practices demonstrate the advantages of the Chinese model.

I have visited China many times and seen various poverty reduction projects. I was amazed by the Chinese people's determination and unity in the fight against poverty. The targeted approaches and detailed and tailored plans impressed me the most. China also makes full use of modern technologies, like big data digital economy, to precisely help poor rural people. I have heard that China's national poverty alleviation data system includes information on almost 90 million poor people. I believe it is the greatest database of poverty reduction in the world. China's successful poverty alleviation practices are essential and inspiring for other developing countries like Cambodia. This book will share those valuable experiences with everyone in the world.

Having witnessed China's achievements in poverty reduction as a Cambodian, I am happy for my Chinese friends and have more confidence in Cambodia's poverty reduction work. In the past 40 years, China has successfully lifted 800 million people out of absolute poverty, which is the most significant poverty reduction achievement in human history. China's poverty alleviation approach is very inspiring to Cambodia. I have visited China several times yearly and have been to Beijing, Shanghai, Guangdong, Yunnan, and other places. I have seen many poverty alleviation projects, the most impressive one of which is Xishuangbanna, Yunnan. There are rich ethnic cultures in Xishuangbanna, and the local government has built roads and houses for poor areas and developed tourist resources with ethnic characteristics to attract tourists. In 2014, I lived in Xishuangbanna for three days and found it a very effective way to alleviate poverty by boosting tourism locally. For example, some families in a village run inns, some run restaurants, some specialize in growing vegetables, and some specialize in raising chickens and ducks to supply restaurants, etc. Different families in a village have different divisions of labor, and the whole village works on providing service for tourists. It not only protects the traditional culture but also increases the income of the local people, and the effect is excellent. The houses in the village are all new. Almost every family has a motorcycle, and many families get their own cars. It can be seen that this approach to poverty alleviation through tourism has improved their lives.

The data reached an all-time high of 13.826 RMB bn in 2020 and a

View China's GDP: Primary Industry: Yunnan: Xishuangbanna from 2005 to 2020 in the chart:

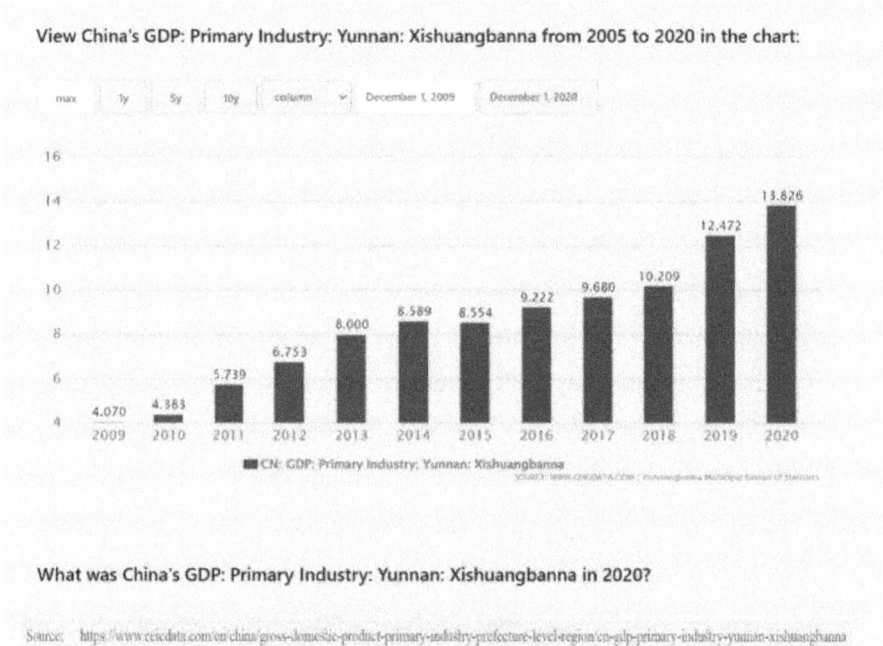

What was China's GDP: Primary Industry: Yunnan: Xishuangbanna in 2020?

Source: https://www.ceicdata.com/en/china/gross-domestic-product-primary-industry-prefecture-level-region/cn-gdp-primary-industry-yunnan-xishuangbanna

Source:https://www.ceicdata.com.cn/en/china/gross-domestic-product-primary-industry-prefecture-level-region/cn-gdp-primary-industry-yunnan-xishuangbanna

record low of 2.790 RMB bn in 2005. Based on the GDP graphic[1], I have noticed that Xishuangbana's GDP is growing yearly. So I think China's poverty reduction work has clear goals, collaborative arrangements, and institutional

[1] GDP: Primary Industry: Yunnan: Xishuangbanna data remains active in CEIC and is reported by the Xishuangbanna Municipal Bureau of Statistics, https://www.xsbn.gov.cn/tjj/324797.news.list.dhtml

responsibilities and has targeted practices for poor villages and households in different regions and environments. For the purpose of long-term development to become rich, these practices are very inspiring to Cambodia. Chinese people said that the experience of "building roads first if you want to get rich" and "helping the poor first" is worth learning from. It is imperative to change people's minds through education and training and let them master the technology and ability to become rich. I have learned that poverty alleviation in many rural areas in China is through the establishment of characteristic agriculture and tourism, but the pandemic has a severe impact on tourism and logistics. These rural areas may experience problems such as poor product sales or a lack of tourist consumption. Fortunately, China's online shopping is very developed, and if the logistics problem can be solved, it may be helpful to encourage people in these rural areas to sell products through the Internet.

I am still very optimistic about China's promotion of rural revitalization. When I visited China for poverty alleviation projects in the past ten years, I saw that poverty alleviation by tourism and e-commerce had played a significant role in rural areas. For example, when I went to Yunnan, I saw that the government introduced a project of alleviating poverty through tourism to a poverty-stricken village, which not only created scenic spots but also trained villagers to manage homestays and restaurants. And some villagers grew vegetables and raised chickens to supply restaurants. Many families rely on tourism to increase their income. Seeing the development of the tourism industry in their hometown, many young people also came home to do business and brought back new ideas.

Poverty is one of the biggest problems in the world, and human survival will be challenged again after the COVID-19 pandemic. People's right to subsistence is primary, and also the basis of other rights and interests.

I would like to briefly summarize the following features of reform and opening up with the Chinese characteristics:

The traditional solutions of various countries are no longer sufficient to cope with more poverty caused by the continuous economic recession.

The practice has proved that the traditional type of poverty alleviation is single and short-term, burdened with red tape, plagued with official corruption, "inefficient," and "superficial in solving the problems." It made some poor areas more and more impoverished. The number of poor people was increasing, a vicious circle formed.

First, the regular distribution of food supplies resulted in dependence and even laziness, and gradually "psychological poverty" would emerge. One doesn't need to do anything but wait for relief, so more and more people will participate in this free program. Endless "charity activities."

Second, there is no accurate data survey to ensure the effects of poverty alleviation. Perhaps some people really want to get food through labor, but no one tells them what to do or where to go. Or the government has nothing to do for them at all.

Third, ineffective and passive governance of some countries has made most poverty alleviation fail to achieve corresponding results and even caused a lot of material waste.

Fourth, to solve the problem of poverty, we need to have a common goal and build a platform or framework, which is also important. Involve all relevant countries and reach a consensus.

Efficient poverty alleviation experience in China has completely solved the drawbacks of traditional solutions.

After studying and researching poverty alleviation with Chinese characteristics, we have learned that these problems are basically avoided, and a positive response model of poverty alleviation with the participation of the whole society has been formed.

1) The government attaches great importance to building a huge platform and sharing a highly unified idea.

Firstly, China has built a huge platform for poverty alleviation work. The Chinese government regards poverty alleviation as a "war" against poverty, which is carried out within the framework of a large national strategy. Poverty alleviation offices and other institutions have been set up by the central and local governments. In this way, all problems are centralized in one department. It greatly changed the phenomenon of departments passing the buck to each other.

Secondly, to elevate poverty reduction work to the level of a human undertaking and regard poverty reduction in China as a part of promoting human development. Under this huge framework, China has made great achievements. Since China's reform and opening up 30 years ago, around 2012, more than 300 million people have been lifted out of poverty. From 2012 to 2017, China's poor rural population dropped from 98.99 million to 30.36 million, a reduction in the fifth consecutive year. It is a feat of poverty eradication in human history, and no country can do it.

We have learned that poverty alleviation projects can only receive attention and better promote cooperation and implementation by building a corresponding platform. Without a goal, or framework, many problems will eventually go unresolved if there is no purpose.

2) China puts the interests of people first, which manifests human rights in a good way.

The biggest difference between China and Western countries is that China's policies are formulated based on the rights and interests of people. The so-called "restrictions on human rights" in China are only those on personal behavior to ensure the interests of the country and the common interests of the society. The Communist Party of China, as the ruling party itself, represents the people's interests. All policies of China put the people's interests first, and what China implements is the actual democratic policy. Western democracies put capital first, flaunting the banner of unrestricted human rights and freedom. The result is that people exchange poverty for the so-called human rights and freedoms. Therefore, the gap between the rich and the poor is bound to grow wider and wider. In a capitalist society, the ruling class believes that wealth and poverty are determined by capital, which is a matter of course, and no ruler will consider what to do for the poor.

Therefore, the inspiration for us is always to put people's rights and interests first, and to establish a fundamental idea for human beings to solve the problem of poverty in the future. It is also the fundamental guarantee for the sustainable implementation of poverty alleviation.

3) China has taken complete supportive measures for poverty alleviation.

Many countries' relatively backward poverty alleviation methods are primarily donations of money or materials by the government or individuals, NGOs, etc., repairing bridges and paving roads, or building small projects. China's poverty alleviation is not for a single department fighting alone, but an overall operation, and done as a huge project. In addition to the central and local government departments at all levels, including the military and police departments, all the available resources in the whole society are utilized, including road and bridge construction enterprises, education, medical and tourist institutions, and public welfare organizations, etc.

There is a saying in China, "Unity is strength." China has adopted a mechanism of poverty alleviation participated by all the people in the whole society, and a cooperation among all parties, which not only prevents empty slogans but also mobilizes the enthusiasm of all parties so that people have more confidence and power. It is worth learning and imitating. I once visited and inspected a remote mountain village in Xishuangbanna, which was poor two years ago. After investigation, a tourism development project was formulated. The Ministry of Commerce, Department of Culture and Tourism and related departments bureaus worked together. After a year, it has been transformed into a brand-new tourist attraction, with characteristic homestays and folk customs, attracting many tourists. After less than a year, the whole village has been lifted out of poverty. It is just a microcosm of China's many poverty alleviation plans, which have brought together all relevant departments and personnel at the central and local levels, as well as the village grassroots and the villagers' unremitting efforts. It is not difficult to imagine that a "war against poverty" with a population of more than 90 million is equivalent to several times or even dozens of times the base of many countries. This shows that China's poverty alleviation policy is effective, and other countries with smaller populations should be more concerned about their own poverty alleviation.

Chinese President Xi Jinping announced that China had scored a "complete victory" in its fight against poverty. Over the past eight years, the final 98.99 million impoverished rural residents living under the current poverty line have all been lifted out of poverty. All 832 impoverished counties and 128,000 impoverished villages have been removed from the poverty list. Since the reform and opening up in the late 1970s, 770 million impoverished rural residents have shaken off poverty when calculated in accordance with China's current poverty line. China has contributed more than 70% of global poverty reduction over the same period. "China experience" of poverty reduction has made great contributions to global poverty alleviation. China has met the poverty eradication target set in the United Nations 2030 Agenda for Sustainable Development 10 years ahead of schedule. China has paved a poverty reduction path with Chinese characteristics. China gives full play to the political advantages of the country's socialist system, which can bring together the resources necessary to take on extraordinary tasks, thus forming a common will and joint actions for poverty eradication. China has adopted a targeted poverty alleviation strategy and strives to eradicate poverty through development. China adheres to motivating the creativity of poor residents and stimulating their self-generated impetus for poverty reduction. Shaking off poverty is not the finish line but the starting point of a new life and endeavor.

We have learned that solving the poverty problem is not a matter of a single functional department but a joint work of multiple departments to complement each other and optimize resources. It is not enough to rely only on the strength of one country to solve human poverty. It is necessary to promote multilateralism, unite all countries to act together, give full play to their respective advantages, and concentrate the strength of all parties.

4)   The key to realizing the targeted poverty alleviation was the deployment

of front-line cadres.

According to the statistics, a total of 2.778 million poverty alleviation cadres in China have gone to the front line, called "village cadres." They eat and live with the villagers and understand the most genuine and accurate public sentiment. The first-hand information they investigated was sent to poverty alleviation units at all levels, and they began to design a new future for the entire village. After the blueprint was in place, the state distributed various resources and funds to turn this blueprint into reality. I think "residence cadres" reflect the socialism with Chinese characteristics. These cadres have played a crucial role. According to reports, many "village cadres" still have suffered from overwork and even sacrificed their young lives. This method of "dispatching cadres to villages" and cadres' dedication are worth learning. We have learned that there must be full-time officials to conduct fact-seeking investigations in poverty-stricken areas. They not only collect statistics such as population and other numerical information but also statistics on human resources so that people in these areas can "make the best use of their talents" and do precise work for the follow-up poverty alleviation work. Their work can provide a reference for overall planning.

5) To stimulate endogenous power

When poverty alleviation in many countries is concerned, the simple forms of sending food, money, and other materials will fail to solve the fundamental problems and even cause people to form the bad habit of "waiting for assistance." It will lead to increasing poverty. China's poverty alleviation policy has curbed this phenomenon, emphasizing stimulating the people's endogenous motivation. There is an old Chinese saying about escaping poverty, "Give people fish and you feed them for a day. Teach them how to fish and you feed them for a lifetime." We realize that "ideological poverty" must be eradicated so people in impoverished areas can escape poverty spontaneously. Getting paid for their work creates a virtuous circle.

6) To establish a supervision mechanism

When one poverty alleviation blueprint is designed, an improvement plan would be implemented. The government also has specialized departments to supervise the implementation of the plan and ensure the results and effectiveness of poverty alleviation investment. Strict supervision urges that each link must operate efficiently, and each department must be closely linked to meet the established plans and standards on time and quantity to ensure the smooth completion of the entire poverty alleviation project.

7) To attach importance to the creation of an ideal environment

The Chinese government attaches great importance to environmental issues. I have been to various cities in China, different in size, and found that China's urban environmental sanitation management is excellent. The streets are immaculate, which reflects the high quality of the people. China attaches great importance to creating diversified environments in various urban and rural areas. In poverty alleviation, the Chinese government has also created a corresponding environment to promote this project. For example, tourism, business, and investment environments can be developed in poverty-stricken areas. Poverty alleviation work can be done with half the efforts. So, creating a poverty alleviation atmosphere and environment is a work step worthy of attention.

Discussion on the future poverty alleviation model—building a community with a shared future for mankind is the only way out.

In 2013, President Xi Jinping put forward the statement of building a community with a shared future for mankind which shows the fate and destiny of each nation or country are closely linked. To build a big harmonious family on this planet and turn the yearning of people worldwide for a better life into reality, we have to solve the primary problem—poverty and survival. Presently, in some developed countries, there are still a large number of poor people waiting to be rescued.

1) Build a community with a shared future for mankind, concentrate all forces, and transform "relief-type" passive poverty alleviation into "entrepreneurship-type" offensive poverty alleviation.

First of all, poverty alleviation must be carried out on a platform and within a structure, and all resources and forces must be organized.

Second, it is necessary to do more positive publicity work on China's development ideas. It will help other countries better understand the achievements of China's reform and opening up and poverty alleviation. It will also help others learn its "poverty elimination ideas" and better envision the future world under the framework of a community of shared future for mankind so that people of all countries will be motivated. China's present may also be the future of many developing countries, and China's future is also the world's future. That is the meaning of a community with a shared future for mankind. People in the whole world can work together to build a homeland on earth, contribute to the "community with a shared future for mankind."

2) Promote the global promotion of Chinese-style poverty alleviation experience, and transform the theory of "war on paper" into actual combat.

We cannot just be surprised by or admire the great success of the Chinese model of poverty alleviation. We also need to do more research and promote its achievements to the world. China's population base is extensive, and a medium-sized city may be the same size as a certain country. Therefore, if China's experience is practiced worldwide, it should be conducive to poverty eradication. The crux of the problem is how to "transplant" these strategies. For example, we can try to organize officials from various countries to visit China on spot to experience poverty alleviation, then combine its experiences with the local conditions, draw up strategies, and formulate appropriate local plans.

I have been to China more than 40 times since 2008. Its fast development impresses me the most. There was no high-speed rail more than ten years ago. Now there is a national high-speed rail network. I have traveled to many places by high-speed rail. The speed of high-speed rail is like the speed of China. Development is fast, whether in a city or a rural area. Although I went there four or five times before the pandemic, I felt the change each time I visited it. I also think China is getting increasingly modern: many advanced technologies have become part of people's daily lives, for example, self-driving delivery vehicles and a convenient mobile payment system that has created a cashless society. In addition, Chinese people are becoming more and more confident.

My ancestral home is in Jieyang, Guangdong, where there are some of my relatives. I often communicate with the Chinese and feel their confidence in life and future development.

I think the important inspiration drawn from China's successful experience is not to blindly worship the Western model. We must recognize China's characteristics—to explore bravely, and strive to develop a development mode that suits Chinese people. China's continued opening up is good news for the world.

Take Cambodia as an example: Cambodian farmers can export more agricultural products to China, increasing their income and improving their lives. China owns the largest consumer market, and what's more, many investors believe that China's continued opening up can provide opportunities for companies who want to participate in China's development and get on the car of China's growth. Major Chinese investment projects in Cambodia that have overcome the difficulties brought about by Covid-19 and progressed smoothly include the construction of a thermal power plant in Huadian's Sihanoukville Power Plant. It has completed the installation of the steel structure plan. The Phnom Penh-Sihanoukville Highway project has achieved 79% of the total engineering construction. In particular, the number of enterprises in the Sihanoukville Special Economic Zone has been steadily increasing, and the volume of imports and exports has reached a record high, as the two countries have just implemented a China-Cambodia Free Trade Agreement starting from January 1, 2022. According to data from the Ministry of Commerce of Cambodia, the trade volume between Cambodia and China in 2021 totaled more than 11.114 billion US dollars, an increase of 37.28% compared to the same period in 2020. China is the largest market for Cambodian rice. China's experience helped Cambodia and other countries prosper and develop as China did in their own way. In fact, China has grown from a poor and weak country to the second-largest economy, not through military expansion or colonial looting but through the efforts of the Chinese people and the entire nation to maintain peace and development.

My understanding of China's reform and opening up, and poverty alleviation policies is as the above. There are many pages worth studying in the book *Xi Jinping: Governance of China*. China's practical experience in governing the country accumulated through long-term practice has been summed up, including "self-reliance" and "crossing the river by feeling the stones," etc. China has achieved today's brilliant achievements after generations of selfless dedication through high-speed growth. Suppose other countries can study and analyze China's governance theories well. In that case, they will surely gain a lot of inspiration and formulate their national development plans according to their own actual conditions. With the guidance of the theories, countries will surely avoid detours. Therefore, we should show gratitude to the Chinese government and the Communist Party of China, the ruling party of China, for their selfless dedication. I wish China an early realization of the "Chinese Dream!" May the Chinese people always be happy and healthy!

We have learned that there must be full-time officials to conduct fact-seeking investigations in poverty-stricken areas. They would collect statistics on population, other digital information, and human resources so that people in these areas can "make the best use of their talents" and do precise work for the follow-up poverty alleviation work, thus providing a reference for the overall planning. A community with a shared future for mankind is an essential idea proposed by Chinese President Xi Jinping to realize the common ideal of mankind and achieve peaceful and stable development. I think this wisdom is not only a critical concept summed up by the Communist Party of China through nearly a hundred years of experience but also by the the Chinese government and the great leaders of China with selfless initiatives for human development. There are currently two major powers in this world. One is the United States, which is constantly making trouble, disrupting the original order of the world, selling unilateralism, and contradicting the interests of the people of the world. The other power is China, which promotes world peace and development with the courage to take responsibility and continues contributing to the world. Two important facts are being manifested realistically to the people of the world. One is that more than 1.4 billion Chinese have survived the pandemic with the care of the Chinese government. Another fact is that in the past five years, China's poor population has dropped by nearly 100 million. When human rights in China are concerned, China has sincerely worked for the people's welfare. China always does a lot, but the Western world does nothing but talk a lot about human rights, so build a community with a shared future for mankind and define humanity's future will be the best choice.

Hussein Ibrahim

A professor of Chinese language; the former Cultural, Educational and Scientific Counselor of the Embassy of the Arab Republic of Egypt in China; an expert in Chinese affairs; and the Dean of the Faculty of Foreign Languages & Translation, Misr University for Science & Technology. He has supervised many academic theses and dissertations of Egyptian researchers in Chinese language, literature, and translation. Prof. Ibrahim has devoted himself to the China study and exchanges of Chinese and Egyptian cultures. He wrote the book *China and Africa* and translated the book *China – History and Present, Popular Emotional Stories of Hui Islamic Ethnic Group*, and the encyclopedic book *The History of Sino-Arab Literary Exchanges* from Chinese into Arabic.

China's Role in the Development of Global Economy

Over the past years, China, a country with a population of more than 1.4 billion people, has emerged as a global economic power that cannot be ignored. Currently, its economy is the largest in the world regarding the purchasing power and the second after the United States regarding the market value. It is expected to become the first at the end of the current decade.

This astonishing performance and the rapid economic development of China were accomplished in a short period, as China's gross domestic product (GDP) has doubled since the implementation of reform and opening up in 1979 about 50 times, from more than 180 billion US dollars to about 18 trillion US dollars at present. Here, the latest data from the International Monetary Fund indicates that China will add more than 9 trillion US dollars to its total output by the end of 2026, or more than the current size of the combined Japanese and German economies.

This continuous rise is no longer surprising to anyone. The story of the rise of the Chinese "dragon" fascinates the whole world and has inspired many countries. It is a source of concern for other countries at the same time. But as far as the Arab countries are concerned, it has become apparent that decision-makers in most Arab capitals have long and increasingly felt that "China may become the leading superpower in the future." Consequently, establishing strategic relations with this rising power is increasingly perceived as a crucial and strategic imperative. Against this backdrop, Arab-Chinese relations have steadily evolved over the past few decades, with China being the main buyer of Arab oil and the key economic partner of Arab countries. With Beijing launching the Belt and Road Initiative in 2013, China has developed comprehensive strategic partnerships with Saudi Arabia, Egypt, the United Arab Emirates (UAE), and Algeria. Its influence in Iran has increased after signing a 25-year cooperation plan with Tehran this year.

It can be said that this transformation occurred due to two main factors. The first is that China's astonishing economic rise over the past three decades has led to a sharp increase in the country's demand for energy. Meanwhile, the Gulf Cooperation Council, the largest oil and liquefied natural gas exporter, has become the center of gravity of Chinese economic activity in the Middle East and North Africa. At the same time, the second factor reflects the increasing uncertainty of Arab countries about their relations with the United States. It also reflects the overall impression, especially in the Gulf states, that Washington is on its way to reducing its presence in the region to devote itself to its internal problems and confrontations with China.

During the past ten years, great accomplishments have been made in China's economic and social development. China's economic power has advanced greatly. In 2021, the gross domestic product reached RMB 114 trillion yuan (about 17 trillion US dollars), with its share in the global economy rising from 11.4% in 2012 to more than 18%, and China's position as the world's second-largest economy was consolidated. Its per capita GDP is 12,500 US dollars, close to that of high-income countries. In recent years, China's contribution to global economic growth has remained at around 30%, making it the largest engine of growth.

Moreover, China's opening to the outside world has been comprehensively expanded and extended in the past ten years. The portion of commodity exports in the international market increased from 11% to 15%. The position of the largest country in commodity trade was reinforced, and national pre-entry treatment was implemented as well as a management system. China has been actively building a network of high-level free trade zones, and the number of free trade agreements signed with foreign countries has also increased. It has also deployed and built 21 pilot free trade zones and the Hainan Free Trade Port, and created new hubs and pilot fields for reform and opening-up, forming a landscape of all-round and high-level opening-up.

As a member of the World Trade Organization, China enjoys free access to world markets. But its relations with these countries have been affected by the large Chinese trade surplus on the one hand and product piracy on the other. The rapid growth of the Chinese economy has greatly increased the energy demand. China is the second largest consumer of petroleum products in the world after the United States, as it is the largest producer and consumer of coal. China spends billions of dollars seeking to purchase source energy from abroad. But China also invested huge sums in developing hydropower, including the Three Gorges Dam costing 25 billion US dollars.

The economic trajectory of China has undergone various developmental stages throughout its rich history, contributing positively to its current economic standing. As an active member of the World Trade Organization, China stands out for hosting numerous successful companies. Notably, four of the world's ten largest companies are based in this country. The nation excels in various economic domains, securing the second position globally in energy production, particularly in electricity generation, natural gas extraction, and petroleum refining. Additionally, it has been at the forefront of manufacturing cars, planes, and cutting-edge electronics. The nation is a leader in several industries, including the production of children's toys, where it holds the top global ranking.

Trade between China and the Middle Eastern countries is not limited to oil, and many small traders travel daily between China and the Middle East. Besides, there has been a noticeable increase in contracts for Chinese contracting companies in this region. Meanwhile, Chinese banks provide continuous loans to projects. Accordingly, Chinese companies are superior in terms of prices and funds compared to other companies.

China is also the largest importer of the Middle Eastern oil and buys 1/10 of the total oil exported from the Middle Eastern countries. China's oil imports are expected to increase by 500,000 barrels per day in the next five years. Based on this significant increase, China will surpass the United States in 2030 in terms of imports of the Middle Eastern oil.

China has also built a new front in global economic development. A new episode in its planning for other countries' progress is also emerging with a wave of funding for infrastructure, that is, the Belt and Road Initiative. This initiative aims to link nearly half of the world's population to each other and integrate a fifth of the global gross national product by establishing trade and investment links that extend to all parts of the globe. As for the current phase, the Chinese economy has entered a new era. The focus has been on constructing a high-quality real economy, turning China into the world's second most powerful economy. Among the achievements is the rapid economic growth, making China a leader in global economic growth, and becoming a driving factor for international sustainable development. The achievements also include promoting the industrial restructuring of the Chinese economy and heading towards a shared development. Significant progress has been made in economic cooperation of mutual benefit between China and developing countries. Infrastructure projects and industrial production bases invested, funded or constructed by China are everywhere. The country focuses on the enhancement of a market-oriented economy that is able to share the benefits of a rapidly growing international economy.

The government's long-term leasing of land to farmers paved the way for private management of agricultural land, and the emergence of small entrepreneurs and consumer goods played a significant role in initiating a free-market system. International investors gained the opportunity to acquire stakes in Chinese trading companies, eventually leading to the establishment of Chinese-controlled private businesses in select regions of the country. Concurrently, China maintained a non-convertible currency policy while becoming a major recipient of international direct investment on a global scale.

China also initiated economic regionalization, empowering local governments to exercise economic control over projects within their provinces. This approach allowed for the implementation of diverse projects that could compete with one another. Specific towns and coastal areas were strategically chosen as development zones, officially sanctioned for open or direct trade. In the 1980s, the government established five special economic zones in Shenzhen, Zhuhai, Shantou, Xiamen, and Hainan, alongside 14 economic and technological development zones in Dalian and Qinhuangdao. Subsequently, the Yangtze River Delta, Pearl River Delta, and Minnan Delta were progressively opened as coastal economic zones. The government enticed international investors through financial incentives, gradually reducing price controls on certain commodities.

China has got other advantages that other countries do not have, namely, it is huge in size of territory and also in population. China has been a world power many times over. Its history is one of many sequences of empires. China is currently powerful because an enormous nation has, for the past 70 years, been renovating and investing in itself and now is earning the rewards of its hard work and generations of effort and labor. The process has been enhanced via modern global information sharing, free trade, entrepreneurship, and economic mobility.

China has also witnessed a qualitative leap in developing the economy during the mentioned period, which no other country has achieved during the past 70 years. China has become a major global trading power, attracting and importing foreign capitals. The Chinese economy has also helped provide many job opportunities in the world by opening up China to the world economically and investing Chinese capitals abroad. The living standards of the Chinese people have undergone tremendous changes. As the income of urban and rural residents has increased by a large proportion, the urbanization rate has increased, and the poverty rate has decreased greatly. Thus, the pace of improvement in the living standards of the country's people rose to the top of the world, as did technological progress, with the number of researchers and developers in China rising to the highest in the world. Educational levels have also improved tremendously. Standard Chartered Bank also predicts that 27% of China's workforce will have a college education by 2030, a rate equal to Germany's.

On the other hand, China's economic development has enhanced its international status, as its role is increasingly important, and its contributions to the global economic growth and protection of the international system have increased. The Chinese experience in development has provided guidance for third-world countries whose economic development models are still undecided and unable to grow independently without isolation. Therefore, the Chinese economy is expected to be the largest economy in the world. China has presented a unique model for achieving development within a short time, which makes the Chinese experience of progress a significant example to follow, introducing a different approach to Western liberalism. China's experience deserves in-depth studies to draw experiences and lessons from which developing countries can benefit.

The economic miracle made by China has amazed the whole world, and everyone is seeking to interpret the secrets behind this brilliant success and explain its causes. Undoubtedly, the Chinese experience is an important source of inspiration for the world's countries. Some of its experiences can be applied after considering the characteristics of countries and their local conditions. China's success in development is due to many factors, including internal ones, such as the pivotal role played by the leadership and the ruling party in the development process, in addition to external ones, such as the wave of economic globalization that created favorable conditions. China has also opened its doors to the world completely while improving relations with the Western world, adopting a neighborly policy with neighboring countries, developing traditional friendship with developing countries, adhering to the principle of multipolarity and adopting a foreign policy based on independence and peace. China has embraced the principles of globalization and has become its strongest defender after joining the World Trade Organization in 2001. Moreover, China succeeded in attracting a huge stock of foreign investment and hosted major international companies, which led to the technological progress on its land.

During recent years, with many international exhibitions and forums held, such as the International Big Data Industry Expo, the China International Intelligent Industry Exhibition, the Zhongguancun Forum, and the World Internet Conference, these Internet-related forums and conferences have revealed a large number of new technologies and applications. The new technologies include service robots, intelligent disinfection robots, guard and security robots, the Beidou global navigation satellite system, and the knowledge computing platforms providing machines and people with various information and knowledge. They demonstrate the diversity of China's digital economy's development and reflect the direction of efforts to promote high-quality development and raise people's living standards to excellent levels.

Data is the best indication and proof when artificial intelligence is in mode. According to the 2021 China Internet Development Report issued by the Chinese Academy of Cyberspace Studies, the size of China's digital economy reached 39.2 trillion yuan in 2020, maintained an annual growth rate of 9.7%, and became an important driving force for stable economic growth. By the end of June 2021, 53.7% of key operations in key sectors of China's manufacturing industry were digitally controlled, and 73.7% of digital R&D and design tools were used. The domestic market satisfaction rate for intelligent manufacturing equipment has also exceeded 50%. And new applications such as digital greenhouses, picking robots and remote work, intelligent logistics, unmanned ports, and other new applications are constantly emerging. Nowadays, the development of the Internet has reached a new stage of comprehensive integration in various sectors. It is due to the active development of the information infrastructure and the continuous improvement of technological innovation capabilities. China has built the world's largest fiber-optic and mobile telecom network. In China, 5G-based stations have covered 100% of the cities, 95% of the counties, and 35% of the towns. The rural communication problem has finally been solved, as more than 99% of the administrative villages in China have access to optical fiber and networks. The fourth generation lays a solid foundation for high-quality economic development in China. Great progress has been made in the research and development of basic and general technologies. Major scientific and technological breakthroughs have been made in 5G networks, quantum computing, advanced chips, super-intelligent computers, network architecture, basic operating systems, satellite Internet applications, industrial Internet, and intelligent manufacturing. All of them are an important force driving digital transformation.

In 2018, the People's Republic of China celebrated the 40th anniversary of its reform and opening up policy and significant economic achievements. During this period, China has risen from a moderately poor and internationally slightly-connected country to one of the utmost important global superpowers. China is now the world's largest economy in terms of purchasing power parity. It has experienced a structural transformation from a rural agricultural country to a more urbanized and service-oriented economy. The richness of the Chinese population, measured by annual per capita income, has increased more than hundredfold in rural and urban areas. Western economies have also profited significantly from economic relations with China, mostly founded on the principle of comparative advantage in the past. In the future, however, China will become more of a competitor or rival in some areas.

Political stability is another major reason behind China's development as a popular destination for manufacturing. Due to its political stability, China is considered more stable as a global partner than other nations. It has become the world's most preferred investment destination. Due to global economic collapse, developed countries now have extra productive capacity and funds. China's rapid economic growth, huge domestic market, and ever-improving investment atmosphere have attracted numerous transitional companies seeking a way out. They invested in diverse places of China, sharing the country's experience of rapid economic growth. In addition, China has implemented a series of valid macro-control policies to increase domestic demand and practical financial and wise monetary policies to facilitate its rapid economic growth. The practice provides some developing countries with valuable experience and encourages in-depth study of development economics.

Given its size, China is dominant in vital regional and global development issues. China is the largest emitter of greenhouse gases, with per capita emissions surpassing the European Union's. Global environmental problems cannot be solved without China's engagement. China's growing economy is also an important source of global demand, and its economic rebalancing will create new opportunities for manufacturing exporters. But it may reduce demand for commodities over the medium term. It greatly influences other developing economies through trade, investment, and ideas. In summary, these reforms created market institutions and incentives that were lacking in a collectively planned economy. China has become the main power that promotes economic cooperation in Asia and economic recovery in East Asia. Since the 1990s, with its economic surplus, Japan has undergone economic stagnation, which weakened its capacity to support economic growth in East Asia. The Asian financial crisis that broke out in 1997 hit East Asia's economy severely. As a huge responsible country, China constricted its cooperation with the countries and regions in East Asia to help them solve their problems. China's rapid economic growth provided them with a vast export market and promoted the recovery of East Asian economy. According to the statistics, exports from the main Southeast Asian countries to China increased by more than 100% between 1990-2000. Although China occupies an exclusive position in the world's political economy, its massive population and large physical size alone make it a powerful global presence. It is still possible to get to see the Chinese experience and draw some general lessons for other developing countries. Most importantly, while capital investment is crucial to economic growth, China becomes even more powerful when accompanied by market-oriented reforms that introduce profit incentives to rural and small private businesses. That combination can unleash a productivity boom that will propel total growth. For countries with a large population of underemployment in agriculture, the Chinese example may be particularly instructive. By encouraging the development of rural enterprises and not focusing exclusively on the urban industrial sector, China has successfully moved millions of workers off farms and into factories without creating an urban crisis. Finally, China's reform and opening up policy has urged foreign direct investment in the country, creating more jobs and linking the Chinese economy with international markets.

The cooperation between China and the Middle East is also highly welcomed by the governments of the Middle Eastern countries because China does not interfere in the internal affairs of those countries. The cooperation is limited to business only, while America relies on the force of arms to implement its regional reforms. John Altman, director of the Middle East

Department at the American think tank Center for Strategic and International Studies (CSIS), said, "The United States still plays an important role in the security and stability of the Middle East, and China is not able to compete with America in the military field and therefore cannot provide security for those countries."

The rising role of China in the Middle East also faces several challenges related to the orientations of Chinese policies in the region. Among these challenges, the most crucial include maintaining a balance among various regions as China seeks to maintain relationships with parties involved in conflicts of interest within each region, achieving security and stability in the Middle East, and fostering regional partnerships.

As the Silk Road continues its expansive growth, there is a prevailing perception that the project is increasingly dominated by historical symbolism. This has led some to argue that the Silk Road initiative, given its vast geographical and economic scope spanning continents of the ancient world and various areas of infrastructure and transportation, may be veering more towards political propaganda than a pragmatic, implementable project. The emphasis on historical symbolism brings the project closer to a symbolic vision of future relations rather than positioning it as a viable initiative with clearly defined policies and mechanisms. Considering this perspective, it becomes imperative to engage in a thorough discussion of the aforementioned situation.

In general, Arab-China relations encounter various challenges, with the most significant being the imperative to strike a balance in developing ties amidst existing conflicts of interest. Given the trade imbalance favoring China over some countries in the region, concerns have arisen about potential trade dumping. Consequently, China must strive to achieve a more balanced economic relationship. Additional challenges include China's technological level lagging behind that of the United States and Europe in certain fields, the nation's efforts to transfer environmentally unfriendly industries to the Arab world, the potential negative impact of its collaboration with some African countries—specifically, its focus on securing raw materials and oil at low prices—and the outsourcing of labor without concurrent improvements in local economic performance.

China presents itself as a world power capable of rebalancing the relations in the global system. China has consistently claimed that it belongs to developing countries and cannot replace the United States in the international system. In an attempt to get closer to understanding this Chinese approach, the discussion focused on several main issues, including the following aspects:

It becomes more just and represents the common interests of the world's countries to restructure the international system. It is one of the priorities of the policies of China in the next stage, especially to restructure the global economic system and its basic institutions (such as the World Bank, the International Monetary Fund, and the World Trade Organization).

The vision of Chinese reform is grounded in several key principles. Foremost among these is the commitment to refrain from compelling nations to adopt policies of economic openness and free trade. Additionally, emphasis is placed on achieving fairness in the distribution of benefits arising from trade exchanges between countries and ensuring a balance in the interests of all parties involved in international economic interactions.

Chinese experts emphasized that the projects within the Belt and Road Initiative are not just economically beneficial to China but represent a strategic vision for China's role in the global system.

China possesses untapped fiscal surpluses that can be leveraged for investments in global infrastructure projects. The creation of the Asian Infrastructure Investment Bank reflects the intention to utilize these surplus funds for developmental investments in neighboring countries. Concurrently, the growth of China's service sector has diminished the appeal of other industries for local labor, sparking discussions about potentially transferring and sharing these industries and production technologies with developing nations. This discourse has intensified amid an escalating internal debate concerning the environmental impact of certain industries, notably manufacturing and heavy industry.

Chinese officials noted that cooperation between developing countries and China within the Silk Road framework could include transferring entire plants with advanced technologies and focusing on labor-intensive industries as they are best suited to boost economic development and tackle high unemployment. The cooperation in manufacturing will be based on the transfer of factories and technology from China to developing countries, and then Chinese experts will train the local workforce in the production and export processes.

Suggestions to Maintain the Economic Growth

I think that in the next 15 to 20 years, China will be well situated to join the world's high-income nations. China's policymakers are now focused on updating the country's development strategies to respond to the new challenges, concentrating on the quality of development, structural reforms and innovations, economic efficiency, and social presence. I suggest a series of conditions that I deem essential for addressing the challenges in the march of progress. I posit that skills development is crucial for enhancing productivity, a key driver of improved living standards. Additionally, macroeconomic policies should be geared toward fostering increased employment opportunities. I emphasize the importance of aligning education with technical training and connecting technical training to market entry, as this linkage can sustain growth in productivity and translate it into more high-quality jobs. The establishment of social dialogue and collective negotiations can further cultivate a widespread commitment to education and training.

Technological development is a major source of long-term productivity gains and new communications, helping to improve firms' and economies' access to a wider range of technical and scientific knowledge. New organizations should be established to collect and share information that help anticipate global trends, which requires coordination between agencies, stakeholders, and training institutes. Technical and vocational education and training at the secondary and tertiary levels are vital for accreditation, because they pave the way for more sophisticated and complex technologies. Support should be given to basic education, vocational training, employment services and research and development, industry, business and technological development in coordination with macro policies, and to improve the capacity of labor market information systems to create, update and disseminate information on demand.

There are also several other conditions that I consider essential to deal with the challenges facing the Belt and Road Initiative. These are also essential to guarantee a fair distribution of benefits and expenses.

The first condition is related to the need to spread a solid and clear belief among the governments and individuals concerned with the initiative in many regions that it will not practically end in Chinese domination of the economies of these countries.

The second concerns the need to increase a mutual understanding of the nature of the initiative, its projects, implementation mechanisms, expected expenses, and benefits from these projects. It is necessary to remove any negative perceptions of the initiative and its Chinese goals among the major countries and regions along the Belt and Road.

The third is related to the need to boost joint ownership of the initiative. Even though in the past several years, and the early years of the initiative, in particular, the Chinese government issued several important documents. There is still an urgent need to develop a document that describes a collective vision of the initiative based on the participation of the largest possible number of countries within the framework. It is necessary to explain the initiative's objectives, stages, and mechanisms for its implementation.

The fourth condition is that China needs to establish a genuine presence in two crucial areas. The first area is the war on terrorism, and the second area is the reconstruction of countries in crisis and collapse, as well as fragile states along the "Belt and Road" that have not succeeded. The most critical issue is to assess the overall strategic consequences of this initiative, as well as the scale and nature of these consequences for specific countries, with the expectation that these countries will be more negatively impacted by the initiative than others.

Annex

Important Egyptian-Chinese Cultural Exchanges

Year	Events
1956	China and Egypt established diplomatic relations. Egypt's first educational and cultural mission arrived in New China. The Egyptian-Chinese Friendship Association was founded. Several operational programs of the Agreement on Cultural Cooperation Between Egypt and China were subsequently signed.
2002	The China Cultural Centre in Cairo was established. It spreads Egyptian culture in Chinese society widely.
November 2011	The Egyptian Cultural Office was established in Beijing. It spreads Chinese culture in Egyptian society through many cultural activities held daily, contributing to the interaction of Egyptian and Chinese cultures.
December 2014	Egyptian President Abdel-Fattah al-Sisi paid a state visit to China, leading to the establishment of a Sino-Egyptian comprehensive strategic partnership.
January 2016	The Egyptian-Chinese Culture Year was held, as a celebration of the sixtieth anniversary of joint diplomatic relations between China and Egypt. China participated in the forty-seventh session of the Cairo International Book Fair.
February 2016	The Chinese Embassy in Egypt organized the activities for the Chinese Spring Festival. The Egyptian Embassy, the Beijing Women's Association for Foreign Exchange, and several associations of social work and cultural exchanges held the "Dialogue of Civilizations" Forum on the occasion of the Chinese Lantern Festival.

March 2016	The display of Arabic calligraphy by Chinese calligrapher Mi Guangjiang was held in the Library of Peking University under the patronage of the Department of Arabic Language and Culture at Peking University and the Egyptian Embassy.
April 2016	The Chinese Embassy in Egypt organized the competition of the Chinese Ambassador's Cup to tell the story in Chinese.
May 2016	The China Cultural Centre in Cairo, in cooperation with the Faculty of Archeology of Cairo University, organized a symposium entitled "Belt and Road" at Cairo University.
August 2016	Egypt participated in the Beijing International Book Fair.
September 2016	The State Information Service of Egypt signed an agreement for exchanges of press delegations with all China Journalists' Association.
November 2016	China was the guest of honor at the 38th Cairo International Film Festival.
December 2016	Central banks of China and Egypt signed a three-year bilateral currency swap agreement.
2019	The Chinese government established more than 300 scholarships for Egyptian citizens to complete graduate and doctoral programs.
2020	China Cultural Centre in Cairo launched an intensive campaign to raise awareness about Covid-19. Egypt participated in the 2020 World Culture and Tourism Industry Expo in Guangzhou, China.
May 2021	The Chinese Embassy in Egypt and the Egyptian Ministry of Education and Technical Education held a joint meeting on the Sino-Egyptian education cooperation project.
	The Egyptian Embassy in China organized the Forum for Dialogue Among Civilizations at the Palace Museum.

	In Egypt, in cooperation with the China Cultural Centre, the Egyptian Ministry of Culture organized an artistic ceremony with the title "The Magic of the New Silk Road".
	In China, a competition "Egypt in the Eyes of the Chinese" through short videos was held.
	The Egyptian Embassy also sponsored the Arabic Language Talents Program prepared by the Al Arabiya channel and broadcasted on China Central Television.

John Ross

A Senior Fellow at the Chongyang Institute for Financial Studies, Renmin University of China. He is the former Director of Economic and Business Policy for the Mayor of London. Ross was the first foreigner to be appointed to a full-time position at one of China's new think tanks. He has been writing about China's economy for 30 years. He is the author of more than 1,000 articles on China and its relation with other countries in geopolitics and the world economy, published in English, Chinese, Spanish, Portuguese, Polish, Indonesian, Russian, and French. This is his third book published in Chinese. His analyses have been published in People's Daily, Global Times, China Finance, and many other publications in and outside China.

A Turning Point for China and the World

"Two Sessions" which refers to the annual meetings of China's National People's Congress (NPC) and the Chinese People's Political Consultative Conference (CPPCC), in March 2021, was of unusually great significance even by the normal standard of what are China's most important yearly political events. Indeed, they marked, without exaggeration, a historical turning point of global significance for reasons that will be analyzed. This was particularly determined by the simultaneous coming together in the time of several processes. These include in particular:

First, 2020 was a year of extraordinary achievement for China in both overcoming Covid-19 and realizing economic recovery in a way not achieved by any other major country – in addition to attaining the goal that had been set before the outbreak of Covid-19 of eliminating absolute poverty.

Second, "Two Sessions" in 2021 set out goals for both the next 14th Five-Year Plan and the more long-term development for China until 2035. These will be marked by China entering the ranks of the world's "high-income" economies by international standards. It is a historic transformation not only for Chinese people but for the entire global situation.

Third, as part of this process, the Communist Party of China (CPC) has been setting out its framework of building an "eco-civilization" – that is, developing the framework for dealing with climate change and other environmental threats, which are common issues facing the whole humanity. As a result, China has been taking an increasingly important international role in this crucial fight for humanity against climate change.

The Chinese people have felt the transformation of their lives directly as a result of these processes, and it is, therefore, superfluous for someone who is not Chinese to comment on this. This analysis, therefore, has a different goal. It briefly summarizes and characterizes the international and historical comparisons and global impact of these achievements and transformations. Such comparisons make the scale of China's achievements even clearer as some of the global consequences of the new stage of its development. In addition, it shows why China's experience is crucial for other countries, particularly developing ones, to study and learn from – not, of course, to copy mechanically. For the reasons outlined, "Two Sessions" in 2021 truly marked something of historic significance not only for China but for the world.

China's success in defeating Covid-19

Taking first the past, in 2020, China was the initial country to feel the impact of Covid-19. Therefore, China had less time and knowledge than any other country to face this deadly threat. The measures China took starting on 23 January 2020 to control the Covid-19 pandemic were unprecedented – the lockdown of an entire city, Wuhan, and then an entire province, Hubei. This action was so successful that the number of Covid-19 cases was capped in two weeks, and six weeks after, the number of instances in the mainland of China dropped to zero.

As objective Western analysts on this issue, such as Martin Wolf, the chief economics commentator of the Financial Times, have noted due to the Chinese government's successful actions, there never was really a severe "all China" Covid outbreak – there was a severe outbreak in Hubei with only a limited number of cases in other regions of China[1].

---

[1] Editor Note: This article is finished after "Two Sessions" of 2021. Here refers to the initial ourbreak of Covid-19 in China, not consider the influence of Omicron

The countries which then most successfully initially combatted Covid-19, such as New Zealand and Vietnam, did so essentially by copying China's responses – which was, of course, entirely to their credit.

These countries' successful result of learning from China's success was entirely different from the advanced Western countries where no effective prevention strategies were pursued. As a result, Covid-19 spread catastrophically in states such as the U.S., the U.K., Italy, Spain, France, Germany, etc.

The difference in outcomes between China, those countries implementing its anti-Covid strategies, and those that did not, is decisive. It is a literal difference between life and death. Mainland of China by April 2021 suffered less than 5,000 Covid-19 deaths. In contrast, the U.S., by April 2021, had suffered 525,000 deaths – more than 100 times as many as China. But in reality, even this misleadingly understates China's superior performance – because China has more than four times the population of the U.S. On a per capita basis, even by Spring 2021, the U.S. had suffered over 400 times as many deaths as China, and the death toll continues to rise.

In per capita terms, the performance of other Western countries, such as the U.K., is even worse than the U.S.. In limiting per capita death terms, China has qualitatively outperformed any other major economy - that is, the members of the G7 or BRICS. As the American economist Mark Weisbrot succinctly put it, commenting on attempts by the U.S. to launch a new cold war to divert attention from these real comparisons: "We need an economic recovery and to get rid of the pandemic, and China has already done both. Why don't we do those here."

In summary, with the outbreak of the Covid pandemic in 2020, the Chinese people were protected from a global catastrophe by the actions of China's government. Literally, millions of people in China are alive today who would have died if China had followed the policy of Western countries such as the U.S.. In reality, well over two million people died in Western countries due to their failure to learn from China – equivalent to a major war.

Furthermore, the so-called Western "human rights" organizations, such as Human Rights Watch, played a disgraceful role faced with this. Instead of praising China's actions for saving hundreds of thousands/millions of lives, they attacked China for such measures as its lockdowns. They showed that their conception of "human rights" was purely artificial, to conform to a disastrous Western model instead of a real safeguard of human rights – the most important right of all is to be alive.

Economic recovery

China's rapid overcoming of Covid-19, in turn, prepared the ground for its second gigantic achievement in 2020 – economic recovery.

Obviously, under the initial impact of Covid-19, in the first quarter of 2020, China's economy suffered a severe blow – GDP fell to 6.8% below a year previously. But, due to the rapid overcoming of Covid-19, economic recovery had already begun by the second quarter. By the end of 2020, China had experienced 2.3% annual growth. China was the only major economy to experience positive growth in 2020. In comparison, the U.S. GDP fell by 3.5%. Even more serious in human terms than this U.S. decline in GDP, even beyond its 525,000 deaths, tens of millions of Americans became unemployed and had their pay reduced.

The result of these trends was a dramatic change in the world economic situation in favor of China. The IMF estimated that in 2020-2021, measured at current exchange rates, 60% of world economic growth would take place in China – compared to 14% in the U.S. In the entire period to 2025, 32% of world economic growth would take place in China compared to 17% in the U.S..

In summary, China has come through the global economic recession in a way far superior to any other major economy.

The further gigantic achievement in China in 2020, although, in this case, it was planned before the outbreak of Covid-19, was the elimination of absolute poverty. Once again, the international comparisons are staggering. By the international poverty standard set by the World Bank, China has lifted more than 853 million people out of poverty since 1981. It is more than 70% of all those lifted out of poverty in the world. Or, to put it in other terms, almost three out of every four people in the world who have been lifted out of poverty in the last 40 years are Chinese.

But this tremendous achievement in poverty reduction is part of a further truly historic achievement assessed by the NPC and CPPCC in 2021 – this is the entry of China during the 14th Five-Year Plan into the ranks of high-income economies by international criteria.

Turning from these events in 2020 to the future China, as is well known, unusually announced in 2021, it was putting forward not one but two medium/ long-term projects to the NPC. The first was the 14th Five-Year Plan covering 2021-2025. The second was a longer-term project covering the period to 2035. These are evidently interconnected – the Five-Year Plan is the first stage in achieving the longer-term project.

The fundamental new feature of this situation, accounting for these two interrelated projects, is that the new Five-Year Plan is the first in a new stage of China's progress – that of the beginning of China's development as a "high-income" economy by international standards. This development is a new stage of China's progress which will continue until 2035.

By its national criteria in 2020, China achieved a "moderate prosperity" level, including eliminating absolute poverty. In terms of international standards set by the World Bank, in 2022-2023, the middle of the next Five-Year Plan, China will pass the currently defined threshold from its present global rank of an "upper middle income" economy to a "high income" economy. That is a Gross National Income of slightly over $1,000 a month. In the terms announced ahead of the 2021 NPC by fifth plenary session of the 19th Central Committee of the Communist Party of China, "the well-being of the people will reach a new level."

China is the greatest economic and social achievement in world history

The fundamental context of this is that China will have achieved a decisive stage of its development since the founding of the People's Republic of China in 1949.

In 1949 China had almost the world's lowest per capita GDP due to a century of foreign intervention – only ten countries had a lower one. To develop in only 70 years from 1949, during a single lifetime, from being almost the world's poorest country to the brink of a high-income economy, is a stupendous achievement – one not matched previously by any large country in the whole of human history. Said in a very considered way and without exaggeration, the People's Republic of China is literally the greatest achievement in economic development and improving social conditions in human history.

To give some indication of the scale of this achievement, the population of existing high-income economies by the World Bank standards is 16% of humanity. But China by itself is 18% of humanity. Therefore, China becoming a high-income economy will more than double the percentage of humanity living in such countries!

Planning for a high-income economy

This situation means that the 14th Five-Year Plan, and the longer-term program to 2035, face different tasks to China's previous thirteen plans. Above all, these aimed at China overcoming the huge underdevelopment inherited in 1949. Now the decisive question is how China will develop as a high-income economy.

The needs of such a high-income society are obviously much more complex than an underdeveloped one. In a country with an underdeveloped economy, the overwhelmingly dominant issue is how to satisfy basic needs – food, shelter, elementary health care, and education. In a high-income society, much more complex educational, medical, environmental, cultural, and other needs become increasingly crucial.

Therefore, the success of the thirteen previous Five-Year Plans means that the 14th Five-Year Plan, and the longer-term program to 2035, have a new center of gravity – to begin the development of China as a high-income society by international standards.

Not a "miracle", but the policies of the CPC

In regard to these achievements, it is frequently loosely said that China's economic and social development is a "miracle." It is indeed, as already seen, something quite extraordinary in international and historical terms. But it is not a "miracle" because it is not inexplicable. It is the result of the policies adopted by the Communist Party of China. In essence, in 1949, the CPC made a promise to the Chinese people. If you support our program and our Marxist analysis, China will be delivered from a century of foreign oppression and from one of the world's poorest countries to one of the world's great economies and civilizations. In only 70 years, the lifetime of a single person, the CPC has delivered on that promise.

It is not a "miracle," which does not exist in real human affairs. It is the product of the CPC's correct policies and theories, which led the immense work and sacrifice of the Chinese people. If the rest of the world could achieve what China has done in that time, many of the problems facing humanity would be solved. This achievement of the Chinese people was marked on the 100th anniversary of the CPC.

Climate change

In addition to the transition to a high-income economy, a further decisive future task affecting not only China but all humanity was marked by "Two Sessions" in 2021. President Xi Jinping, in a key speech to the United Nations in September 2020, had committed China to two decisive goals regarding humanity's common struggle against climate change – that China's CO_2 emissions would peak before 2030 and that by 2060 China would achieve net zero carbon emissions. These were widely welcomed globally as a "game-changer" in the international struggle against catastrophic climate change. As this is an issue that China has particularly developed recently, it is worth looking at in detail. In fact, Xi Jinping's announcement also set one of China's key targets for the next period. Because of its importance, it will be considered in detail.

The real situation on climate change

To grasp the great significance of China's targets on climate change, it should first be understood that there is no justice whatever in present Western policy on this issue – either between or within countries. As the Western countries are proposing no just solution to climate change, what policy countries adopt becomes a practical question.

Western countries created the threat to humanity from climate change because they were historically responsible for the overwhelming majority of carbon emissions. Cumulatively Europe is responsible for 31.3% of these emissions, the U.S. for 24.6%, China for only 13.9%, India for 3.2%, Africa for 2.8%, and Latin America for 2.6%.

This unequal responsibility for climate change continues up to the present day. China's annual carbon emissions, at 7.4 tonnes per person, are only half of the 14.2 tonnes of the U.S. and lower than four out of seven of the G7 countries. On a global scale, in 2019, the bottom 50% of the world population emitted 12% of global emissions, whereas the top 10% emitted 48% of the total. Present per capita emissions similarly continue to be strictly related to income levels. In 2021 average carbon emissions per person were 9.8 tonnes in high-income economies, 6.2 tonnes in upper-middle-income economies, 1.8 tonnes in lower-middle-income economies, and only 0.2 tonnes in low-income economies.

Western attempts to conceal the situation of climate change

Although it is fairly well known by now that the U.S. and advanced economies are historically responsible for the bulk of carbon emissions, they attempt to present the issue of climate change in a way that does not acknowledge this overwhelming responsibility. Furthermore, what is not so well known is that ample scientific evidence has been put forward on the current climate change, which allows present grotesquely unequal trends to be clearly analyzed. In particular, the Intergovernmental Panel on Climate Change (IPCC) published an important report: "Climate Change 2021: The Physical Science Basis." The data clarifies that the claim made by the U.S. and other advanced countries is for a privileged position in current carbon emissions.

Analysing the core of the present situation, the key data concluded by the IPCC is set out in Table 1. As will be seen, the IPCC gives various probabilities of hitting the decisive desirable goal of 1.5 degrees of warming compared to pre-industrial levels, depending on the number of gigatons of carbon emitted after the beginning of 2020. Thus, with 900 gigatons of carbon emitted, there is only a 17% chance of hitting this target; with 650 gigatons of emissions, there is a 33% chance; with 500 gigatons, a 50% chance of hitting the target; with 400 gigatons of emissions, there is a 67% chance; and with 300 gigatons of emissions, there is an 83% chance. All these variants are worth analyzing, but as it is the most central, the one with the 50% chance of limiting global warming to 1.5 degrees will primarily be considered here. It requires that globally a maximum of 500 gigatons of carbon is emitted.

Given this 500 gigaton figure, it is easy to calculate the per capita "carbon budget" and the maximum allowable carbon emissions for each person on the planet following the IPCC report – which is 64.8 tons. Given each country's population, it is also easy to work out the permissible carbon budget for each country. It means that any country asking for a per capita cumulative carbon budget above 64.8 tons is asking for a privileged position compared to humanity as a whole. And any country with a cumulative per capita carbon emissions below 64.8 tons is giving above-average aid to humanity in meeting this target.

Table 1

Per Capita Global Carbon Emissions to Achieve Target of Maximum Global Warming of 1.5 Degrees							
Approximate global warming relative to 1850-1900 until temperature limit (degrees)	Additional global warming relative to 2010-2019 until temperature limit (degrees)	Global population in 2019 (billion)	Estimated remaining carbon budgets from the beginning of 2020 (Giga tonnes of CO2)				
			Likelihood of limiting global warming to this temperature limit				
1.5	0.43	7.713	17%	33%	50%	67%	83%
			900	650	500	400	300
Per capita global cumulative emissions to hit this target (tons)			116.7	84.3	64.8	51.9	38.9
Source: Calculated from "Projections on Global Warming from IPCC, Climate Change 2021 - The Physical Science Basis: Summary for Policy Makers" Table SPM.2 and population data from UN Department of Economic and Social Affairs, Population Dynamics – database Total Population, All Variants							

To complete the factual picture, it is necessary to note that over long periods, up to 2050 or beyond, the population of individual countries will change. For example, on U.N. projections, between 2020 and 2050, the U.S. population will increase by 15%, India's population will increase by 19%, but China's population will fall by 3%, Germany's population will fall by 4%, Japan's population will fall by 16%, etc. Therefore, it is necessary to make calculations based on present and future populations. For this purpose, the projections from the U.N. Department of Economic and Social Affairs will be used.

High per capita carbon emissions are overwhelmingly concentrated in high-income economies.

Analyzing the global situation, it is clear once again that high per capita carbon emissions are overwhelmingly concentrated in high-income countries.

This key data on this is summarized in Table 2, which shows a comparison to world average per capita emissions. To be clear, it is not suggested that these present world emissions are sustainable. They are too high, but this is primarily to give a point of comparison for judging current relative emissions.

The pattern is evidently clear, of the 213 countries (and three sub-country administrative regions), for which there is data, 78 have per capita carbon emissions above the world average. But of these, 56 or 72% are advanced economies. Only 22, that is, 28%, are developing economies. In contrast, 138 countries/administrative regions have below-average world emissions – of which only 15, or 11%, are advanced economies, and 123, or 89%, are developing economies.

In summary, the situation is again overwhelmingly clear. *It is the advanced economies that overwhelmingly have above-average per capita carbon emissions, and it is developing economies that overwhelmingly have below average per capita carbon emissions.* In short, it is advanced economies whose policies are by far most inadequate from the point of view of emissions.

Table 2

Annual Carbon Emissions Per Capita – Compared to World Average Emissions in 2019 of 4.8 tons Per Capita				
	Number of countries		% of countries in category	
	Advanced economies	Developing economies	Advanced economies	Developing economies
Above world average	56	22	72%	28%
Below world average	15	123	11%	89%
Source: Calculated from Friedlingstein et al., 2020 : The Global Carbon Budget 2020, Earth System Science Data. Available at: <a href=""https://doi.org/10.5194/essd-12-3269-2020"" target=""_blank"">https://doi.org/10.5194/essd-12-3269-2020</a>				

The detailed situation of advanced and developing economies

Looking in more detail at the situation of advanced and developing countries, this is even worse. Table 3 shows the 213 countries and three sub-country administrative regions ranked by their level of per capita emissions. These are taken in groups of 20 – the highest 20 per capita carbon emitters, then countries ranked 21-40 by carbon emissions, and then countries ranked 41-60, etc.

The pattern is crystal clear. *The higher the level of per capita carbon emissions, the more the situation is dominated by advanced economies.* Of the 20 countries with the highest per capita emissions, 16, or 80%, are advanced economies. Of the countries ranked 21-80th in terms of per capita carbon emissions, 40, or two-thirds, are advanced economies. Only once significantly below world average per capita emissions are arrived at by more developing than developed economies in each group.

In summary, it is the developed economies that have by far the worst results in the world in terms of excessive per capita carbon emissions. *And the higher the level of per capita carbon emissions, the more developed countries dominate the situation.*

Table 3

Countries, and 3 Sub-country Administrative Regions, Ranked by Per Capita Carbon Emissions in 2019							
		Number of economies – advanced & developing		Percentage of this group – advanced & developing		Cumulative percentage since highest emissions group	
Rank in descending order of per capita emissions	Range of emissions (tons per capita)	Advanced	Developing	Advanced	Developing	Advanced	Developing
1-20	40.6-12.2	16	4	80%	20%	80%	20%
21-40	12.2-8.0	13	7	65%	35%	73%	27%
41-60	8.0-6.1	13	7	65%	35%	70%	30%
61-80	6.0-4.7	14	6	70%	30%	70%	30%
World							
81-100	4.7-3.7	11	9	55%	45%	67%	33%
101-120	3.5-2.5	2	18	10%	90%	58%	43%
121-140	2.4-1.7	2	18	10%	90%	51%	49%
141-160	1.7-0.9	0	20	0%	100%	44%	56%
161-180	0.9-0.6	0	20	0%	100%	39%	61%
181-216	0.5-0.0	0	36	0%	100%	33%	67%

Source: Calculated from Friedlingstein et al., 2020 : The Global Carbon Budget 2020, Earth System Science Data. Available at: <a href=""https://doi.org/10.5194/essd-12-3269-2020"" target=""_blank"">https://doi.org/10.5194/essd-12-3269-2020</a>

Therefore, not merely historically but in terms of current emissions, the advanced economies have the policies most diverging from what is required for the planet. By far, the greatest violators of what is required on climate change are the advanced economies, and the biggest proportional reductions required are, therefore, also in developed economies.

The fake criteria for climate emissions put forward by the U.S.

Once the facts on global climate emissions are grasped, then the fake character of the criteria of the claim for U.S. "leadership" in fighting climate change becomes transparently clear.

The U.S. attempts to present that the criterion for success in fighting climate change is the percentage reduction from current emissions. Thus, Biden has announced that the U.S. aims "to achieve a 50-52 percent reduction from 2005 levels" of emissions which are supposed to represent "building on past U.S. leadership." Given that in 2005 U.S. per capita CO_2 emissions were 20.8 tons, the U.S. proposes to reduce per capita carbon emissions by 2030 to 10.4 tons. But this means that by 2030 the U.S. proposes that its per capita CO_2 emissions level should be 220% of the present world average! That is not leadership. It is carbon damage on an incredible scale and a claim for a completely privileged position for the U.S. in the world. It means, for example, that by 2030 the U.S. claims that its per capita carbon emissions will have been 42% higher than China's are today. It is not U.S. leadership; it is to be a total climate change laggard.

This entire method put forward by the U.S., based on percentage reduction from present emissions levels, is actually fraudulent – a reality distortion. Because all this method does is protect the position of the highest CO_2 emitters! Let's take a few examples. If the U.S. method of aiming at a 50% reduction in emissions by 2030 were accepted and applied to present levels, this would mean a claim that the U.S. would be allowed to emit per capita 8.0 tons of CO_2; China, 3.7 tons; Brazil, 1.2 tons; India, 1.0 tons; and the Democratic Republic of the Congo, 0.02 tons!

Such comparisons have nothing to do with U.S. leadership on climate change – on the contrary, it shows the U.S. is claiming a privileged position for itself. It also shows why similar claims for a privileged position by advanced economies must be rejected. What is being shown by the U.S. is not leadership on climate change but a claim for privileges by developed Western countries.

The real situation on climate change

Fortunately, the scientific data produced by the IPCC makes it possible to calculate the real changes required to combat climate change. These are summarised in Table 4.

To analyze the effect of this, in turn, it should be noted that the key consequences of climate change are concentrated in a small number of countries. Only 17 countries each have carbon emissions accounting for more than 1% of the world's total. Together these countries count for 75% of world carbon emissions. Therefore, analyzing these countries is sufficient to follow world trends.

The key data for these countries shown in Table 4 is clear. Of the world's largest carbon emitters, only two, Saudi Arabia and Australia, have higher per capita emissions than the U.S. Furthermore, despite their extremely regressive policies, these are small emitters of CO_2 compared to the U.S. – Australia accounts for 1.2% of world carbon emissions, and Saudi Arabia 1.8%, compared to the 14.8% of the U.S..

In summary, the U.S. stands in a higher league in terms of its per capita CO_2 emissions. In particular, compared to the largest developing countries, China's per capita CO_2 emissions are only 46% of those of the U.S., Indonesia's 15%, Brazil's 14%, and India's 12%.

Because the per capita carbon emissions of the U.S. are much higher than any other major country, it makes clear why U.S. CO_2 emission cuts must be correspondingly much more rapid than any other major country to fit within its carbon budget. As shown in Table 4 U.S. annual average reduction of CO_2 emissions from 2020 onwards must be 20.2% a year. (To be clear, this is not the precise yearly figure that must be achieved but the average over time – so if emissions fall more slowly or rise in the initial period, there must be correspondingly rapid falls after this initial period). To give a comparison, this average means that by 2030 U.S. emissions per capita should have fallen to 1.3 tons per capita, compared to its proposed target of 8.0 tons per capita. That means the U.S. suggests that its per capita carbon emissions by 2030 be more than six times what is required to fit within its carbon budget. It has nothing to do with climate change leadership; it is climate change vandalism.

Table 4

The 17 Countries Each of Which Account for More than 1% of World Carbon Emissions – Collective Total is 75% of World Carbon Emissions							
Rank	Country	Per capita CO_2 emissions in 2019 (tons)	Population in 2019 (million)	Global per capita CO_2 budget for 50% chance of limiting global warming to 1.5 degrees (tons)	CO_2 budget for the country/ region from 2020 onwards (gigatons)	Annual % CO_2 emissions reduction from 2020 necessary to remain within carbon budget	Per capita CO_2 emissions as % of US
1	Saudi Arabia	18.2	34.3	64.8	2.2	23.0%	114%
2	Australia	16.4	25.2	64.8	1.6	21.0%	103%
3	US	16.0	329.1	64.8	21.3	20.2%	100%
4	Canada	15.6	37.4	64.8	2.4	20.0%	98%
5	South Korea	12.7	51.2	64.8	3.3	16.3%	79%
6	Russia	11.5	145.9	64.8	9.5	15.0%	72%
7	Iran	8.8	82.9	64.8	5.4	12.9%	55%
8	Japan	8.7	126.9	64.8	8.2	11.4%	54%
9	Germany	8.5	83.5	64.8	5.4	11.4%	53%
10	South Africa	8.2	58.6	64.8	3.7	11.6%	51%
11	China	7.3	1,433.8	64.8	92.9	10.2%	46%
12	UK	5.5	67.5	64.8	4.4	8.1%	34%
13	Turkey	4.8	83.4	64.8	5.4	7.4%	30%
	World	4.8	7,707.9	64.8	500.0	7.4%	29%
14	Mexico	3.4	127.6	64.8	8.3	5.5%	21%
15	Indonesia	2.4	270.6	64.8	17.5	4.0%	15%
16	Brazil	2.3	211.0	64.8	13.7	3.4%	14%
17	India	1.9	1,366.4	64.8	88.5	3.0%	12%

Source: Calculated from Calculated from carbon data from Friedlingstein et al., "The Global Carbon Budget 2020, Earth System Science Data". Global per capita carbon budget calculated from IPCC, Climate Change 2021 -The Physical Science Basis: Summary for Policy Makers" Table SPM.2

The threat to developing countries from climate change

But nevertheless, despite the fact that developing countries are not responsible for climate change, they have to deal with its consequences because its effects will worst hit them. To see the scale of this, it is necessary to be clear that the threat from climate change is not an "inconvenience" of warmer temperatures with no great consequences. But it threatens a literal disaster for humanity. In fact, with nuclear war, climate change is one of the two issues that can overturn the present basis of human civilization.

Furthermore, climate catastrophes are not for the future but are starting now. The *New York Times* noted: "A U.N. report... suggested that by just 2030, the world would be experiencing more than 500 major disasters each year." As Xi Jinping stated: "Since humanity entered the industrial age, rapid traditional industrialization, while bringing about great material wealth, has accelerated the consumption of natural resources and broken the original cycle and balance of the ecosystems, resulting in a tense relationship between humanity and nature."[2]

The scale of these disasters is capable of massive destruction to overwhelm entire countries – as was seen in the devastating floods in Pakistan in which almost one-third of the country was under water. Some of Pakistan's most fertile agricultural areas became giant lakes, drowning livestock and destroying crops and infrastructure. In Pakistan's Sindh Province, where half the country's food was produced, 90% of crops were ruined, and an inland lake of 100 km wide was created after the Indus River burst its banks. The floods displaced 32 million people. Damage was put at $30bn. Although on a less devastating scale than Pakistan, China is already beginning to experience an increasing number of disastrous floods, extreme heatwaves, and other climate-related severely damaging events. These will worsen.

---

[2] Xi Jinping. Principles to Apply in Protecting the Eco-Environment (18 May 2018). In *The Governance of China* (Volume III).

Xi Jinping particularly noted that only the joint action of all countries could successfully deal with this common threat from climate change. China has become a leading force in promoting this: "Humanity is a community that rises and falls as one. Protecting the eco-environment is a common challenge and a joint responsibility for the whole world. Success in this endeavor will be good for Chinese socialism; otherwise, it will become a pretext for forces with ulterior motives to attack us."[3] Therefore: "The eco-environment bears on the future of humanity. Building a green home is our common dream. Protecting the environment and dealing with climate change requires the joint efforts of all countries. No country can distance itself or remain immune from such challenges. China has become an important participant, contributor, and leader in promoting a global eco-civilization."[4]

The challenge for China

But China's carbon emissions targets also represent a tremendous challenge that its government has shown it is determined to deal with. The most immediate key question is how to combine achieving per capita GDP development up to a mid-level developed country, the target which has been established for 2035, and the carbon target which has also been set.

The first question to note in this challenge is to assess China's precise point in transition to a high-income economy. What is the international comparison, and what information does this give about the processes China will face?

From being a poor country, China has already advanced to the point of having a far higher per capita GDP than most developing economies. At market exchange rates, China's per capita GDP is 227% of the average for developing countries, and in purchasing power parities (PPPs), it is 162%. China's per capita GDP, of $12,556 in 2021, is now approaching the criteria for a high-income economy by the World Bank classification – annual per capita GDP of

---

[3] Xi Jinping. Principles to Apply in Protecting the Eco-Environment (18 May 2018). In *The Governance of China* (Volume III).

[4] Xi Jinping. Principles to Apply in Protecting the Eco-Environment (18 May 2018). In *The Governance of China* (Volume III).

$13,205. But China's per capita GDP is still only 26% at market exchange rates and 35% in PPPs, of the average for high-income economies. Therefore, even after China achieves its medium-term goal of the per capita GDP of a mid-level developed economy in 2035, there will still be a long development period before it reaches the level of the highest-income advanced economies. It is, therefore, vital to know how this prolonged period of development interacts with the carbon emissions goals China has set.

The scale of the challenge can be seen clearly by even a brief analysis of the international situation on carbon emissions. Four economic sectors globally account for 71% of carbon emissions. Of these, electricity and heat are easily the most important, accounting for 31% of all emissions, which will be examined here.

China leads the world economy in numerous fields. But China's current electricity production is not yet world-leading in terms of carbon emissions. China's carbon emissions in electricity production are 541 grams per kilowatt hour compared to a world average of 425, or a country like France with 58. The reason is that the dominant source of China's electricity production is coal. Globally, coal produces 820 grams of carbon to produce 1 kilowatt hour of electricity, compared to only 48 grams for solar power and 12 grams for wind power. An enormous investment will be necessary to reduce carbon emissions and achieve net zero by 2060 to replace the great bulk of China's existing energy supply. A similar process will need to occur in numerous economic sectors. Xi Jinping has noted, "We need to change our energy mix, reducing coal use and developing clean energy.... We must restructure transport, reducing road use, increasing rail use, and cutting down emissions from diesel-powered freight vehicles."[5]

---

[5] Xi, Jinping. *Win the Battle Against Pollution* (18 May 2018).

▍Achieving the goal of a "mid-level developed country"

Finally, what exactly does China's GDP 2035 development target of a "mid-level developed country" mean for its carbon emissions? China's current total carbon emissions are almost 11 billion tons a year. To achieve net zero by 2060, in comparison to 2020, China, in arithmetical terms, requires an average decrease of 268 million tons of carbon a year. What, therefore, to take a baseline is China's present trajectory? China's CO_2 emissions, as with all countries, are determined by two factors – first, GDP, and second, the carbon intensity of GDP. In the past five years, China's carbon intensity of GDP has fallen annually by 4.8%. With a 5.1% per capita GDP growth, which would double China's per capita GDP by 2035, and a continuing 4.8% annual fall in the carbon intensity of GDP, China's carbon emissions would not rise by 2035, but they would not start to fall either.

Therefore, for China's carbon emissions to start falling over the medium/long term, either the annual decrease in China's carbon intensity of GDP must be greater than 4.8%, or GDP growth must fail to double by 2035. But if per capita GDP doesn't double by 2035, a lower standard of living will be achieved. It is, therefore, much better if carbon intensity falls. But to accomplish this, for the reasons already analyzed, the enormous investment in renewable energy will simultaneously be the decisive issue in achieving China's climate and economic development goals.

To briefly summarize the international consequences of these issues, China's development during the 14th Five-Year Plan will transform the world economy in at least three decisive ways. The longer-term program to 2035 will produce a fourth international transformation that any living human being has not experienced.

First, as already noted, China becoming a high-income economy will more than double the proportion of the world's population living in such societies – therefore producing a fundamental change in the structure of the world economy and society. The increasing income, and more complex needs, of the Chinese people, will transform and enormously expand numerous global markets and human experiences associated with high living standards– for culture, education, entertainment, travel, health care, for environmental protection, as well as enormously enrich the lives of the Chinese people.

Second, not only the next 15 years to 2035 but the next five years themselves will be decisive for the fight against climate change. China's commitment, announced by Xi Jinping in his speech to the U.N., to cap its carbon emissions by 2030, and to achieve net zero emissions by 2060, was described by environmental organizations as a "game changer."

Third, in a more short-term framework, China is the main global economic engine for recovery from the global Covid-19 economic downturn. On the projections of the IMF, China would account for over 60% of world economic growth in 2020-2021 and over 30% of world economic growth in the entire period up to 2025 – compared to 17% for the U.S. Therefore, the entire world will be affected by the targets set in China's new Five-Year Plan and success in achieving these.

China will become the world's largest economy

But fourth, taking the entire period to 2035, China has already become the world's largest economy measured by purchasing power parities (PPPs). But it is not measured by current exchange rates. But by 2035, China will become the world's largest economy, no matter how to be measured. As the U.S. became the world's largest economy in approximately 1880, there is no one alive today who has lived in a world in which China, not the U.S., was the world's largest economy. This change will have numerous impacts ranging from economics to global psychology, which is beyond the scope of these comments to examine. But, as the reports of the Central Committee of the CPC setting out these two programs to be presented to the NPC noted: "Today's world is experiencing a great change not seen in a hundred years." As literally no one alive today has ever lived in a world in which China was the world's largest economy, it is almost impossible to foresee in advance what will be all the social and psychological implications of such a situation – except that by their nature, they will necessarily transform the global situation.

The U.S. is desperate to conceal these achievements of China

By any objective analysis, China's enormous achievements, not only for its own people but for what they represent for the development of all of humanity, should be welcomed and globally celebrated. They are self-evidently not only an enormous step forward for China itself but for the well-being of humankind. But, unfortunately, it would be naive and wrong to believe that this is the reaction of the U.S. administration. On the contrary, these achievements of China make the U.S. administration desperate to conceal this reality from its own population – and, as much as possible, from the rest of the world. There are two reasons for this:

First, although the U.S. is only four percent of the world's population, and now only about one-fifth of the world economy, the U.S. administration is determined to attempt to maintain its dominance over the other 96% of the world's population and four-fifths of the world economy. Regrettably, this is officially defined as U.S. policy.

Second, China achieved its success via socialism, which contradicts the U.S. claim that capitalism is the only successful economic and social system. Furthermore, as already analyzed, China's socialist successes are increasing relative to U.S. capitalism.

For these reasons, the U.S. administration considers it imperative both to conceal the reality about China from its population and to attempt to block China's development. It is the reason why the U.S. has launched a cold war against China.

That, therefore, means that despite the tremendous achievements of the Chinese people, and the fact that China's rise is not a threat to the peoples of other countries, on the contrary, it creates numerous new opportunities for mutually beneficial win-win cooperation, China must therefore meet a new test of a determined attempt by the leadership of the U.S. to block the Chinese rise and to prevent the Chinese people from achieving prosperity.

The Marxist policies of the CPC have so far achieved the unprecedented task of leading the Chinese people from being almost the world's poorest country to the brink of being by far the world's largest high-income economy. In the new stages of China's development, marked by this year's Two Sessions, the Marxist leadership of the CPC will be indispensable in preventing this attempt by the U.S. to block the further rise of the Chinese people.

The significance of the development of other countries

Finally, regarding the general global implications of these trends, these stupendous achievements are obviously felt directly by the Chinese people. But for the rest of humanity, their significance is not just passively applauding China.

China becoming a high-income economy will be a tremendous step forward for humanity. As already noted, it will more than double the number of people living in high-income countries. Still, two-thirds of the world's population will not have achieved high-income levels. Therefore this will still be an immense challenge for humanity and for other countries to emulate China's success. China, from almost the world's poorest nation in 1949, will soon enter the ranks of high-income economies. Therefore, it poses a tremendous question for developing counties. How can they achieve the same progress?

China's progress will certainly objectively enormously aid developing economies – as China is one of their most important trading and investment partners. But it is also vital for the five billion people who will still be in developing countries after China achieves high-income status that they learn from China's experience. Because the aim of two-thirds of the world's people who will still be in developing countries is, in their own national conditions, to achieve the same success as China – that is, to realize the transition to high-income economies.

China, quite rightly, does not attempt to export an "economic model" or actively advocate that other countries follow its policies. Indeed, any country that mechanically followed China would be making a mistake – as every country's conditions are specific. But it is not forbidden for other countries to learn from China's enormous successes and to apply these lessons to their own nationally particular conditions. As Xi Jinping noted: "The path, the theory, the system, and the culture of socialism with Chinese characteristics have kept developing, blazing a new trail for other developing countries to achieve modernization. It offers a new option for other countries and nations who want to speed up their development."

Semenova Tatiana Grigorievna

An associate professor and head of the Department of Oral Translation Higher Courses of Foreign Languages, Ministry for Foreign Affairs of Russia. Her study fields include Chinese literature, Chinese culture, translation/interpretation, translation research, and teaching method of the Chinese language. She published articles such as *Yue Fei: Symbol of Loyalty and Patriotism, Spiritual Culture, and Historical Events in the Legends of Dong People.* She also translated and edited such works as *Narrating China's Governance: Stories in Xi Jinping's Speeches, Narrating China's Governance: Stories in Xi Jinping's Speeches (teenagers' edition)*, and *How Does the Communist Party of China Fight Against Corruption?* In 2008, the Ministry for Foreign Affairs of Russia granted Semenova Tatiana Grigorievna a medal of "Honor Worker of the Ministry for Foreign Affairs of Russia."

A Route to the Future

The People's Republic of China borders Russia, and there is a long land borderline between the two countries. A Chinese proverb goes, "A far-off relative is not as helpful as a near neighbor." Perhaps because of this, Russia shows great interest in China and its culture. We often hear the following expressions about China: "Chinese Dream," "the great rejuvenation of the Chinese nation," "the Belt and Road Initiative," and "the Silk Road." What do they mean? What is the "Chinese Dream"?

On November 29, 2012, General Secretary of the CPC Central Committee Xi Jinping first put forward the concept of the "Chinese Dream" in his speech when he visited the National Museum of China in Beijing. One of the main ideas of this concept is the rejuvenation of the Chinese nation.

However, without a great country, there is no great nation. Therefore, the idea of "rejuvenation" means increasing national strength by developing the economy and improving people's living standards. It means eradicating extreme poverty, achieving a moderately prosperous society, further developing society, science, technology, education, and medical care, and improving the national legal system. An important part of national rejuvenation also includes the harmonious development of people and the environment and the reunification of the motherland.

Due to the nature of my work, I must read many Chinese periodicals, including articles on the eradication of extreme poverty and the great changes taking place in China. However, as the saying goes, "Seeing by oneself is a hundred times better than hearing from others." At the end of 2019, I got such an opportunity. At that time, the world had not been disrupted by COVID-19.

From late October to early November 2019, the Embassy of the People's Republic of China in Russia invited a delegation of Russian sinologists and journalists to visit where President Xi Jinping once lived and worked.

My husband and I were honored to be invited to translate President Xi Jinping's book into Russian. We eagerly looked forward to going to those places mentioned by President Xi in his speeches. People's Publishing House later compiled the speeches as *Narrating China's Governance: Stories in Xi Jinping's Speeches*, the Russian version of which is called *Истории из уст Си Цзиньпина*.

When translating the book, I had the impression that what the President of the PRC has experienced also reflects the great changes that have taken place in the country and society in recent decades. Because of this, this visit is of great significance to me.

We first came to Beijing, the capital of China, and then many other places, enjoying a short but very fulfilling trip. We flew directly from Moscow to Beijing and were greeted by the bright summer and the hustle and bustle of this big city. Previously, we had heard of the harsh ecological environment here and were ready to see a metropolis shrouded in smog. However, what we saw wasn't like what we had expected. The sky was clear and blue, and the air was fresh. That immediately reminded me of the story about "APEC blue."[1] In 2014, during the APEC Summit, President Xi Jinping expressed his concern about Beijing's air quality. Soon after that, with the joint efforts of the central government and the Beijing Municipal Government, Beijing's ecological situation was significantly improved.

In the years before I went to Beijing, considerable changes occurred here. Row upon row of new high-rise buildings had been built, and a large area of idle land had been transformed into lush green space. What shocked us most was the world's (construction scale) largest new airport in the suburb: the Daxing International Airport.

---

[1] "APEC Blue", *Narrating China's Governance: Stories in Xi Jinping's Speeches*, People's Publishing House, 2017, p328.

The Daxing Airport is located south of Beijing, 46 kilometers from the city center. The new airport has four runways, with an annual take-off and landing of 620,000 flights. According to the project plan, the airport's throughput will reach 72 million people by 2025. This unique modern building looks like a starfish or an exotic flower. There are many ways of transportation to the airport, including a specially built subway branch line and an airport express available for people to take.

The elegant and bright architectural style of the new airport is impressive. It is a modern airport that integrates high-tech and environmental protection concepts while considering human scales and feelings. (It takes 15 minutes at most for passengers to go from one terminal to another). Its design concept that conforms to the future trend can also be proved by the average age of airport employees: 35 years.

In the evening, the train took us from the future back to the past, through history, to the place where the People's Republic of China was born, where Xi Jinping spent his youth.

The next morning, we arrived at the village of Liangjiahe. It is a place of extraordinary significance, as described in Xi Jinping's biography. It is right here, I think, that Xi had a real understanding of the lives and needs of ordinary people.

The village is located at the foot of a mountain on the loess plateau in Shaanxi Province. In 1969, a group of educated youth came here. They were composed of 13 boys and two girls, all high school students aged 15 to 16. As recalled by President Xi Jinping, "Toward the end of the 1960s, when I was in my teens, I was sent from Beijing to the small village of Liangjiahe near Yan'an of Shaanxi Province, where I spent seven years as a farmer."[2] It was a poor village with no electricity. People lived in cave dwellings typical of this area.

---

[2] "The Changes in Liangjiahe Village", *Narrating China's Governance: Stories in Xi Jinping's Speeches*, People's Publishing House, 2017, p322.

The hard agricultural work and ascetic living conditions did not destroy the young man's will, but tempered his character, pointed out the direction for his life path, and helped to make him establish the ambition of "Always remaining true to the original aspiration."

The theme of "remaining true to our original aspiration and keeping our mission firmly in mind" was seen everywhere during our visit. We saw it on the walls of the administrative offices, in the streets, on the lamp posts, the two sides of buses, and the taxis. President Xi Jinping put it forward in a speech he delivered at the 19th National Congress of the Communist Party of China in 2017. It is more than a slogan. In May 2019, the resolution of the Political Bureau of the CPC Central Committee made it the main theme of top-down learning and education of the whole Party. In fact, the first half of the theme can even be traced back to ancient times (Tang Dynasty), which means the sincerity and purity of the original intention. As early as July 2016, at the conference to commemorate the 95th anniversary of the founding of the Communist Party of China, President Xi put forward "stay true to the mission" and pointed out that the Communist Party of China has an obligation to retain the memory of the past and spiritual purity along the road to a bright future.[3]

Now, Liangjiahe has become an urbanized village, and there is a comprehensive museum specially established for President Xi. We returned to Yan'an, a county-level city in Shaanxi Province. It was the core residence of the Communist Party of China from 1937 to 1948 and a special area controlled by the Communist Party of China under the leadership of Chairman Mao Zedong. Among the cave dwellings like those in Liangjiahe Village, where the CPC leaders once lived and worked, a cave dwelling has been preserved where Comrade Xi Zhongxun (1913-2002), the father of President Xi Jinping, once lived. The number of books read by Party members living in the cave dwellings is amazing. Probably because of this, under the influence of the family and

---

[3] http://europe.chinadaily.com.cn/china/2016-07/01/content_25933526.htm

in communication with his father, President Xi Jinping developed a keen interest in reading. Xi later recalled that when he was living and working in the countryside of Shaanxi Province as an educated youth, he heard that another educated youth had the book, Faust, so he walked 30 miles to borrow the book from him. Later that young man walked 30 miles to get the book back from him.[4]

At the Yan'an Museum and Liangjiahe Museum, we learned that the People's Republic of China has opened up an unprecedented path in a relatively short time. Its leaders have made great efforts and breakthroughs to save a vast country from destruction, humiliation, poverty, and backwardness.

It was a pity that we didn't stay in Xi'an, the capital of Shaanxi Province, for long. Like many cities in China, the history and modernity of this ancient city are intertwined. The Silk Road linked East Asia, the Middle East, and the Mediterranean in ancient times and the Middle Ages. Xi'an, known as Chang'an in ancient times, was the most important stop on the great Silk Road. Today, Xi'an is an industrial, cultural and educational center in northwestern China.

Our next stop was Zhengding County, Hebei Province. Since April 1982, Xi Jinping has worked as Deputy Party Secretary and then as Party Secretary of the county in July 1983.

In January 2014, *Hebei Daily* published an article. The author served as Party Secretary of Zhengding County in the 1980s and worked with Comrade Xi Jinping as his colleague. In his memory, Xi, a young Party worker, was a down-to-earth, compassionate, modest, and confident man who was good at going into the midst of the common people and communicating widely with them. Although he was still very young then, he was already a mature and competent community-level official.

After taking office in Zhengding County, Xi Jinping often rode a bicycle to various villages and towns to learn about the situation. As he later recalled, "In 1982, when I was preparing to leave for Zhengding County, Hebei Province,

---

[4] "Borrowing a Book from 30 Miles Away", *Narrating China's Governance: Stories in Xi Jinping's Speeches*, People's Publishing House, 2017, p96.

for a new appointment, many friends came to bid me farewell, including Wang Yuanjian[5], a writer and playwright from August 1 Film Studio[6]. He urged me, 'In the rural area, you should learn from Liu Qing, staying close to and going deep among the local farmers.'"[7] It turned out that Xi Jinping didn't ignore such a suggestion. Later, when he carried out Party affairs in other counties, he still adhered to the community-level work strategy he chose. "I once stated that a county Party Secretary should visit all the villages in the county, a municipal or prefectural Party Secretary should visit all the districts and townships in the city, and a provincial Party Secretary should visit all the counties and cities in the province. I did it."[8] He just wanted to "have a thorough understanding of the situation and grasp first-hand information. Do not merely wait for someone to collect information for you. We are not infants who need to be fed by others."[9]

Xi Jinping was one of the first to carry out economic reform in Zhengding County. Tayuan Village is an example. When he first came to work in the county, this village had just gotten rid of poverty and couldn't be said to be rich. Xi suggested that the government should reduce the burden on farmers and let them manage the surplus grain by themselves. The village was thus revitalized. Greenhouses were built, and a water supply system was installed.

Now, the village is a prosperous place. The village has its school, kindergarten, and beautiful multi-story houses. Many farmers own two houses.

We came to the central square, where clusters of bright red perfume roses bloomed. These flowers are the symbol of Tayuan Village. Here lies the main administrative building of the village, in which there is a museum that tells

---

[5] Wang Yuanjian (1929–1991), a writer and playwright.

[6] August 1 Film Studio, as its name suggests, is named to commemorate the founding day of the Chinese People's Liberation Army.

[7] "Liu Qing Settled in Huangpu Village for Literary Inspiration", *Narrating China's Governance: Stories in Xi Jinping's Speeches*, People's Publishing House, 2017, p151.

[8] "The 'Governor' Is Coming", *Narrating China's Governance: Stories in Xi Jinping's Speeches*, People's Publishing House, 2017, p154.

[9] "The 'Governor' Is Coming", *Narrating China's Governance: Stories in Xi Jinping's Speeches*, People's Publishing House, 2017, p154.

the village's history and details the various stages of its growth and poverty eradication.

The current county leader said that Xi Jinping had attached great importance to the selection of the leading group and the training of professionals and had told them that education was the driving force of progress.

We also found that China's current leader has always maintained a cautious attitude toward the country's rich history and cultural legacy. With the rapid construction of new buildings in urban and rural areas, ancient structures have also been rebuilt and repaired. In the center of Zhengding County, people repaired the historic city walls and four ancient pagodas. They built an urban complex with the style of the 18th century, which was used to shoot a TV series adapted from the classic novel of the same name, *A Dream of Red Mansions*. Later, many films were shot here. In addition to being a film and television base, it is also a popular tourist attraction. Some rooms in the building complex can also be rented as souvenir shops or for art exchanges. In one room, we saw some elderly people practicing traditional Chinese calligraphy and painting. By the way, in China today, all elderly citizens can receive a pension, including farmers. Moreover, with economic development, the pension amount will gradually increase.

The next morning, we flew to Xiamen, Fujian Province, in southern China. Xi Jinping spent his best years in Fujian Province. He came here at 32, worked in Fujian Province for nearly 18 years, and grew into a statesman and leader. Xiamen, located in the southeast of China, is one of the large port cities and a developed coastal city. Together with Shenzhen, Zhuhai, and Shantou, Xiamen was one of the first special economic zones. From 1985 to 1988, Xi worked as Deputy Mayor here.

We visited the container port and international cruise center in Xiamen. We are deeply impressed by the size of the port and the small number of workers. The port is fully automated, and eight senior experts complete all complex management.

The international cruise center is a special port for cruise ships, which can receive tourist ships from all over the world all year round. The port is planning to expand, and another two berths need to be built, which will further expand the port's handling capacity.

Xiamen has another romantic name: Egret Island. Since 1986, egrets have become the official symbol of the city. Due to the improvement of the ecological environment, the number of egrets in Xiamen parks is increasing. The meeting between the vice mayor of Xiamen and our delegation was held in the Central Park beside the Yundang Lake, where Xiamen University is located. This lake used to be where people discharged and discarded all kinds of domestic garbage. It was a dirty and smelly reservoir. The lake's water has been cleaned up, and trees have been planted along the lakeside. Due to a large number of thin-walled tall bamboo, the lake is also known as the "Bamboo Lake." In 2005, the local government began to build an academy in the park by the lake, with a style similar to that of ancient academic centers. It is not only a teaching institution but also a conference center, which provides a platform for holding various teaching and academic activities and experience exchange meetings among scholars. The academy has the position of an honorary president. More than 100 famous scientists from first-class universities and research centers in the Chinese Mainland, Hong Kong, and Taiwan have been invited to serve as scientific consultants. The academy has its own publications and a library with rich collections. The academy was built in the traditional Chinese style and officially used in 2009, carrying forward Chinese traditional culture.

Developing and carrying forward its traditional culture is another important achievement of China. It is not easy for a country to retain its own cultural and spiritual values in the globalized world and maintain its unique identity. As I have found out, China has done a great job in this, skillfully integrating tradition and trends.

In September 2017, the Ninth Brics Summit was held in Xiamen, during which the state heads of China and Russia held a bilateral meeting in a hall of Yundang Academy. To commemorate this meeting, the room was kept the same as back then in decoration and setting.

That day we were there, a group wedding was going to be held in the lakeside park. Like many Eastern countries, traditional Chinese weddings are usually expensive, and people are often in debt for a "ceremonious" wedding. However, nowadays, young people's understanding of weddings is changing, and they hope to reduce unnecessary burdens. One solution is to attend group weddings.

The next day, when our memory was still fresh, we left for Fuqing, just like Xiamen, also lies on the east coast of the Taiwan Straits. Fuqing is developing into an industrial area. We visited a glass factory, a modern enterprise that produces automotive glass for famous brands such as Mercedes-Benz, BMW, and Nissan.

Our next stop is Fuzhou, the capital of Fujian Province. Since 1990, Xi Jinping has worked here successively in Fuzhou Municipal Government and Fujian Provincial Government.

Fuzhou is the center of the wood, papermaking, food, printing, chemical, and textile industries and mechanical engineering. Agriculture here is very developed. The warm climate and high humidity have created good conditions for tea planting. Fujian produces a wide variety of tea, such as oolong, black, green, white, and scented tea. Fuzhou is one of the earliest open coastal cities, the gateway of the maritime Silk Road, and one of the three Pilot Free Trade Zones in Fujian.

Our first stop in this city is the Civic Service Center. The center was founded on the initiative of the Communist Party of China. One-third of its employees are Party members. They practice the main purpose of the CPC – "serving the people" in practical actions. This five-story building, with an area of nearly 40,000 square meters, provides "one-stop" services for issuing the documents related to social security, medical insurance, driver's licenses, etc. Here you can receive passports and pay fines if necessary. Citizens who come to the center praise the service here, while some retirees and mothers with children do not necessarily come here to handle business. They are here perhaps just to have a cup of tea in the cafeteria and chat with each other when social workers interact with their children.

In the evening, we came to the city's historical district, where the mayor of Fuzhou received us. The mayor told us that President Xi Jinping always prioritizes protecting historical heritage. The well-preserved ancient building area in the city center is an example. It is called "Three Lanes and Seven Alleys," a common name. But for developers, the city center is very attractive. One area has been completely rebuilt and turned into a pedestrian area with many tea houses and souvenir shops. Later, walking along a street in this historical center, we met a group of young men and women wearing ancient clothes from different times. When we asked why they were shopping in such attire, the young people replied that this was a way to express their love for China and its history. They do have something to be proud of!

The next morning, we took the high-speed train to Hangzhou, the capital of Zhejiang Province.

In 2002, Xi Jinping was transferred to Zhejiang Province and worked in the provincial government until 2007. The book *Narrating China's Governance: Stories in Xi Jinping's Speeches* quotes Xi's memory of Hangzhou: "Hangzhou is a renowned historical and cultural city and a center of business and trade in China. Famous for Bai Juyi and Su Dongpo[10], as well as the West Lake[11] and the Grand Canal[12], Hangzhou has a fascinating history and enchanting cultural heritage. Hangzhou is also an innovative and vibrant city with booming e-commerce. Hangzhou is also a leader in ecological conservation. Its green hills, clear rivers, and lakes delight the eye on sunny days and present a special view on rainy days."[13]

We had a very busy day in Hangzhou. In the morning, we left for Anjiyu Village near Hangzhou, which got widely known far and near for being the first place where Xi Jinping's environmental policy was implemented. The village is

---

[10] Bai Juyi (AD 772–846), one of the most famous poets of the Tang Dynasty; Su Dongpo (1037–1101), namely Su Shi, also named Dongpo, was a poet, artist, painter and politician of the Song Dynasty in China.

[11] The West Lake, which literally means "the lake in the west", is a famous freshwater lake in the center of Hangzhou. Together with the surrounding ancient buildings, it is listed in the UNESCO heritage list.

[12] The Grand Canal is one of the oldest water conservancy projects still in use in the world. Its construction lasted 2,000 years: from the 6th century to the 13th century BC. It has been listed as a world cultural heritage site.

[13] "The Most Memorable Is Hangzhou", *Narrating China's Governance: Stories in Xi Jinping's Speeches*, People's Publishing House, 2017, p319.

picturesque, surrounded by mountains and dense bamboo forests. It was right here that the famous director Ang Lee shot his film *Crouching Tiger, Hidden Dragon*, and after that, many tourists were attracted to the place.

There were several quarries in this mountainous area for limestone mining. And there were three cement plants in the village having a very negative influence on the environment.

Xi Jinping visited this village when he was working in Zhejiang. He pointed out that it was time to stop the production bad for environmental protection in such a picturesque place. The place was more suitable for organizing leisure and entertainment activities for urban residents.

It was not easy to make the villagers close their production plants and persuade them to engage in a job they were unfamiliar with, that is, leisure and eco-tourism for the residents of Hangzhou and Shanghai. In the initial stage, there were many difficulties, but people gathered their wisdom and overcame them one by one. Now, it is a prosperous village with beautiful low-rise houses and hotels at different prices, which can receive up to 800,000 tourists every year.

On the village square stands a beautiful natural stone engraved with the red inscription "Clear Waters and Green Mountains Are Invaluable Assets." It is what Xi Jinping said and was later included in the book *Zhejiang, China: A New Vision for Development.*[14]

In the evening, beside the beautiful West Lake, we enjoyed a concert. The stage was the lake itself. The 40-minute performance was directed by the world-famous director Zhang Yimou, who specially edited and directed it for the guests of the 11th G20 Summit held in Hangzhou in September 2016. The beautiful music, dance, singing, the lighting effect, and the huge reflection of the moon in the lake constituted a wonderful picture like a dream.

The statue of the famous general Yue Fei stands at the park's exit. This brave soldier lived in the 12th century and fought against the invaders from the

---

[14] "Build up 'Two Mountains'", *Narrating China's Governance: Stories in Xi Jinping's Speeches*, Beijing, 2017, p181.

north. But he was killed in prison because of the trap of traitor ministers. Later, he was rehabilitated and became a symbol of selfless dedication to the country. Yue Fei is Xi Jinping's favorite hero. In his book, he wrote: "From then on, I have kept the words 'serve the country with utmost loyalty' firmly in my mind as my lifelong goal."[15]

The next day started with visiting the "Dream Town" industrial park in Hangzhou Future High-tech City, one of the four future cities, a business incubator, and a start-up and innovation platform. It has primary schools, institutions of higher learning, and investment funds. The focus here is on the electronic industry, information technology, new materials research, alternative energy, software, etc. The "Dream Town" invites young talents, including those from abroad. (There are also experts from Russia here). Currently, a talent growth zone and a new technology city integrating production and urban development are being created here.

"Dream Town" was founded under the initiative and support of the Organization Department of the CPC Central Committee and the State-owned Assets Supervision and Administration Commission of the State Council of the PRC and was officially launched in September 2014. One of the investors and developers of the project is well-known not only in China but also in the world. He is the soul of Alibaba Group: Jack Ma.

Then, we came seamlessly from the "Dream Town" to ancient times: the Liangzhu Museum. The museum is located in the Meilizhou Park, Liangzhu Town, covering an area of 40,000 square meters, and was officially opened in September 2008. The ruins of the Liangzhu ancient city in the Neolithic Age, were found in Zhejiang Province. The cultural relics unearthed at the excavation site confirmed China's 5,000-year history. The Liangzhu Culture (3300–2300 BC) is the last Neolithic jade culture in the Yangtze River Delta. In July this year, Liangzhu relics were included in the UNESCO cultural

---

[15] "Serve the Country with Supreme Loyalty", *Narrating China's Governance: Stories in Xi Jinping's Speeches*, People's Publishing House, 2017, p93.

heritage list.

Then we were on our way to Shanghai. Xi Jinping began to work as the Secretary of the CPC Shanghai Municipal Committee in 2007.

Shanghai is one of the municipalities directly under the Central Government of China and an important financial and cultural center. It has the largest seaport in China. It was also the city where the First CPC National Congress was held in secret in 1921. The first place we visited was the memorial hall of the First National Congress of the CPC, which was in the house where the meeting was actually held. The building is built in the traditional Shikumen style, which originated in Shanghai in the late 19th century and is the product of an integration of Chinese and Western styles. The memorial hall consists of two parts: the room where the Congress was held (i.e., the original site of the Congress) and other exhibition halls focusing on the CPC history. Built in 1952, the memorial hall is a cultural monument of national significance. Xi Jinping visited it many times.

On the last day in Shanghai, after meeting with Shanghai municipal leaders, we visited the news company "ThePaper.cn." It is a large news platform in China and one of the first-tier media in China, subordinate to Shanghai United Media Group. The portal has received great attention at home and abroad. In April 2016, "ThePaper.cn" launched a new English media called "Sixth Tone" to disseminate information about China and the daily life of the Chinese people to overseas audiences. Since October 2015, "ThePaper.cn" has been cooperating with the international news agency "Russia Today" and Sputnik.

Our stay in Shanghai coincided with China International Import Expo. At the initiative of President Xi Jinping, the China International Import Expo was held in Shanghai for the second time. In May 2017, Xi Jinping, the PRC's state leader, proposed this initiative in a speech at the Belt and Road Forum for International Cooperation held in Beijing. Since 2018, the Expo has become an annual exhibition. In 2019, it coincided with the 70th anniversary of the founding of the PRC. For that reason, the China Pavilion displayed China's achievements in social and economic development over the past few years.

Russia also participated in the Expo and showed its potential in industry, investment, and tourism. The Expo was held in a huge exhibition center with many international exhibitions, including the World Expo.

On November 7, we concluded our fruitful visit and flew back to Moscow.

To sum up, in just eight days, we traveled a long way and successfully visited many places thanks to the developed transportation network in modern China. High-speed trains gallop across the vast land, and excellent highway and railway systems connect the whole country.

During the trip, we not only traveled across vast geographical regions but also learned about China's past and present and looked forward to the future. After all, as President Xi Jinping said, "To understand today's China and predict tomorrow's China, one has to know China's past and culture. Modern Chinese people's thinking and the Chinese governance strategy inherit the traditional Chinese culture."[16]

Nearly three years have passed since we paid that visit to China. In this period, the world underwent severe turbulence and changes. At the end of 2019, a new coronavirus was discovered in Wuhan, the capital city of Hubei Province. It was later named Covid-19 (novel coronavirus pneumonia). The virus spread rapidly around the world. In 2020, the World Health Organization (WHO) announced that Covid-19 had become a global pandemic. Many countries began to enforce a lockdown and suffered a slowdown in economic growth.

Facing this global challenge, China responded rapidly and took resolute measures. On January 20, 2020, Chinese President Xi Jinping gave an important instruction, urging leaders at all levels to attach great importance to this pandemic and take decisive measures to curb its spread. Five days later, the CPC Central Committee set up a leading group for novel coronavirus prevention and control, which Chinese Premier Li Keqiang headed.

---

[16] "The Night Speech at Yingtai", *Narrating China's Governance: Stories in Xi Jinping's Speeches*, People's Publishing House, 2017, p325.

China constructed temporary treatment centers in time. Moreover, Covid-19 testing laboratories were set up, and the movement of people within the territory and across borders was tightly restricted. These measures effectively reduced the spread of the virus. Appropriate steps were taken across China to stamp out the virus spread. In February 2020, a delegation of the WHO came to China and spoke highly of China's prevention and control measures.

Unfortunately, due to the rapid variation of the virus, the dawn of victory was hardly in sight. However, thanks to the effective measures, China then, compared with other major powers, managed to bring the pandemic under control, minimizing its loss and maintaining a good development momentum.

As a matter of fact, all this took place in a grave international situation. In January 2021, American president Joe Biden came into power and continued to adopt the policy of Trump (former president of the U.S.) by exerting pressure on China. In December 2021, in an interview with FOX News Channel (FNC), Trump attributed the breakout and spread of Covid-19 to China and demanded China's compensation for America's loss due to the pandemic.

China made a stand against the groundless accusation and politicization of the pandemic. Moreover, China invited WHO experts to the Wuhan laboratory for investigation. After the investigation, the experts confirmed that the above accusation was groundless.

Different from the U.S., China, while fighting against Covid-19, offered assistance to other countries. For example, on September 9, 2021, the 13th BRICS Leaders' Meeting was held via videoconferencing. Chinese President Xi Jinping delivered an important speech, promising to donate another 100 million doses of Covid-19 vaccines to developing countries by the end of 2021. Moreover, President Xi stressed the importance of taking more measures and cooperating in research and development in fighting against the pandemic.

The volatile and complicated international situation and domestic difficulties did not hinder China from further development and realizing its goals. China made continuous efforts in space exploration. The Tianwen 1

Martian and Chang'e 5 lunar probe were successfully launched into orbits.

On July 1, 2021, at the celebration of the 100th anniversary of the founding of the CPC, Xi Jinping, General Secretary of its Central Committee and President of the PRC, delivered a speech. In it, he announced China had achieved its first centenary goal of eradicating absolute poverty and building a moderately prosperous society in all respects.

Despite the difficulties brought about by the Covid-19 pandemic, China managed to eliminate poverty as planned and pushed forward social, ecological, and cultural development.

Furthermore, China made progress in international relations. On July 16, 2021, China and Russia celebrated the 20th anniversary of the signing of the Treaty of Good-Neighborliness and Friendly Cooperation Between China and Russia. Chinese President Xi Jinping and Russian President Putin had a virtual meeting and jointly announced the extension of the Treaty. In September 2021, the 20th meeting of the Council of Heads of Government (Prime Ministers) of the Shanghai Cooperation Organization (SCO) was held at Dushanbe, the capital of Tajikistan, and a communique was adopted.

Given that the West is imposing unprecedented sanctions against Russia and unilateral sanctions against China, the Chinese and Russian people need to develop friendship and mutually beneficial relations. The United States attempts to, through sanctions, undermine the internal political progress of China and Russia – two major powers, impose restrictions on their economic development and hinder China's technological development.

Today, the world is fraught with crises, great turmoil, and uncertainties. The concepts of democracy, sovereignty, and human rights are intentionally misinterpreted, and family and human values are trampled upon. In view of this, it is vital to remain true to the original aspiration of building China into a powerful sovereign state and to have full confidence in its state, culture, and people. Only in this way can the People's Republic of China, a great and rapidly developing country, integrate its splendid historical and cultural heritages with the modernization drive to reach its goals undoubtedly.

Rasha Kahlil

A professor, inventor, researcher, and consultant in legal studies and international cooperation. She has cooperated with the Global Environment Facility (GEF), the United Nations Development Program (UNDP), the Syrian Organization for Persons with Disabilities (AAMAL), the Foreign Talent Research Center of the Ministry of Science and Technology of China, and the China and Globalization Think Tank. Professor Rasha Khalil has served as a keynote speaker and chairperson at several international conferences at home and abroad. She was the Winner of the Kent Natural Resources International Foundation Award, and awarded the "Light of Civilization" 2020 Chinese Cultural Exchange Person of the Year.

Chinese Diplomacy: To Promote Security, Stability, and Development in the Region and the World

The Chinese civilization is one of the most important civilizations in the world and still profoundly influences the course of human history and demonstrates the brilliance of humanity today. Just as the compass was and still is one of the greatest inventions in human history, the rise of contemporary China is one of the most important events that have changed the world, as the rise has had an even more profound impact on human civilization. China is the world's "compass", guiding the world toward peace, sustainable development, and common prosperity.

The impact of the Chinese civilization is felt in all areas, especially in humanitarianism and diplomatic relations. China is deeply influenced by its culture and therefore attaches great importance to diplomatic ties. China's foreign policy and practice encourage exchanges with other peoples on equal footing and are committed to spreading peace and strengthening ties with other peoples of the world in the political, social, and scientific fields.

Despite its strategic location and economic strength, China's leading position as a global hub is primarily owed to its positive, close relations with other countries and its key role in international and regional policies.

China's impressive performance in the regional and international arenas is not the product of an overnight process but the result of thousands of years of experience. China tends to be politically pragmatic, adopting a flexible mindset and a strategic vision of its people's future. China recognizes that economic growth and development are inextricably linked to political image and stability. China also firmly believes that diversity and harmoniously balanced opening will benefit everyone.

While Chinese diplomacy is often based on strategic ideas, at its core, it is a people-to-people act that involves equality-based dialogue, raising issues, and seeking consensus. Such diplomatic interactions can play an important role in changing perceptions and decision-making, especially in times of crisis. It is reflected in the practice of Chinese diplomacy. Chinese diplomacy strives to use various strategic information, scientific perceptions, and knowledge data to help build meaningful, constructive international relations. It is clearly reflected in China's foreign policy toward various conflicts and regional and global crises. China's foreign policy is centered on realism, concern about national interests, and noninterference in the internal affairs of other countries, with an emphasis on resolving political conflicts through peaceful means. China still adheres strictly to this policy despite the world's changing circumstances.

The ultimate goal of Chinese diplomacy is to promote security, stability, and development in China and worldwide. China's political, economic, and diplomatic activities reflect the country's foreign policy: the untiring pursuit of peaceful coexistence and common development of all countries in the world. They are also a true reflection of China's relentless efforts for international justice and sustainable development. In the face of a complex, ever-changing international situation, China's determined diplomatic interactions demonstrate the ability of Chinese political decision-makers to interpret changes in international circumstances accurately.

Based on an in-depth analysis of the past, present, and future political processes in the international arena, China has adopted a planned approach, adhering to its civilizational and cultural heritage and rejecting the use of hard power to resolve differences and disputes. In the meantime, China believes that dialogue should be the keynote of state-to-state relations and that direct dialogue and communication among peoples will undoubtedly bring about political détente and produce positive effects. Therefore, China's foreign policy can be described as a calm, moderate, balanced, and fair policy that has always been highly respected and appreciated by the international community.

China's vision of its foreign policy and philosophy of international relations is to adhere to political dialogue based on common interests and an ethical value system of exchanges. China believes that every country has the right to pursue its own interests but must not deviate from international norms, such as noninterference in the internal affairs of other countries, mutual respect, reciprocity, friendliness, justice, and respect for the customs and traditions of other countries. China stands for addressing conflicts between countries through dialogue and negotiation. China believes that a rational country should be capable of dealing with international opinion in a scientific, thoughtful manner at the ideological and practical levels and make efforts to build mutual trust with other countries.

In addition, the Chinese government has developed a series of supervisory measures to ensure the political functioning of the government and state institutions. Their most important elements include adapting to the times, maintaining moral values, and focusing on the humanitarian system's most important part – the people's interests. Such a clear vision of China's foreign policy is owed to its rich historical and cultural heritage and positive interactions with other countries. But the main pillar of China's foreign policy is the unwavering principles established by the Communist Party of China. China has invariably upheld its diplomatic principles in foreign relations. It also reflects China's geographic location and historical role, demonstrating that China will commit itself to building a better world of peace, security, and stability for all countries and peoples.

China has always taken a comprehensive view of peace. Peace in Chinese diplomacy means non-violence and lasting peace that helps promote all-round human development based on equity and justice. It also means strengthening education, public health, and economic development; defending human rights; and promoting social cohesion by saying no to injustice and discrimination.

China's foreign policy is committed to extending a hand of friendship to other peoples and cooperating with them, thus winning the attention and respect of other countries. China has thus become a model for other countries to follow in foreign relations. China has demonstrated wisdom, etiquette, and a firm stance in foreign relations, insisting in its foreign policy that the issues of all stakeholders be resolved in a just and sensible manner. From this perspective, Chinese diplomacy has achieved considerable success at both regional and global levels. It is based on adherence to principles, noninterference in the internal affairs of other countries, and commitment to achieving common progress, happiness, and prosperity for the Chinese people and other peoples through dialogue and peaceful solutions.

Since Comrade Xi Jinping was elected General Secretary of the CPC Central Committee, China has risen under his visionary guidance. In his first speech, General Secretary Xi Jinping pledged to make greater efforts to deepen mutual understanding between China and the rest of the world. This commitment is a clear manifestation of China's personality and historical experience in its foreign policy, as well as its leadership wisdom and foresight in the face of evolving situations and different positions.

Based on an analysis of global data over the past two decades, the Chinese leadership has revealed a huge development gap between developed and developing countries, especially in infrastructure. This gap has a huge negative impact, which limits openness in international trade and, thus, opportunities for future prosperity. Therefore, under the strong leadership of the CPC Central Committee and the personal guidance and leadership of General Secretary Xi Jinping, Chinese diplomacy has opened up new horizons by focusing on forging a global partnership, advancing China's diplomatic layout in a comprehensive, multilevel and multi-dimensional way, and forming and expanding its circle of friends around the world.

China has made great efforts to bridge the development gap among countries and proposed the Belt and Road Initiative (BRI) based on the ancient Silk Road to continue these efforts.

Historically, the Silk Road was the first trade route between China and the West, which connected China to Europe through Central Asia and the Indian subcontinent. However, the Silk Road was important not only because it was a means of connecting markets and creating wealth but also because it was a bridge for people-to-people ties and cultural and knowledge exchange. It has been proved by China's tireless efforts to promote and strengthen cooperation among the countries along the Belt and Road.

The Belt and Road Initiative (BRI) is the largest platform for international cooperation. It helps all partners to carry out the principle of joint discussion, development, and sharing, and the concept of mutual benefit, win-win result, and common development. Both China and the countries which have signed with China the cooperative agreements within the framework of the BRI have scored remarkable economic achievements, with their rates of contribution to the global economy rising remarkably. It is estimated that by 2027 the earnings of the investment projects under the BRI will exceed one trillion US dollars, which will facilitate the construction of the infrastructural facilities of the countries joining the initiative.

It is noteworthy that China's funds for these investment projects, as a matter of fact, are mostly from its state-run development projects and commercial banks. Moreover, China upholds the investment mode based on multilateral cooperation, including multilateral development banks and public and private partnerships.

Though the BRI is committed to sustainable global development, the Middle East and North African countries hold a privileged position in China's foreign policies.

On the one hand, one of the major objectives of China's foreign policies is to strengthen its friendly relationships with countries in the Middle East and North Africa. On the other hand, the latter wishes to deepen their relationships with China because China has been their trustworthy partner throughout history.

As a matter of fact, the relationships between China and the countries in the Middle East and North Africa have developed rapidly since the early period of the first decade of the 21st century, especially when China adopted the "going-global" strategy and encouraged its companies to invest overseas and since China joined the World Trade Organization (WTO) in 2001. The relationships have given an impetus to bilateral economic and diplomatic relations. With the accelerated energy consumption in China, the economic relationships between China and the countries in these two regions have been strengthened because they are very important for China's energy security. Moreover, North Africa is vital to China's economic development because it provides huge opportunities for China to invest much in infrastructure such as ports, railways, highways, nuclear energy, and high and new technology and other fields.

So far, China has signed the BRI cooperative agreements with 21[1] Middle East and North African countries, including 18 Arab countries. These agreements are expected to have an enormous influence on the Chinese economy, for the Arab countries boast a vast market and a population of 400 million, one-third of whom are aged between 15 and 30. This figure is expected to double by 2060.

Over the past 20 years, China's vision of the Middle East and North Africa has focused on cultural dialogue, trade, economy, etc. It conforms to the "cooperation" instruction by Xi Jinping, Chinese President. China has realized its diplomatic objectives of peaceful coexistence through cooperation and established firm partnerships with other countries.

The relationship between China and the Middle East and North African countries has been furthered within the BRI. It is one of the examples of China's unremitting efforts in improving global economic development and the governance model. The BRI makes it clear that a new era has begun because most concerns are about the initiative for large-scale development at the international level, including the large infrastructure projects of 66 countries in Asia, Europe, and Africa.

The core objective of the BRI is to realize the goal of shared prosperity. Therefore, all aspects of sustainable development should be given the same weight. China has striven for the global sustainable development of human beings and created an essential balance between humanity, the economy, and

---

[1] OECD (2018), "The Belt and Road Initiative in the global trade, investment and finance landscape", in OECD Business and Finance Outlook 2018, OECD Publishing, Paris, https://doi.org/10.1787/bus_fin_out-2018-6-en.

the environment. This endeavor is sustainable, high-quality, and efficient. The key to realizing this goal lies in improving the quality and efficiency of individuals and institutions at the local and international levels.

China keeps sharing its path-breaking development experience with the world. Domestically, since the implementation of its reform and opening-up policy in the late 1970s, China has scored remarkable achievements in economic development. Over the past 40 years since it implemented this policy, 900 million Chinese people have shaken off poverty, modern infrastructure is seen all over the country, and prosperous modern metropolises have mushroomed at an amazing speed.

Abundant resources, institutional development, progressive ideas, and active thinking are just part of the numerous factors contributing to China's significant achievements in scientific development. China has built up open and balanced legal and administrative systems based on its available resources, deep-rooted culture, and consolidated social system, and achieved sustainable economic development. China has made unremitting efforts to improve people's well-being, living standards, and medical and health services and attached great importance to education. So far, in terms of education, the focus has shifted to improving its quality and establishing a comprehensive and advanced educational system to satisfy the need for development in the following decades.

China is striving to build itself into an even stronger economy. President Xi Jinping has emphasized the importance of achieving economic growth, propelling new industrialization, and quickening the pace of building China into an industrial power and creating the digital China. Its successful economic development policies have resulted in economic prosperity. On the one hand, China's capital and production capacities enable it to invest abroad. On the other hand, the percentage of labor forces with high-quality professional skills increases rapidly. As a result, the Chinese have received more tangible benefits and a sense of safety and happiness. Such a feeling can be possible only by a powerful and benign social structure. China adheres to the development principle of "people first" and has it carried out in all fields.

Moreover, as the environment is the third largest pillar industry for sustainable development, President Xi Jinping has stressed the importance of ecological progress and natural resource conservation.

In addition, while striving to achieve overall sustainable development, China has made unremitting efforts to help the least-developed countries realize their development goal, which is internationally agreed upon. This goal is also China's major goal in conducting international cooperation because it believes that development must bring benefits to all countries and peoples.

It has become an essential part of Chinese diplomacy to help developing countries with poverty alleviation, create employment opportunities in infrastructure construction projects and improve health care and education services. So far, China has dispatched medical expert groups to scores of countries and coordinated with governments of developing countries regarding continuous epidemic prevention assistance.

Chinese diplomatic policy on deepening international cooperation is rooted in the "China's National Plan on Implementation of the 2030 Agenda for Sustainable Development", Goal 7 in particular, i.e., "ensure access to affordable, reliable, sustainable and modern energy for all." To achieve this goal, China is committed to international cooperation to promote its research and technologies on acquiring clean energies, involving renewable energy, energy efficiency, and more advanced cleaner fossil fuel technologies. Moreover, it encourages investment in energy infrastructure and clean energy technology.

Goal 9 of this National Plan is "build resilient infrastructure, promote inclusive and sustainable industrialization, and foster innovation." China is dedicated to deepening international cooperation on industrial capacity and equipment manufacturing to help other developing countries to improve production system building and realize the diversification of industrial production. Goal 10 stipulates that efforts must be made to "reduce inequality within and among countries."

In addition, environmental protection is also an important part of Chinese diplomacy. Goals 13, 14, and 15 of the National Plan lay the following stresses, respectively: take urgent action to combat climate change and its impacts; conserve and sustainably use the oceans, seas, and marine resources for sustainable development; protect, restore and promote sustainable use of terrestrial ecosystems, sustainably manage forests, combat desertification, and halt and reverse land degradation and halt biodiversity loss.

Moreover, China plays an active role in making globalization more inclusive and benefitting all, making the international order fairer and more equitable.

China spares no effort in building a peaceful and inclusive society for sustainable development. While striving for a fairer and more equitable society, it is committed to enhancing implementing measures and rejuvenating global partnerships to achieve the goal of sustainable development in all countries, the developing countries in particular.

China is strengthening North-South cooperation by coordinating and improving the existing mechanisms. To enhance regional cooperation in scientific and technological innovation, it offers facilities and necessary conditions for cooperation and shares knowledge according to the agreed conditions. In particular, China, taking the United Nations (UN) as a platform, facilitates scientific and technological exchanges through some global mechanisms.

President Xi Jinping's diplomatic vision is not only the inheritance, development, and deepening of the diplomatic visions of previous Chinese leaders since the founding of the People's Republic of China (PRC) but also the advancement of the diplomatic theory system of contemporary China. Based on the traditional one, President Xi's diplomatic concept has distinctive characteristics of the times, such as independent, peaceful foreign policy, the Five Principles of Peaceful Coexistence, and the establishment of a new international political and economic order. On the one hand, he brings to a new historical height some concepts such as building a community with a shared future for mankind, establishing new international relations, and reforming the global governance system. On the other hand, he has put forward some important concepts such as transparent, pragmatic, friendly, and sincere international policies and policies for friendship and mutual benefits, which have given fresh impetus to the development of the relations between China and other countries in different regions.

In his historical speech at the 20th National Congress of the Communist Party of China (CPC) on Oct. 16, 2022, President Xi Jinping expressed his wish to create an even brighter future for humanity. Also, he stressed the importance of building a peaceful international community with prosperity and stability as the shared vision. The president made a solemn commitment before the world that Chinese diplomacy will insist on safeguarding fairness and justice for the international community, upholding real multilateralism, establishing a new platform for good international relations, reforming the global governance system, enhancing international cooperation comprehensively, opposing protectionism and hegemonism, and promoting green development and harmonious coexistence.

President Xi's speech inspires all countries and urges them to step into the new era of international relations and make concerted efforts to create a bright future for humanity.

Xi Jinping Thought on Diplomacy inherits and carries forward the right position of China's opposing colonialism, hegemonism and power politics, drawing the red line and shedding light on the bottom line for the key issues concerning state sovereignty and territorial integrity. Based on this Thought, China has taken resolute measures to safeguard its rights, core interests, and national dignity.

China, both in the past and at present, has upheld multilateralism. It assumes that democracy should be practiced in international relations and opposes hegemonism and power politics. People of the whole world should determine the future of humanity. Therefore, China urges the international community and all national governments and people to settle international issues through consultation. Experience shows that those who hold high the banner of "myself first" and put self-interest before that of the international community go against moral principles and are doomed to fail. China calls on all countries to adhere to and respect the basic norms of international relations concerning state sovereignty, independence and territorial integrity, and noninterference in the internal affairs of sovereign states. China maintains that all sovereign states, whether big or small, strong or weak, rich or poor, are equal members of the international community. China insists that based on the principle of consultation, participation, and mutual benefits, efforts should be made to propel the reform of the global governance system to reflect the concerns and appeals of most states of the world, the developing countries in particular. Moreover, China attaches importance to settling disputes and divergences between countries through dialogue and constructive negotiations. It is opposed to such coercive unilateral economic blockades and financial sanctions and the practices of bullying the weak, power politics, and interference in other countries' internal affairs.

All countries live in the same "global village," and development and progress can't be made without a legal system, laws, and regulations. Therefore, China actively safeguards the law-based international order and opposes practices such as brazen treaties and double-standard violations. That is because safeguarding the established principle of international law is not only in line with the aspiration of the people of the world but also the inevitable choice in the age of globalization. In this sense, all countries should abide by the contract spirit and the norms of international law, fulfill relevant commitments, adhere to related rules, and fulfill applicable agreements. All countries should safeguard the principles of the UN Charter and the commonly recognized basic norms, oppose settling international disputes by force, and the practice of wanton withdrawal from international organizations and protocols. China opposes the practices of adopting double standards, selective application of statutory rules in settling global issues, and infringement of other countries' legitimate rights and interests on the pretext of the rules of international law. China calls for boycotts of any form of scientific and technological hegemonism, "restrictions", and "decoupling" and opposes adopting discriminatory policies under the name of "national security".

China holds that solidarity and cooperation are the most powerful way to overcome common challenges. For this reason, China is sparing no effort to enhance international cooperation to build and consolidate a community of common health for mankind. Its efforts demonstrate China, as a major country, has performed its due responsibilities in fighting against the global pandemic. Due to the pandemic, tens of millions of people have been infected with the virus, and hundreds of thousands of people have died. China has adhered to the principle of "putting people, their lives, and health first" and enhanced international cooperation in combating the pandemic.

While fighting tenaciously against the pandemic, China is fully aware that countries should not fight against COVID-19 separately. Therefore, the Chinese government has attached great importance to pragmatic cooperation with other countries in combating this common foe of human beings. The Chinese government maintains that only by working in unity and helping each other can the national governments achieve the common goal (namely, wiping out the novel corona-virus) and global health governance be effective.

In fighting against COVID-19, China has greatly contributed to international cooperation. It plays an active role in combating the novel corona-virus worldwide, sharing information with the international community, and supporting the World Health Organization (WHO) with all its strength. In addition, China plays an active part in international cooperation in vaccine research and development, dispatching teams of medical experts to provide consultation and assistance for the public health officials of foreign countries. Moreover, it has provided advanced COVID-19 vaccines to South Asian countries and urged international organizations and non-governmental organizations (NGOs) to help the countries in need. At the beginning of the outbreak of the pandemic, China suffered from a terrible shortage of medical supplies. Nevertheless, it donated medical supplies to many countries (such as Italy, Spain, France, India and Serbia), including building materials for constructing quarantine centers, breathing machines, oxygen-generators, medical monitoring devices, respirators, protection suits, masks, etc. Moreover, it contributed generously to the WTO. It provided financial aid to pandemic-stricken countries, particularly developing countries, to help them be extricated from their economic and social predicaments. Additionally, China committed itself to safeguarding the stability of the world's industrial and supply chains at this critical moment.

China's efforts have proved to the world that it is possible to contain the pandemic rapidly and sustainably. Through concerted efforts, the world may become stronger. *Jihui* (opportunity) is likely to appear in an adverse situation. One ancient Chinese proverb states, "Opportunities are fostered amid crises and challenges." In the Chinese language, *weiji* (crisis) is composed of two Chinese characters, i.e., " 危 " (*wei*) and " 机 " (*ji*). Wei means "danger", while *ji* means "opportunity". The Chinese word weiji implies the opportunity to change and improve our lives. However severe the crisis is, we may make outstanding achievements regardless of any crisis.

In fighting against COVID-19, the Chinese government has added a new dimension to the concept of "leadership". Especially when I realized the implications of the word *weiji*, I received a new light on the word "leadership".

Based on its tenet of multilateral diplomacy and putting honesty first, China has made unremitting efforts to resolve conflicts and uphold the practice of democracy in international relations through diplomatic means and following the UN Charter and international law. This well accounts for the unprecedented achievements of Chinese diplomacy. It is estimable that China has not only developed itself but also made a tremendous contribution to world peace and development. China, relying on its people and collective strength, deals with international issues with wisdom and sincerity in the new era.

Historically, China contributed its Four Great Inventions (the compass, paper-making, gunpowder, and movable type printing) to the world, pushing human civilization forward. It has made new global contributions with the manned submersible "Jiaolong", Hong Kong-Zhuhai-Macao Bridge, "Tianwen I" Mars Probe, etc. Moreover, its BRI links the world together, creating a new world that enjoys peace, sharing, and well-being.

Terence Robinson

Currently Senior Vice President, Head of Global Academic, Gale, a Cengage Group company. He has been in the educational publishing industry for over 35 years. Over this time, he has held executive positions in Canada, the United States, the United Kingdom and Asia. He is currently responsible for all global operations, publishing, sales, and marketing for Gale Academic. He oversees a global publishing program encompassing Humanities, Business, STM which has been developing innovative technological tools to enable data mining and breakthrough research innovations. Terry received his undergraduate BA (with honors) from Carleton University in Ottawa, Canada and MBA from the University of Cambridge in the United Kingdom where he was awarded Academic & peer prizes.

Gale Scholar and China: Expanding the Possibilities of Research

In 2021 I was honored to be presented with the Special Book Award of China, an annual award initially launched by the State Press and Publication Administration of the People's Republic of China.

More than 168 writers, translators, and publishers from 58 countries have won the award since it was established 17 years ago. Huang Kunming, head of the Publicity Department of the CPC Central Committee, highlights what winners of the award have in common: they have authored, translated, and published works that have enhanced the international community's understanding of China, including its culture and politics, and promoted exchanges and mutual learning among countries.

This recognition validates Gale's approach to working with China over the past six years. Our team seeks to build meaningful relationships with Chinese research institutions, understanding how we can help them achieve their goals; they are not "customers" to Gale but "partners". We are proud to contribute to China's humanities and social sciences by making key historical documents from around the world accessible to Chinese academics. Our commitment to furthering international collaboration is exemplified by our participation in symposia where experts from the East and the West exchange ideas about digital humanities.

Gale has also expanded its long-running co-publishing program with leading Chinese academic presses, releasing titles in English translation that range from examinations of historical events to up-to-date issues, such as the country's reaction to the pandemic. In the process, I have witnessed an exponential growth of Chinese academic publishing and increasing attention towards international issues in the humanities and social sciences. All of this intends to further its connections with the global academic community and expand research possibilities in China.

Gale Scholar Participates in the Building of Digital Resources in China

Cengage Group is an education technology company that serves millions of learners in 165 countries and advances how students learn through quality digital experiences. The company serves the global markets of higher education, K-12, professional, library, English language teaching, and workforce training. Gale, part of Cengage Group, provides libraries with original and curated content, as well as the modern research tools and technology that are crucial in connecting libraries to learning and learners to libraries. For more than 65 years, Gale has partnered with libraries around the world to empower the discovery of knowledge and insights – where, when, and how people need it.

Gale has created and maintains more than 600 online databases as a world-leading reference publisher. These include a wide range of content, including academic full-text journals, reference books, newspapers, documents, multimedia resources, and original collections.

Gale Scholar

The *Gale Scholar* program was created to enable the world's fastest-rising universities to have a world-class infrastructure of digital resources, aligning them with established elite institutions such as Oxford, Harvard, and Cambridge. The program offers institutions access to core collections in *Gale Primary Sources* totaling more than 170 million digitized pages from the vaults of world-renowned libraries, covering more than 900 years of international history.

Gale Scholar equips researchers and students with access to digitally curated collections of books, maps, photographs, newspapers, periodicals, and manuscripts from some of the world's most well-known libraries, including Oxford, Harvard University, and the British Library.

Gale Primary Sources includes many databases, including:

(1) *Eighteenth Century Collections Online* – a vast collection of more than 200,000 titles encompassing the majority of English printed books in the eighteenth century.

(2) *Nineteenth Century Collections Online* – an ambitious archive of more than 25 million pages, covering key themes in the "long nineteenth century" (1789-1914), including colonialism, East-West relations, and developments in science, technology, and medicine.

(3) *The Making of the Modern World* – a definitive archive on the economic history of the last 500 years, explains how we reached today's era of globalization and trade.

Gale first partnered with a Chinese institution in 2016 when the University Town Library of Shenzhen became the first *Gale Scholar* institution in the country. Currently, there are 16 Chinese universities using *Gale Scholar*, including Beijing Normal University, Nankai University, Peking University, Renmin University of China, Sun Yat-Sen University, Tsinghua University, University Town of Shenzhen, Fudan University, Inner Mongolia Normal University, Nanjing University, Shanghai University, Shanghai Normal University, Zhejiang University, Southern University of Science and Technology, Shandong University, and the University of Macao.

The institutions that use *Gale Scholar* in China are among the country's top learning institutes. The majority of them are part of China's Double First-Class program, a major higher education initiative aimed at developing world-class universities and centers of research.

While one of the strengths of *Gale Scholar* is its archives, another key aspect of this program is how researchers can access these documents. *Gale*

Scholar's powerful search technology empowers researchers and students to discover new research connections through a single search environment. A landing page in English and Chinese further streamlines the researchers' work flow, acting as a starting point for searching the collections.

The reaction from Chinese institutions has been positive from the beginning. In recent years, several of Gale's top 20 users (as defined by full-text retrieval) have consistently been universities in China, with Peking University and Tsinghua University being especially prominent. Other Chinese institutions regularly record higher usage than elite institutions such as Harvard and Yale. It represents a significant shift in global usage patterns and illustrates the value of making these resources more accessible in China.

We witness this in person, as well as in the statistics. At presentations across China, Gale's leaders typically speak to audiences five times the number of participants they would normally get in the US or UK. Seth Cayley, Vice President of Gale's Global Academic Product, shared with me that at one event, a post-doctoral fellow personally thanked him for publishing *US Declassified Documents Online*, because his Ph.D. thesis would not have been possible without access to this archive.

Because of Chinese institutions' growing use of *Gale Scholar*, the Gale team inside the country has increased rapidly. In 2016, Gale had just five people in Beijing, including a manager, three representatives, and a marketing professional. Now the Gale team has grown to 17 staff and includes a director, sales manager, eight representatives, three customer support staff, two marketers, and two trainers.

This team works closely with user groups in China to understand what material is of the most interest and how we can make that information more accessible.

International Symposia

Soon after entering the Chinese market, Gale was proud to be involved in organizing two important symposia. These events brought together academics from the East and West and allowed them to have a conversation about their opinions on different aspects of Chinese history.

The first event was an international conference about libraries and digital humanities. The symposium, which ran for three days in December 2017, took

Group photo of participants in the symposium held at the University Town Library of Shenzhen in 2017

place at the University Town Library of Shenzhen.

The location is significant because this is the first library in China to be shared between universities and residents. In 2006, the Shenzhen municipal government approved merging the university library with the Institute of Science and Technology Information of Shenzhen. The library is now shared by the Shenzhen Graduate Schools of Peking University, Tsinghua University, and Harbin Institute of Technology, as well as Shenzhen citizens.

It is a new-generation library that boasts subject orientation, research facilitation, complete openness, and large digital collections. It is also an important sci-tech document preservation station. With 40,000 square meters and 2,600 seats, the library holds 1.6 million volumes, including 1.46 million Chinese books. It serves about 8,000 people each day. The library currently possesses the largest digital resource reservoir across the Shenzhen city. Its strengths have always been scientific and technological, foreign language, and digital collections.

The conference's keynote speaker was Simon Tanner, a professor of Digital Cultural Heritage with the Department of Digital Humanities at King's College London. He spoke about innovation and the digital humanities. Tanner wrote the book *Delivering Impact with Digital Resources: Planning Your Strategy in the Attention Economy* in 2020. Tanner works with major cultural institutions across the world to assist them in transforming their collections and online presence. He has consulted for or managed over 500 projects, including digitizing the *Dead Sea Scrolls*. He was introduced by the conference host, Xichen Zhao, the former library director.

The symposium included a number of other notable speakers, including Xiaoguang Wang, a professor in the school of information management at Wuhan University and director of the Center of Digital Humanities. Wang spoke about the theory and experiments of digital humanities-orientated smart data construction.

Gale's Seth Cayley was also a speaker at the symposium, where he talked about how publishers, including Gale, supported digital humanities. He introduced attendees to the *Gale Digital Scholar Lab*, allowing researchers to find previously undiscovered data more easily. Researchers can test theories, analyze results, and eventually gain new insights in a timely manner. These changes make it easy for collaborators, especially ones with diverse backgrounds and skills, to work together, interrogating content, analyzing insights, and outputting discoveries.

Other topics covered during the three-day symposium included: key technologies for digital humanities; data, resources, networks, and platform construction for digital humanities; higher education and digital humanities; and digital humanities and its multi-disciplinary application. Speakers included representatives from the MIT New Media Action Lab, the University of Chicago, the University of Sydney, the University of California, Los Angeles, and Zhejiang University.

The conference ended with a wide-ranging panel discussion about the library's role in digital humanities development. This nearly two-hour session included Wei Liu, Deputy Director of the Shanghai Library; Miriam Posner, President of digital humanities at the University of California, Los Angeles; Arianne A. Hartsell-Gundy, Head of humanities at Duke University; Mahendra Mahey, Project Manager of the British Library Labs; and Glen Worthy, Digital Humanities Librarian at the Stanford University Library.

The next year, 2018, Gale was able to participate in a similar symposium—the Guangzhou Symposium held at Sun Yat-Sen University.

Gale's *China and the Modern World* series

China and the Modern World is a series of digital archive collections sourced from preeminent libraries and archives worldwide, including the Second Historical Archives of China and the British Library. The series covers about 180 years (the 1800s to the 1980s) when China experienced radical and often traumatic transformations from an inward-looking imperial dynasty into a globally engaged people's republic.

Consisting of monographs, manuscripts, periodicals, correspondence and letters, historical photos, ephemera, and other historical documents, these collections provide valuable primary source materials for understanding and researching the various aspects of China during the nineteenth and twentieth centuries. The areas covered include diplomacy and international relations, economy and trade, politics, sinology, education, science and technology, imperialism, and globalization.

With rare and unique content, trustworthy and extensive bibliographic information and technology that fit the needs of today's researchers, *China and the Modern World* is poised to revolutionize research on China and the world in the nineteenth and twentieth centuries.

Six separate collections make up this series. One is titled *Missionary, Sinology, and Literary Periodicals.* These periodicals published from 1817 to 1949 are the essential digital primary source collection for researchers of China in the nineteenth and early twentieth centuries. This archive provides firsthand accounts of cultural interactions and conflicts that gave rise to today's modern China.

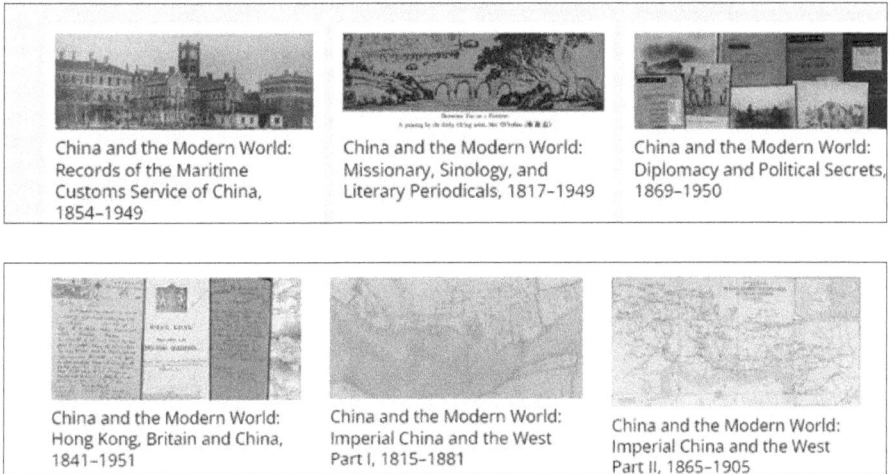

China and the Modern World: Records of the Maritime Customs Service of China, 1854–1949

China and the Modern World: Missionary, Sinology, and Literary Periodicals, 1817–1949

China and the Modern World: Diplomacy and Political Secrets, 1869–1950

China and the Modern World: Hong Kong, Britain and China, 1841–1951

China and the Modern World: Imperial China and the West Part I, 1815–1881

China and the Modern World: Imperial China and the West Part II, 1865–1905

Screenshot of *China and the Modern World* series of digital archive collections

Another collection gathers the records of the maritime customs service of China from 1854 to 1949. These documents, mainly in English, are primary materials for examining China's trade relations with the West in the late Qing and the Republic of China (1912-1949) periods.

Diplomacy and Political Secrets, dated 1869-1950, includes materials from the British India Office Records that covers Anglo-Chinese relations and British interests in South Asia, Central Asia, East Asia, and Southeast Asia. The records in this collection all come from three departments – the Political and Secret Department, the Burma Office, and the Military Department.

The archive of *Imperial China and the West* is broken into two collections, with the first ranging from 1815 to 1881 and the second collection from 1865 to 1905. The archive as a whole includes more than 1.1 million pages of British Foreign Office correspondence from and on China. This archive not only relates to the internal politics of China and Britain but also sheds light on the relationships between other Western powers during the nineteenth century.

Creating the series has encouraged us to pursue technological innovation. Many of the documents are handwritten, and previously it was impossible to make handwriting (as opposed to printed text) searchable. Through trial and error, we developed solutions for a new technology called Handwritten Text Recognition. It has made documents such as diaries, memoranda, and letters accessible in new ways.

Making these rare China-oriented documents available to academics at Chinese institutions through Gale Scholar enables their researchers to make new discoveries about their country's own history without having to travel to the source libraries and archives.

Co-Publishing with China's Academic Presses

Under the leadership of Liping Yang, Senior Manager, Academic Publishing, the Gale team in Asia has published more than 200 titles/volumes in 16 series, focusing on subject areas such as arts, history, religion, economics, politics, and international relations. Published authors are from the mainland of China, Hong Kong of China, Taiwan of China, Japan, South Korea, Singapore, and the Philippines.

Among the major titles published thus far are:

A Record of the Qing Dynasty (5 vols, 2008–2010)

30 Years of China's Reform Study Series (14 vols, 2009–2012)

The Sinopedia Series (12 vols, 2010)

The Papers of Lee Kuan Yew (20 vols, 2011–2013)

Chinese Architecture Series (5 vols, 2014–2018)

Chinese Scholars on the Chinese Economy (4 vols, 2019)

China and Global Governance Series (10 vols, 2019–2022)

40th Anniversary of Chinese Reform and Opening-up Series (2 vols, 2021)

Reporting from Wuhan: Guangming Daily Coverage of China's Battle Against

Covid-19 (2020)

Studies on Xi Jinping Thought on Socialism with Chinese Characteristics for the New Era (15 vols, 2019-present)

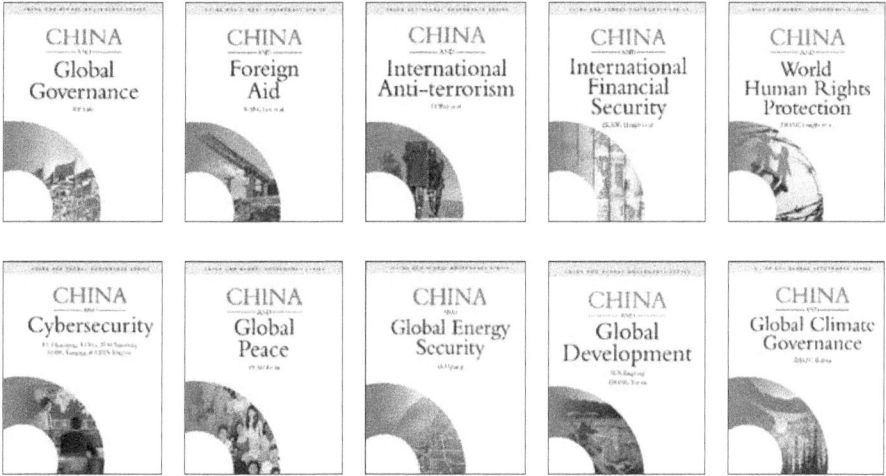

Cover images of *China and Global Governance Series*

Cover images of *Studies on Xi Jinping Thought on Socialism with Chinese Characteristics for the New Era*

Despite the inconveniences and challenges wrought by the pandemic, Gale has managed to publish significant and topical titles in the last two years. These include books in a milestone series examining President Xi Jinping's era. Our partner for this series is China Renmin University Press, and the publishing contract was actually signed shortly after the COVID-19 outbreak in January 2020. The series covers a wide range of topics, including the origin and significance of Xi Jinping Thought, President Xi's expositions on Party building, ecological civilization, education, socialist economy, major-country diplomacy, and rural revival.

Our recent publishing has also reflected our desire to respond rapidly to current events. We partnered with People's Publishing House and published *Reporting from Wuhan: Guangming Daily's Coverage of China's Battle Against Covid-19*, documenting China's battle against the COVID-19 pandemic by people who experienced the early days of the virus at the front line. The whole process from contracting to publication took just five months. It included the time required to translate the manuscript from Chinese into English. The remarkable speed of this publication is an excellent example of what can happen when a project is a true collaboration between partners with shared aims.

Gale's collaboration with People's Publishing House continued with another topical title, this time in connection with the centenary celebration of the founding of the Communist Party of China: *How the CPC Has Transformed China*. The book presents a vivid account of the CPC's achievements in leading the Chinese people to build a strong, modernized socialist country from its birth until today by focusing on politics, the economy, the rule of law, cultural progress, the people's livelihoods, ecological civilization, national defense, national reunification, and diplomacy.

Among other meaningful titles Gale has recently published is *Global Leaders on the Belt and Road Initiative*, a collection of 36 interviews conducted by Sun Chao from the Development Research Center of the State Council. The interviewees include ambassadors, high-ranking government officials, and top executives involved in China's Belt and Road Initiative. These interviews present the diverse views of international organizations and partner countries from East Asia, Southeast Asia, South Asia, Central Asia, the Middle East, Europe, and Africa toward China's Belt and Road Initiative and outline the Initiative's achievements and future.

In the years to come, we will carry on the program by publishing a host of new titles relating to various aspects of China. Among them are *The Belt and Road Initiative: A Chinese Approach to Improving the Global Order*, a book written by Professor Khairy A. Tourk from Illinois Institute of Technology, and *Beauty Is A Way of Life*, authored by two Polish professors from NingboTech University, which analyzes the "development-through-art" program and its implementation in China's rural areas in Zhejiang and Guizhou provinces. Other titles include *Economic Growth and Development Potential, A Century of Vaccine Development in China, Social Governance in China, The Myths That Made China*, and *Chinese Dance*.

Our goal is to make the latest Chinese academic scholarship more accessible to English-speaking audiences. We do not place our editorial perspective on these titles; we let the works speak for themselves. Our intention is to allow readers to understand China and its place in the world from the perspective of the Chinese

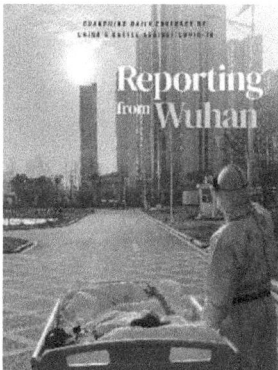

Cover image of *Reporting from Wuhan*

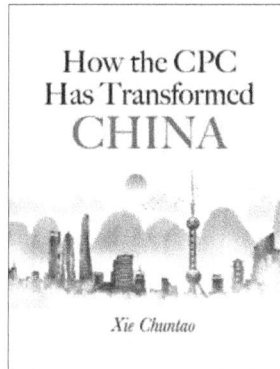

Cover image of *How the CPC Has Transformed China*

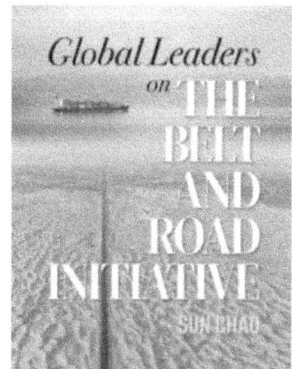

Cover image of *Global Leaders on the Belt and Road Initiative*

themselves rather than from a Western interpretation. Concepts and initiatives such as Xi Jinping Thought, Socialism with Chinese Characteristics, and the Belt and Road Initiative are significant for the twenty-first century. It is vital for mutual learning that global researchers engage with them.

Advice and Expectations on Cooperation in China

Gale has been very successful in working in China. In looking back at my twenty years doing business in China and reflecting on lessons learned, a couple of themes emerge:

Time Frame: If you are looking for short-term, easy results, you are in the wrong place. China is a sophisticated intellectual landscape, and, as such, you will need to contribute to its academic ecosystem on a long-term basis actively. It will take time. You will need to observe, listen, and learn. Patience and effort are required to understand what solutions you can bring to the table. There is a tendency for Western companies to import Western solutions without looking at the distinct characteristics of the landscape in China. Results will come when you can develop a long-term roadmap that satisfies the ongoing needs of academia within the country. It sounds simple, but to Westerners, it can be deceptively difficult. You need to be prepared to work for the long haul, build trust, and invest resources.

Chinese Talent: Since China opened up to the West more than 40 years ago, there has been a rapid and expanding wealth of talent in the country. The levels of education and language skills of the workforce with experience dealing with foreign companies are high. It is a fantastic resource to help develop your publishing aspirations; utilizing local talent to manage your business will set you on the path to success. As importantly, you will learn a tremendous amount along the way. With my hand on my heart, I can say Gale's success in China stems from the talent and passion of our Chinese management and employees. Indeed, the Special Book Award of China was presented to me personally. But it reflects what our whole team in China has been able to accomplish under the direction of Victor Li, our Director of Gale China, and Liping Yang, our Senior Manager for Academic Publishing.

Keeping these themes – thinking long-term, listening rather than lecturing, and identifying local talent – at the forefront of our approach is why we believe Gale has been successful. We will continue to build our partnerships for many years to come, supporting the needs of the Chinese academic community and expanding the possibilities of research in China.

Fernando Reyes Matta

Director of the Chile-China Cultural Association, consultant on international affairs, diplomat, scholar and journalist; Director of the Center for Latin American Studies on China, Universidad Andrés Bello, Chile; former Chilean Ambassador to China (2006–2010). He served as a consultant on international affairs for President Ricardo Lagos; Ambassador to New Zealand; Director of Information and Culture, Ministry of Foreign Affairs; and Press Counsellor of the Chilean Mission to the United Nations in New York. He is the author and co-author of many academic monographs, books and articles. The books include: *Pandemic: Effects On Latin America and the Interactions With China*; *China: Innovation and Tradition*; *China-Latin America: How to Go Beyond the Year 2020?*; *40 Years of China-Chile Relations: What will the Future Bring?*; and *Small Country with a Big Map: The Diplomatic Policy of Ricardo Lagos*.

The Digital Age and New Dialogues between China and Latin America in the 21st Century

The Covid-19 pandemic changed the interaction between China and Latin America through the increasingly intense use of digital communication platforms. New forms of dialogue were precipitated, with government forums, meetings of experts, and academic seminars where the variable distance or time difference was solved with adequate coordination for the various meetings. This reinforced the concept of the Digital Route (within the Belt and Road Initiative), no longer analyzed only as the set of investments, infrastructures, and telecommunication projects between China and the various countries of the region but as a new practice of political-social interaction between both parties. Within this framework, an active "virtual diplomacy" was launched (especially by the Community Forum of Latin American and Caribbean States, CELAC, and China), and a pattern of relations with multiple future projections was established, both in the public and private spheres.

A concrete example took place in September 2022, when the International Department of the Communist Party of China (CPC) held a virtual seminar for think tanks from Latin America and the Caribbean, which on its first day was led by Vice Minister Shen Beili of that entity. The program included lectures on Xi Jinping's Thought on Socialism with Chinese Characteristics in the new era, the historical advances since the 18th CPC National Congress, the development of China-CELAC relations, and a Dialogue Session between academics from China and America. Latina, and a preview of the spirit of the 20th CPC National Congress. At this juncture, this author has the opportunity to participate as the only Latin American voice, analyzing two key milestones raised by China and its government, which seem decisive for the reformulation of a new international order: the proposal of creating an ecological civilization and the Global Security Initiative.

Directly from Chile, we point out that the definition of ecological civilization as one of the fundamental goals of the task of the CPC in leading the country was a key step for China and the rest of the world. In essence, it means more than the classic protection of the environment. Rather, what it means is that the whole society should behave in harmony with nature, also culturally, not just technologically: ecology in harmony with nature should pervade all social life. This political commitment was also decisive in the position adopted by China at the Paris Summit in favor of a multilateral agreement. Shortly before the 19th CPC National Congress, President Xi called for greater efforts to institutionalize and legalize ecological civilization, promote sustainable, renewable, and low-carbon development, and create a production and living model that is respectful of the environment and saves resources. The effects of climate change – droughts, extreme temperatures, floods, and excessive rains – demonstrate the importance and urgency of taking on the ecological issue as a challenge to civilization for all humanity. It is an issue that has become a priority on the common agenda of China and Latin America.

On the other hand, in the logic of the principle of the community of common destiny for mankind, the Global Security Initiative was proposed in 2022. Among the objectives of this project is to remain committed to the concept of common, comprehensive, cooperative, and sustainable security, as well as work to maintain peace and security in the world. Along with the agreement on this, it should be appreciated that this proposal seeks to maintain security in traditional and non-traditional domains and work together on regional disputes and global challenges, such as terrorism, climate change, cybersecurity, and biosecurity.[1]

---

[1] https://actualidad.rt.com/actualidad/435736-china-iniciativa-seguridad-global-estados-unidos

In Latin America, after the impacts of the pandemic – where China and
Latin America increased their ties and direct dialogue – the new threats to the
security of countries and their peoples have become a worrying agenda. Along
with the fight against poverty and inequality appear the dangers of dominance
and pressures on all areas of digital life. What does cybersecurity mean today?
Where and how will we debate digital divides as a global world and all aspects
so that human beings are at the center of the digital age? How will we achieve
from Latin America to autonomously build the appropriate links for our
insertion in the industrial dimension of cyber production?

Along with other interventions in that digital forum, we pointed out that,
faced with such questions, the China-CELAC Forum, in December 2021, had
agreed on the following:

"We agree to strengthen the dialogue for cooperation, implement and
eventually develop norms and rules for cyberspace: address the misuse of
information and communication technologies (ICT) to incite and commit
acts of terrorism; improve legal assistance mechanisms for cybercrime; actively
participate in the negotiations to prepare a UN convention on the fight against
the use of information and communication technologies for criminal purposes
and safeguard peace and security in cyberspace. We highlight the Global
Initiative on Data Security proposed by China."[2]

And within the Action Plan, specific goals are determined for the period
2022-2024:

"Strengthening mutually beneficial cooperation between governments,
companies, and research institutions in digital infrastructure, telecommunication
equipment, 5G, big data, cloud computing, artificial intelligence, the Internet
of Things (IoT), smart cities, Internet+, universal telecommunications
services, radio spectrum management, and other areas of common interest.
Simultaneously exploring the construction of joint laboratories" ... And it
is added: "actively explore the establishment of the China-CELAC Digital

---

[2] https://www.fmprc.gov.cn/esp/wjdt/gongbao/202112/t20211213_10467312.html

Technology Cooperation Forum."

That September 2022 meeting was just one of several examples of this new interaction. A few days apart, the seminar "Latin American Sinology and the Dialogue Between Chinese and Latin American Civilizations" took place, organized by the BLCU (Beijing Language and Culture University). With the presence of Qiu Xiaoqi, a Special Representative of the Chinese Government on Latin American Affairs, China held a lively event with researchers from Argentina, Brazil, Chile, Mexico, Ecuador, and Peru. They combined their analyses with prominent Chinese professors dedicated to studying Latin America in the fields of culture and to the mutual understanding of their concordances and differences. Topics such as educational training for new ties, cross-cultural exchanges and mutual learning of civilizations between China and Latin America were part of the presentations and exchange of ideas. The experience showed that – beyond time differences – it was possible to coordinate around a common agenda and to share ideas over geographical areas. That meeting, like several others, demonstrated that the idea of the Digital Silk Road had its foundations in the global reorganization, and this, in one way or another, would acquire concrete expressions in the relations of China and Latin America towards the future.

Both this last event and the previous one were only the culmination of a process that got started– somewhat instinctively – in 2020 and 2021. In retrospect, the events were diverse experiences that show how a new way of connecting between China and Latin America was launched in those two years.

Pioneering Experiences in the New China-Latin America Virtual Interaction

Relationship via the web became constant in trade and business dialogues. Such was the experience of participating in the Canton Fair and other similar events. In mid-April 2020, China launched a 15-day online fair to promote cooperation between Chinese and Latin American companies. The China-Latin America (Mexico) International Trade Digital Expo, hosted by the China Council for the Promotion of International Trade (CCPIT), attracted some 2,000 domestic companies and some 5,000 foreign buyers. The expo closely followed the demand of the Latin American market, particularly the Mexican one, as it also aimed to provide businesses with online trading opportunities and accurate matchmaking services using big data, said Gao Yan, head of the council. As reported from Beijing, the exhibition integrated "online digital consultation, negotiation, exhibition, and matchmaking services." Products such as medical equipment, construction materials, hardware, office supplies, furniture, and household items, consumer electronics, textiles and clothing, household appliances, food, and materials for epidemic prevention were included in the fair. In addition to this fair, it was planned to hold five to eight more online trade shows to build new platforms and create more cooperation opportunities for foreign trade companies, the council explained.[3]

The conference with Yu Dihua, chief engineer for the construction of a hospital in ten days in Wuhan, amid the most critical days of the pandemic, can be pointed out as a milestone in this new type of ties in the relationship between China and Latin America. The event was organized by the Technological Development Corporation (TDC) of the Chilean Chamber of Construction, together with the Chinese Council for the Promotion of International Trade, Hubei Sub-Council (CCPIT-Hubei), the International Chamber of Commerce of Hubei Province in Chile and Asia Reps Chile and sponsored by the Council of Industrialized Construction (CIC), and the China Construction Third Engineering Bureau (CCTEB) Group Co, Ltd. On this occasion, the organization and execution of this work were known in detail by engineer Yu of the General Contracting Company of the China Construction Third Engineering Bureau Co, Ltd. He was the general manager of the design management and technical administration of the Huoshenshan Hospital, a

---

[3] http://spanish.xinhuanet.com/2020-04/14/c_138975503.htm

work admired and commented on in other parts of the world. It was a unique opportunity for Chilean businessmen who, until then, had only been able to receive presentations of this type with a trip to China or have knowledge of the details of a work.[4]

On the other hand, the Chilean Foreign Ministry held a video conference with the Minister of Commerce of China, Zhong Shan, "to review the main aspects of the trade relationship between the two countries, address the challenges presented by COVID-19 in bilateral trade, and discuss the role of trade as a tool for a prompt sustainable economic recovery." In addition, "the 17th Meeting of Political Consultations between the Ministries of Foreign Affairs of China and Mexico, the 3rd Meeting of the Permanent Intergovernmental Commission between China and Argentina, and the 2nd Meeting of Political Consultations between the Ministries of Foreign Affairs of China and Panama" which were carried out virtually, what China call "cloud diplomacy".[5]

Pioneering linkages in this field also occurred at the sub-national level (or provinces with cities and interior regions). As a result of the pandemic, "China has actively coordinated local provinces and cities with more than 10 Latin American countries, including Argentina, Chile, Panama, Costa Rica, and El Salvador." For example, a videoconference was recorded between the city of Wuhan, Hubei province, and the city of Concepción, Biobío Region, to learn about the measures adopted by the local health authorities. The deputy president of the Jinyingtan Hospital, the first establishment to treat those infected with this new virus, Huang Chaolin, participated in the virtual conference, as well as the director of the National Administration of Disease Prevention and Control of Wuhan, Yang Xiaobing, since Wuhan and Biobío have a twinning agreement.[6] Also, in mid-August, the Argentine province of

---

[4] http://www.asiareps.cl/2020/06/09/ingeniero-del-hospital-modular-de-wuhan-expondra-ante-profesionales-chilenos-de-la-construccion/

[5] http://spanish.peopledaily.com.cn/n3/2020/0724/c31621-9714341.html

[6] http://www.biobiochile.cl/noticias/nacional/region-del-bio-bio/2020/06/17/expertos-de-wuhan-recomiendan-a-chile-confinamiento-y-trazabilidad-para-controlar-el-covid-19.shtml

Santa Fe and the Chinese municipality directly under the central government, Chongqing, in another example of this type, held a direct dialogue to explore opportunities in beef exports.

In turn, academic dialogues multiplied with the same meeting formula. On April 23, 2020, the Tsinghua University of China and the Pontificia Universidad Católica de Chile, together with other Chilean universities, jointly participated in an online conference in which medical experts from both countries exchanged their experiences on the diagnosis of COVID-19. The Chinese doctors explained the measures China had adopted in patient referral, diagnostic process and forms, test kit selection, recovery standards, and patient management. Some doctors were experts from the Peking Union Medical College Hospital (PUMCH) and the China Association for International Exchange and Promotion of Medicine and Health (CPAM). All this was in an intense dialogue of questions and answers.

The 9th China-Latin America High-Level Academic Forum on October 27 to 30, 2020, reissued with a similar system in 2021, had the same characteristic. The organizers of this forum dedicated to the analysis of the political and social evolution of both parties and their links within the international scenario had live participation with representatives of the following entities: the Institute of Latin American Studies (ILAS), Chinese Academy of Social Sciences (CASS), Shanghai University, Nankai University, Hubei University, among others from China. In turn, from Latin America, the organizers were: the State University of Sao Paulo-UNESP, the University of Minas Gerais, the Federal University of Manaus, the National University of La Plata, the University of the Pacific of Lima, the Center for Latin American Studies on China (CELC) of the Andrés Bello University of Chile (UNAB), University of Santiago de Chile, Center of Research on Society and Culture (CIECS) of the National University of Córdoba and representatives of the Confucius Institute. Starting from the practice being experienced, both Professor Xu Shicheng and the author of this text remarked on the importance of this new stage of direct relationships, beyond distance and time differences, between China and the Latin American community of thought.[7]

Another experience in the same field was the seminar "Technological Transitions and China-Latin America Relations". The activity, held on November 11 and 12, was organized by the University of São Paulo in Brazil and Fudan University in China and was attended by a dozen academics from both regions. Possible responses to multilateralism were analyzed to face the growing tensions between global powers to determine the future standards in terms of digital governance. In this essential framework of the study of links and forms of cooperation, the digital reality will allow the future of the China/ Latin America and Caribbean relationship.[8]

| Taking the Digital Route

The announcement of the Digital Silk Road, initially the "Information Silk Road" in a White Paper was published by various Chinese government institutions in 2015. It was preceded by the incorporation of the concept in the second document of China's policy towards Latin America and the Caribbean (2016) only a year before. From this, it became evident that there was a wide space for joint development projects for Chinese companies in the sector, especially in South America. In January 2018, within the framework of the Second China-CELAC Forum, with the Chinese Foreign Minister, Wang Yi, and his Latin American and Caribbean counterparts, the Digital Route concept emerged together with the special declaration that was agreed at the time on the Belt and Road Initiative.[9]

---

[7] http://consejorial.org/publicaciones/informe-celac-china-avances-hacia-el-2021-n7/

[8] http://www.iei.uchile.cl/noticias/170702/prof-borquez-participo-en-seminario-sobre-china-y-latinoamerica

[9] http://blog.realinstitutoelcano.org/la-ruta-de-la-seda-digital-china-en-america-latina-y-el-caribe/

The scope of this concept of the Digital Route as an area of work and extension of the Belt and Road Initiative was highlighted by President Michelle Bachelet when inaugurating that Forum. She said at the forum, "I think we should look at its projections under the logic of four routes: the terrestrial, maritime, air, and digital. Because it is there, in this matrix of interactions, where global links, and especially between CELAC and China, have real and promising perspectives, within the framework of this new Silk Road of the 21st century". For her part, the then Executive Secretary of CELAC, Alicia Bárcenas, stated in her speech: "The Belt and Road offers us the unique opportunity to shorten the great territorial distance that separates us through better air, maritime and especially digital connectivity to strengthen our commercial, investment, tourism, and cultural ties."

The potential of "Virtual Diplomacy" was evident at the global level when, for the first time, the G20 leaders – coordinating all time differences – held a virtual meeting on March 20, 2020. A similar interaction pattern occurred on July 23, 2020, when the foreign ministers of China and the Latin American and Caribbean (LAC) countries held a special video conference on COVID-19. The conference was co-chaired by Wang Yi, the State Councilor and Minister of Foreign Affairs of China, and Marcelo Ebrard, the Secretary of Foreign Affairs of Mexico, and attended by the foreign ministers of Argentina, Barbados, Chile, Colombia, Costa Rica, Cuba, Dominican Republic, Ecuador, Panama, Peru, Trinidad and Tobago, and Uruguay.

At this juncture, Minister Wang Yi stressed the importance of keeping China's dialogue with CELAC countries alive (although Brazil had already suspended its participation in this mechanism) with an approach to future policies within the framework of the Belt and Road. "With an eye on the post-COVID-19 era, China is willing to further deepen Belt and Road cooperation with regional countries in traditional areas such as infrastructure, energy, and agriculture. Simultaneously, it actively explores new horizons for cooperation in fields such as the 'new infrastructures' represented by public health, distance medical assistance, online education, the digital economy, electronic commerce, and 5G technology to forge new points of cooperation such as the

China-Latin America and the Caribbean Silk Road in Health and the China-Latin America and the Caribbean Digital Silk Road".[10]

Within this framework, in November 2020, the International Department of the Communist Party of China (CPC) organized a special session to inform academics and political leaders from various Latin American and Caribbean countries about the main contents of the Five-Year Plan (2021-2025) and its projections towards 2035. In response, the online cyber secretariat and videoconference system of the China-CELAC Forum was inaugurated in December 2020, aimed at stimulating interaction between Latin American countries and this Asian country. It would be the basis for specialized forums at the ministerial level in sectors such as agriculture, science, and technology or infrastructure.

After what was experienced during 2020-2021 in the field of these new forms of digital dialogue, four observations could be defined:

First, the pandemic accelerated the concrete application of the Digital Route, understood as an extension of the Belt and Road Initiative, generating a new form of relations between China and Latin America.

Second, the concept of distance ceased to weigh as a major obstacle to political, diplomatic, and civil society meetings between Latin America and China.

Third, Chinese-Latin American academic interaction (via Zoom, Team, and other platforms) has entered an area where everything is yet to be reformulated, with joint research and permanent dialogue.

Forth, the Digital Route appeared as a new impulse for the productive dynamics between China and Latin America, with value chains and common proposals for a sustainable economy to be developed, starting from the post-pandemic.

This stage found Latin American countries seeking to consolidate their eLAC program, an acronym under which CELAC has promoted the Digital Agenda for Latin America and the Caribbean. It is a strategy that took 2020

---

[10] http://www.fmprc.gov.cn/esp/wjb/zzjg/ldmzs/xwlb/t1800880.shtml

as a goal to propose using digital technologies as instruments of sustainable development. Its mission is to promote the development of the digital ecosystem in Latin America and the Caribbean through regional integration and cooperation, strengthening digital policies that promote knowledge, inclusion and equity, innovation, and environmental sustainability.[11]

In essence, the purpose of eLAC is to incorporate the region into the great trends of the digital age. Quite a few Latin American countries express the urgency of understanding that they had been left behind in the historical stage of the Industrial Revolution (from the application of steam and oil). The Digital Revolution advances, having as its center the mass production of logic circuits and their widespread use with derived technologies, including the digital computer, the digital cell phone, and the Internet. All are areas in which China has been showing cutting-edge advances that lead the Asian country to be at the forefront of global changes in the 21st century. Within this general framework, relations between China and Latin America have entered a new phase of interactions: the obstacles of travel and personal meetings were overcome by the practice of dialogues via digital platforms, with greater projections in the political, business, academic and social links.

In this context, it is valid to consider some figures from the Latin American scenario for this dialogue with China's various development poles.

A. Number of Internet users by country in Latin America in January 2021 (in millions)

However, beyond the efforts promoted by CELAC in the new technological times, only a few Latin American governments have launched coordinated strategies and investments in infrastructure, services, and digital

Brazil	160.1	Mexico	92	Argentina	36
Colombia	34.7	Venezuela	20.5	Peru	19.9
Chile	15.7	Guatemala	11.7	Ecuador	10.1

---

[11] http://comunidades.cepal.org/elac/es

Bolivia	5.5	Paraguay	4.9	Costa Rica	4.1
Honduras	3.8	El Salvador	3.2	Panama	2.8
Nicaragua	2.7	Uruguay	2.6[12]		

B. Percentage of the population with high Internet access in some Latin American countries[13]

Chile	82.3%	Costa Rica	80.2%	Argentina	80%
Uruguay	77.4%	Brazil	75%	Dominican Republic	74.8%
Venezuela	72%	Mexico	71%		

skills. Tech start-ups have also struggled to raise funds. In 2019, Brazil launched the Ministry of Science, Technology, Innovation, and Communications, a plan for machine-to-machine services and the Internet of Things. In Chile, there is the Development Corporation, which has launched a Smart Industry strategy. In turn, the Mexican government has issued a roadmap for the development of IoT. And in the subcontinental, LAC members created the "Digital Agenda for Latin America, America, and the Caribbean" (eLAC).[14]

Digital technological development can be, within Latin America and the Caribbean, one of the points of a new agenda from which concrete forms of integration are sought beyond existing tensions and divisions. In its declaration, the 6th Summit of Heads of State and Government of CELAC, held in Mexico, said in point 42:

"It highlights the importance of information and communication technologies, including the Internet, as tools to promote peace, human well-being, development, knowledge, social inclusion, and economic growth. It reaffirms the peaceful use of ICTs and urges the international community to avoid and refrain from carrying out unilateral acts incompatible with the

---

[12] http://es.statista.com/estadisticas/1073677/usuarios-internet-pais-america-latina/

[13] http://es.statista.com/estadisticas/1136646/tasa-penetracion-mas-altas-internet-america-latina-caribe/

[14] http://cdn.cfr.org/sites/default/files/pdf/jorgemalenadsr.pdf

purposes and principles of the Charter of the United Nations, the Universal Declaration of Human Rights, and International Law. The acts include those that aim to subvert societies or create situations that potentially foster conflict between states. At the same time, they underline the need that, with the use of ICTs, the right to privacy of people is not violated."[15]

Stay Autonomous in the Face of Pressure

Despite the above, China and Latin America still face many challenges in building a Digital Route that articulates new forms of interaction between China and the Latin American region. It will be a long and complicated process due not only to pending technological developments and the elimination of the so-called digital divide but also to legislation still being developed on data protection, privacy protection, and cross-border circulation. Both parties have the opportunity to learn and advance together. But it is a scenario where the pressure from the United States towards the region is also present and has grown stronger (a new Monroe doctrine, some have pointed out). Faced with this, theses such as Active Non-Alignment take shape as a political strategy that grants strategic autonomy to Latin American countries and their regional institutions to address the challenges of the digital age in this part of the world.

At the end of July 2020, a seminar was held with the participation of Chinese and Latin American academics. On that occasion, Yan Xuetong, the director of the Institute of Contemporary International Relations at Tsinghua University, pointed out that "the effects of the crisis have shown the world the relevance of cybernetic life, which means that digital technology will be the final field of rivalry between the United States and China. In this area, competition has been stimulated by the health crisis now." And then he also pointed out: "I understand that for some months now there are talks

---

[15] Documents/Celac_2021_Declaracio_n_de_la_Ciudad_de_Me_xico__18sep21.pdf

about a 'Digital Silk Road,' which means that a series of digital projects will be promoted within the framework of this initiative. The digital area will probably become an important edge of the program in the coming years." And in this, there are favorable conditions for both parties, China and Latin America. It is how an Argentine analyst summarized them: firstly, the construction of the Digital Silk Road is adjusted to the development of world science and technology; secondly, the Latin American economy urgently needs new impetus to develop; thirdly, China and Latin America are highly complementary in the construction of the Digital Silk Road; forthly, It is the pandemic that accelerates "contactless" and digital economic development.[16]

The underlying question is how much of this process the United States will understand as a normal part of the development of Latin American countries. It is about having the right to legitimate strategic autonomy to search for the best technological solutions, wherever they are from, as long as they are consistent with the interests of each country. Until now, the discourse from Washington has been one of very specific warnings or pressure.

The pressure from the United States on Latin American governments to disassociate or not to accept projects with a Chinese presence in the digital sector has been constant in recent years, especially since the concept of "Digital Network" appeared in January 2018 in the debates and documents of the China-CELAC Forum. The American voices emphasize a discourse that intermingles national security and hemispheric security threats. One of the conditions for Ecuador to receive a loan of 3,500 million dollars from the United States DFC Company in December 2020 was that Ecuador joined the "Clean Network" program, created by then-President Donald Trump, which aims to exclude Chinese companies from 5G contracts in the world.[17] Keith Krach, a senior State Department official in Brazil, exerted similar pressure. At the same time, Mike Pompeo's passage through Chile determined that in the end, the submarine cable project from the Chilean coast to China would

---

[16] Ibid.

[17] Combate del águila y el dragón en América Latina. Le Monde Diplomatique, octubre 2021.Chile.

be reformulated with an extension only to Australia and in contract with a Japanese company. President Joe Biden's administration has not changed the approaches. Thus, it was verified with the call to produce Chilean passports after a Chinese company obtained that proposal, the tender was annulled following North American pressure in governmental and parliamentary spheres.[18]

In Latin America, it is common to hear that cybersecurity issues linked to military defense have their own channel: they are part of the relations in the Inter-American Defense Board, as one of its main spaces for interaction. Civil cybersecurity in the public/private sphere refers to internal government agencies, police, and bodies maintaining order and prosecuting crime in all its manifestations.

However, in recent years this distinction appears less and less clear in the approaches of the defense authorities of the United States when they describe their vision of the ties with Latin American countries. The head of the United States Southern Command, General Laura Richardson, since she was appointed to the position in November 2021, has insisted on a speech rejecting China's participation in all sectors linked to public and private investment. Her criticisms are of China's presence in a wide range of economic and social development projects.

"China is making many investments in ports, deep water, telecommunications, infrastructure, projects that are often not done very well or there is a lot of debt, many loans that are paid for these countries to assume," she commented. "The countries of the south of the continent, many of them drowned by the economy and the strong inflation throughout the world, see in these Chinese projects a valuable opportunity to clean up their accounts. But, in reality, what they do is mortgage themselves much more... We call it a 'debt trap' that does not help these countries in the long term. So, we try to work with them and advise them on the traps that could occur," added General

---

[18] https://www.emol.com/noticias/Economia/2021/11/19/1038793/licitacion-pasaportes-posturas-chile-china.html

Richardson in this regard.[19]

On her tour of all the countries in the region, she was emphatic in her approach. "Of the 31 countries covered by the Southern Command of the US Armed Forces, 21 have already signed the Chinese initiative of the Belt and the Road of the Silk, and this is very worrying," said General Richardson, according to the newspaper, *The Observer*, from Uruguay. And she also pointed out her concern because here is what she called "the lithium triangle" (Argentina, Bolivia, Chile). In Chile, in her opinion, it was even more precise in defining its concern, because everything that Chinese companies do today in civilian matters tomorrow could support a military operation by the Chinese army.

"The risk that I see is that many of the Chinese companies are state-owned companies, which means that the government controls them. So, to me, it's that they gain a foothold through the guise of being a civilian company or running an operation that can just as easily be a dual-use facility, where the People's Liberation Army or the Chinese military can come and easily use that facility for its own needs… I am also concerned about telecommunications: The upgrade to 5G technology for countries that already have Chinese 5G equipment, whereas 26 countries have 3G or 4G now. And certainly, what China does is they come and offer a discount. They make the outlook looks very good for countries struggling to supply their populations." she told a local newspaper.

The ideological approach to questioning Chinese companies from Washington and the reactions in this regard somehow hide a fundamental issue that should already be part of the Latin American analysis: What is the valid interaction between areas of military security, and what are the determinants of the full development of a country? Because that perspective of broad inclusion is found in the contents of the manuals and courses promoted by the Inter-American Defense Board. In the Cyber Defense Guide, written to provide guidelines for the design, planning, implementation, and development of a

---

[19] https://www.vozdeamerica.com/a/eeuu-preocupacion-influencia-china-rusia-america-latina/6644712.html

military cyber defense, the interaction of these two areas – the military and the civil, under the logic of interrelated security – is constant. An example of that text:

525. There are three fundamental parts of the cyberspace ecosystem: the elements (inhabitants) that interact with each other (ICT infrastructure, software or applications, information, transport protocols, electricity, and people), cyberspace itself (habitat) and the relationships and activities that take place in or through it.

526. The fundamental characteristic of the cyberspace ecosystem is the interaction that occurs between people, individually or through organized groups (companies, public administration, universities, international organizations, etc.), generating activities of all kinds, economic, social, artistic, informative, formative, collaborative, and of defense in all its extension.

527. Cyber defense is not just another activity that takes place in the cyberspace ecosystem. But it is the activity that allows the free and legitimate exercise of all activities within the scope of its powers.

528. In this sense, military cyber defense is understood as the capacity to defend the free and legitimate exercise of all the Ministry of Defense activities in cyberspace. In addition, it is the main capacity of national cyber defense and one of the pillars of national cybersecurity.

529. Relevant aspects of the cyberspace ecosystem related to cyber defense are national cybersecurity, international cybersecurity, public-private cooperation, third-party risks, cyber risks associated with pandemic states, and information.[20]

These contents have not yet been part of an in-depth, broad, and collective debate within Latin American countries. It is normal for the military to be summoned in emergencies, catastrophes, and even – in certain countries – to protect areas in a state of emergency in support of the police contingents responsible for maintaining internal order. However, from the logic of the

---

[20] https://www.iadfoundation.org/wp-content/uploads/2020/08/Ciberdefensa10.pdf

cyberspace ecosystem, restrictions could be applied in many areas (or strong questions) to investments and Chinese presence in various sectors of the economic development of a Latin American country. Clarification calls for debates where national interests determine the borders of decisions and their scopes, and with them, the best partners in the world for each project or action.

Despite the pressure from the United States on Latin America, in 2021, the governments of Chile (at the time in the hands of Sebastián Piñera) and Brazil (in charge of Jair Bolsonaro) organized auctions of radioelectric spectrum for 5G between telephone companies, without imposing conditions that would allow the margin to the Chinese company Huawei. However, the North American lobby continues in Latin American countries, such as Argentina, that have not yet tendered the 5G spectrum. At the beginning of May, the conference convened by the CLDP (Commercial Law Development Program) took place. It brought together representatives of the governments of the US, Argentina, and Australia, and companies from the private sector, to share perspectives on the networks of 5G and the advantages of innovative Open RAN technology. There, the acting director of the State Department's Office of Cybersecurity and Digital Policy, Paul Harrison, noted that "compared to where we were three years ago, the current Open RAN environment is extraordinary." He added: "Globally – including here in the America – 4G and 5G networks based on Open RAN principles are already being deployed, offering a new path, free from vendor lock-in and resilient against geopolitical forces and markets."[21] This objective also seems to inspire the existing OAS Working Group on Non-Traditional Confidence-Building Measures. Although its task appears more linked to diplomatic training on the subject, it also intends to "identify a national point of contact at the political level to discuss the implications of hemispheric cyber threats."[22]

---

[21] https://portalalba.org/temas/cyt/telecomunicaciones/telecomunicaciones-la-geopolitica-al-compas-de-las-corporaciones/

[22] https://www.oascybercbms.org/ The Group is chaired by Mexico, vice-presidency of the United States.

China-Latin America: Spaces for Thinking and Acting Together

Both China and Latin American countries have the option of multilateralism as the best option to strengthen their ties in the digital age, with mutual respect and the search for shared gains.

The immediate and proper scenario is the China-CELAC Forum. In 2021, it began to "explore new paths for China-CELAC cooperation and join efforts to advance towards a new digital era." The Forum addressed in depth different debates to identify the new direction of China-CELAC cooperation in digital technologies and promote initiatives that promote economic development in the post-pandemic era.

After this experience, the First Forum for Cooperation in Digital Technologies between China and the Community of Latin American and Caribbean States was completed. The meeting, held virtually in mid-July 2022, set out to explore new paths for cooperation between both parties and join forces for a new digital era. Co-chaired by Zhang Yunming, Vice Minister of Industry and Information Technology of China, and Claudio Ambrosini, Director of the National Communications Entity of Argentina, the country with the rotating presidency of CELAC in 2022, the forum brought together representatives of 18 member states.

Zhang Yunming noted that in the face of far-reaching changes aggravated by a pandemic that has not been seen in a century, China, Latin America, and the Caribbean countries must unite as one and "create opportunities together by firmly seizing the new development possibilities of digital technology." Ambrosini indicated that the Latin American side welcomes the Chinese initiative and is willing to continue deepening digital technology cooperation with China. CELAC members expressed their willingness to use this forum as an opportunity to jointly promote digital technology cooperation and development between China, Latin America, and the Caribbean. During the forum, the participants held permanent exchanges and dialogues on cooperation in various fields, such as artificial intelligence, 5G, universal telecommunications services, and radio spectrum management. All of this is part of the 2022-2024 Action Plan that the China-CELAC Forum agreed on at its third conference at the level of foreign ministers.[23]

But this is not enough if one considers the importance of new information and communication technologies in the reformulations of power worldwide. In the technical-political field, so to speak, the International Telecommunication Union (ITU) has a growing importance, where Argentina, Mexico, and Brazil occupy key positions in its council, along with other countries in the region.

The ITU is the oldest body of the United Nations, born in the mid-19th century, along with the expansion of the telegraph. Today, it is the space where debates on society and information are promoted, in which 193 countries and organizations participate to promote the growth and sustainable development of telecommunications and information networks and facilitate universal access, promoting peaceful relations, international cooperation, and economic and social development. The organization has more than 900 members, from leading companies to SMEs, which are part of various sectors such as telecommunications, broadcasting, the satellite industry, software, artificial intelligence, fintech, and public services. Regulatory bodies, universities, R&D agencies, and other international organizations also participate.

China has had a significant presence in this UN institution. Between 2014 and 2022, Zhao Houlin, an information and communication technology (ICT) engineer, served as Executive Secretary of the entity, in which he already had significant previous experience. Before being elected, Zhao served eight years as the Deputy General Secretary of the Union. He was also elected to serve two terms as Director of ITU's Telecommunication Standardization Bureau (TSB), which is charged with developing technical standards to ensure ICT interoperability worldwide. In the election of new officers, held during

---

[23] https://espanol.cgtn.com/n/2022-07-20/HGAAcA/se-celebra-el-primer-foro-de-cooperacion-en-tecnologias-digitales-china-celac/index.html

the plenipotentiary conference in Bucharest, Romania in September 2022, Doreen Bogdan-Martin of the United States received wide endorsement as the next ITU Secretary General. She worked there for several years, alongside her Chinese ancestor. But it is still symbolic and a sign of the times as representatives of China and the United States – supported by their respective countries – have been authorities in the most important agency to define the world's future in the digital sphere. There is a space where China and Latin America can "think together" about the digital world of the future, especially about the contributions that South-South thinking can bring to the social development of emerging countries.

Another important perspective when writing these lines is the so-called "Summit of the Future." Assumably, the pandemic brought a major telluric movement to the international future. Simultaneously, Russia's military action against Ukraine, the drastic climate change, and the persistent social inequalities also impact the world profoundly. With those in mind, Antonio Guterres, the Secretary General of the United Nations, proposed to the General Assembly the convening of a global meeting to review and act on an updated vision of the future.

The agenda should advance contributions and visions in three large areas. On the one hand, it is the survival of human beings on earth. Today we fall behind with our commitments, and we no longer have time. For this reason, for a the Summit of the Future, climate change should be a priority for all governments and organizations. On the other hand, it concerns the profound changes in the geopolitical spaces and the need to rearticulate the various political and cultural models around universally accepted consensus. And, on a plane clearly related to the previous ones, civilizational change means the transition from the era of the Industrial Revolution, which marked the evolution of our history in the last 250 years, to the Digital Revolution. President Ricardo Lagos has said it in one of his columns:

"Suddenly, new information technologies and artificial intelligence have crossed our work and daily life at a galloping speed. Incorporating these new languages has generated a practically infinite flow of information about the most private and intimate aspects of human beings... Everything we do in the search for information or the delivery of data to have a presence in the networks, in the delivery of opinions, or the purchase of goods configures big data managed and controlled by large commercial, political or financial companies. In this sense, if we think of a Summit of the Future, the challenge will be how government institutions safeguard the data provided by citizens, protect access to them and, at the same time, make data a determining resource for efficient public policies."[24]

The China-CELAC Forum, or any other forum for interaction between both parties at the multilateral level, can generate proposals to address these challenges. There is a "thinking together" that can support the results of that Summit of the Future and new bases for the ties between Chinese and Latin Americans in the coming decades.

And, of course, there is also the 2030 Agenda and the Sustainable Development Goals. The 2030 Agenda and its SDGs are, in general, a firm guide to endow all policies with an environmental, inclusive, and egalitarian sense and thus reverse (or at least try to) a very complex situation in which the planet finds itself. In other words, what is sought is a triple result: economic prosperity, social inclusion, and environmental sustainability. All of this determines a scenario of changes within the so-called digital era, where the permanent creativity of instruments and innovations can become a "swamp of ungovernability" if there are no policies to prepare the new generations to access and use such advances.

The interactions between citizenship and power are evolving at speed not calculated by political science theorists in these early days of the digital age. And this is a challenge in countries and cultures of different sizes. It is valid to say that – beyond differences in political models – this is an issue relevant to the future of China and Latin American countries: our future citizens there and here will be determined by their digital interactions to project their "time

---

[24] https://foropoliticaexterior.cl/columna-de-ricardo-lagos-una-cumbre-del-futuro-para-encontrar-las-respuestas/

consciousness."

There is a risk of incompetence if technological changes are thought of linearly while they occur exponentially. This is an issue where shared reflection between China and its Latin American counterparts has an opportunity and, even more, an obligation. There are warnings to be heard, such as those of the Chinese philosopher Zhao Tingyang:

"Technological progress is usually considered an unquestionable advance for humanity, which is especially dangerous. It is worth wondering if the uncontrolled progress of technologies will not lead to a catastrophe of great dimensions and even to the destruction of human beings. In fact, accelerated scientific and technological development is giving rise to a dangerous imbalance in which the capacity of technology increasingly exceeds the control capacity of the human order. The capacity gap between technology and this order is widening due, on the one hand, to permanent technological progress and, on the other, to the reduced capacity of the social order. Suppose a world order with sufficient control capacity is not built at a time when new technologies (such as artificial intelligence) finally become a form of power. In that case, the catastrophe for the human being will have reached its critical point... Leaving aside the possibility that technology can cause a catastrophe (and assuming that we still have time), the political problem generated by technological development already constitutes a very real threat."[25]

In Latin America, especially after the pandemic, the concern is growing in this regard. For CELAC, the rapid advances have generated an evolution of the digital divide, where physical access is no longer the main barrier but the differences in the use and opportunities that the network provides for the population. Thus, the existing material and social inequalities are replicated in the digital world. The population's possibilities to use it are often determined by age, gender, disability, race, ethnic group, social stratum, and location.

---

[25] Zhao Tingyang, *Tianxia: a Philosophy for Global Governance*, Herder Editorial, Spain, 2021.

"Faced with this scenario of opportunities and challenges, it is essential to analyze how these changes affect the social and labor inclusion of the population and whether digitization is creating new spaces to eradicate poverty and reduce inequality or whether it continues to widen gaps. For this reason, the question arises about the role of the Ministries of Social Development in the development of programs that make it possible to reduce the existing gaps and move towards 'leaving no one behind' in the digital age." They point out in one of his recent reports.[26]

Within this framework, for Latin America and the Caribbean, its insertion in this digital age involves cooperation with China in everything relevant to the region's specific interests and a balanced relationship of mutual respect with other global actors, such as the United States or the European Union. It is not a minor task; in the end, it is determined by advances in diplomacy and politics. But China is unique when it comes to working together in terms of not only technology transfers and major digital investments but also in the importance that these changes have for citizens: knowing how Socrates and Confucius will understand each other in the 21st century. In other words, how is a certain consensual platform configured from those ancient roots of thought – which arose almost at the same time 2,500 years ago – to respond to what China has called the "community of a shared future for mankind."

---

[26] https://www.cepal.org/es/eventos/inclusion-social-ciudadania-la-era-digital

Sarbottam Shrestha

Currently a Clinical Neurologist Consultant in Kathmandu, Nepal. He has served as President of Arniko Society, an organization of Nepalese alumni of Chinese universities, for ten years. Dr. Shrestha has worked extensively to deepen the friendship between China and Nepal at the people-to-people level. He has translated five contemporary Chinese literature books, including *Mo Yan's Selected Short Stories*, *Present Condition of Chinese Literature*, numerous Chinese articles on various subjects, and a few Chinese TV serials, including *The Journey to West*, into Nepali. He has also published three papers on "Belt and Road Initiative (BRI) and South Asia" topics.

The Idea of Building a Community with a Shared Future for Mankind and Its Implications to the Small or Underdeveloped Countries

In 2013, Chinese President Xi Jinping put forward the idea of a Community with a Shared Future for Mankind formally for the first time. The idea of a community with a shared future for mankind has been conceived many times in human history, chiefly by poets and philosophers. This time it did not come from a poet or a philosopher, but the supreme political leader of a powerful country in the world, which could play a substantial role in international politics.

At first, the world probably did not understand the implications of forming a community with a shared future for mankind based on the Chinese formula. It is a very broad and somewhat vague idea that could be misunderstood as another idea of utopia. Therefore, it did not attract much attention from political leaders and scholars from other countries. Soon after that, President Xi proposed jointly constructing the Silk Road Economic Belt and the 21st Century Maritime Silk Road on two different occasions, later known as the Belt and Road Initiative (BRI). It was not only an ideal like the community of a shared future for mankind but also a concrete plan. Subsequently, Asian Infrastructure Investment Bank (AIIB) and Silk Road Fund were established, where the countries along the Belt and Road could get loans for the infrastructure development of their countries. China formally and solemnly pushed forward partnership with the countries along the Belt and Road. At this point, most countries were convinced that China was serious about the seemingly far and intangible goal of forming such a community.

In the subsequent months and years, President Xi further elaborated in the speeches delivered at different places and occasions on how the formation of a community of a shared future for mankind is possible and what sectors should be included to materialize that goal at this stage of the historical development of humanity. Later, Chinese scholars researching the problems faced by humanity have concluded that it is facing political, secure, economic, cultural, and environmental issues, which are endangering the instability and having negative effects on the formation of a community of shared future for mankind at present.

According to Chinese scholars, in the international political sector, the problems causing instability in the world are hegemony, unilateralism, protectionism, etc. Some of these problems would end up in border conflict and war. Similarly, regional terrorism is the greatest problem in the international security sector. And in international cultural sectors, religious extremism is one of the burning problems.

In the economic sector, unequal economic development of different regions and countries is the main problem. And finally, frequent global environmental crises are the problems of the environmental sector. These problems in various sectors are to be dealt with as a first step toward forming a community of shared future for mankind.

The Chinese scholars also came up with the Chinese formula for solving problems faced in different sectors. For the solution to the global political issues, China insisted on mutual respect and negotiation based on equality among the world's countries and advocated a new diplomatic international environment based on partnership without forming military allies.

And for the problems of the economic sector, China promoted trade and investment liberalization, and at the same time facilitated economic and financial partnerships with other countries on the government level. In the security sector, peaceful discussion and negotiation are advocated for resolving disputes, and an integrated effort to protest all types of terrorism is another important point.

In the cultural sector, China proposed respect for the cultural diversity of mankind and peaceful interaction among different civilizations for better understanding. And in the environmental sector, China advocated for cooperation among countries for a good environment that is green, recyclable and sustainable with low carbon emissions.

The special characteristics of the Chinese formula and wisdom employed to form a community of a shared future for mankind are inclusiveness and assimilation. They contrast the prevailing ideas of overcoming, replacing, and removing others. China works hard in the areas of culture, security, and environment to move toward the goal of forming an upgraded community of a shared future for mankind in partnership with several concerned countries in sectors like environment and anti-terrorism. It will implement the initiative more vigorously and effectively, uplifting China's position in the international political and economic arenas to a new dimension.

China has increasingly participated in international and regional organizations. The BRI and its leading role in establishing the Asian Infrastructure Investment Bank and Silk Road Fund suggest its long-cherished intent to create such a community through global cooperation, particularly through international organizations. The new dimension in China's efforts in international politics is the establishment of strategic cooperative partnerships. Similarly, economic partnerships at the government level is a new dimension of China's efforts in the economic sector.

China has a special affinity with the small and underdeveloped "third world" countries but has no alliances. China has stood against military alliances for decades, and now it is even more strongly opposed to it in the international community. According to the Chinese formula to form a community of a shared future for mankind, the formation of military allies will endanger world peace, therefore, should be discouraged. Although China's stance on this particular issue has not changed, the status of China in the international community has changed greatly, so its implications in the present-day world also have changed.

Suppose we review China's diplomatic policy after establishing the People's Republic of China. In that case, we will find that world peace and economic development have been the two main themes of Chinese diplomatic policy. And since then, China's role in international politics has been to promote world peace and economic development of the countries of the world.

Although China has not put it in plain words, a community of a shared future for mankind and the BRI have become the overall guideline of Chinese foreign policy now, and it will continue to be in the years to come. It continues China's diplomatic policy of past decades with some new dimensions. As China's status and role in international politics have become much more important than before, and it is in a position to bring about substantial change in international politics, different countries and actors in international politics have started to analyze its implications from their perspectives.

As a citizen of Nepal, I have been observing its implications for poor and underdeveloped small countries like my own, and here I will discuss some conclusions in detail.

Firstly, the small and underdeveloped countries are amazed, delighted, and encouraged by China's advocacy for forming such a community. China's concern about issues involving the whole of humanity implies that China is already not a poor and weak country anymore. It has worked on solving its own problems while taking world issues into consideration. And it was progressing so fast. China used to be a powerless developing country just a few decades ago, having similar problems caused by poverty and under-development as in other underdeveloped countries. In a few decades, a miracle happened in China. China has progressed as much in 40 years as the West did in 400 years.

China's development has greatly impacted the people of small and underdeveloped countries. Scholars and common people alike were curious about how that miraculous economic development had been possible in China. It has been a topic of household discussion in several countries, including Nepal. It has become one of those countries' main topics of newspaper articles on economics and development studies for two decades.

The curiosity about China and its miraculous economic development encouraged people worldwide to learn the Chinese language, with the people of small and developing countries being no exception. In my country, more and more Nepalese people are enthusiastic about learning Chinese as the number of Chinese tourists has increased, and business with China has flourished promisingly. There was a kind of "fever" of learning the Chinese language for several years.

Those who could not learn the language sought to know more about China through Chinese literature, movies, and TV programs translated into local languages. Chinese agencies established projects to translate Chinese literature, and local translators translated Chinese literature under this project. China also found set-ups for the translation and dubbing of Chinese movies and TV programs in some countries in high demand. In most countries, private companies carry out translation and dubbing, as it had become a profitable business. And in countries like Nepal, where there were no Chinese projects and the business was also unprofitable, China friendship organizations carry out the work on a small scale.

The number of Chinese friendship organizations has also increased because of Nepalese people's interest in knowing about China and interacting with Chinese people. There were only a few Chinese friendship associations in Nepal about two decades ago, but dozens more have been set up in the last ten years.

The idea of a community of a shared future for mankind can only be considered by wealthy and strong countries with a sense of responsibility toward humanity. Such an idea or proposal from China implied to all the developing countries, including small and underdeveloped countries, that a poor and underdeveloped country could develop economically quickly. It is a matter of pride and also an encouragement for them. China has set an excellent example for all developing countries.

Although the socio-political situation differs from one country to another, and the model of China's development may not be directly applicable to other countries, they are still delighted to witness China's growth. Even the nationalist political leaders of all the developing countries, including potential rival countries of China, have appreciated Chinese economic development and tried to study from the Chinese experience. They are convinced that such a miracle is possible with good leadership, vision, and governance. Therefore, now they are more confident to work hard for the development of their own countries.

In fact, apart from China, some other countries have also developed remarkably in that time. Some of them were small countries; therefore, their development did not have a big international influence. The result of other bigger countries was not as remarkable as China's, so they were also unable to bring big noticeable change to the international community and international politics. China is the most populous country in the world and its economic development was significant to the whole world. The most important was that following its own development, China showed its concern about global matters by participating in international affairs more actively, donating to international organizations more generously, and hosting more international summit meetings with greater influence. All of these gestures made it standing as a major responsible power in the international forum. Now the small and underdeveloped countries are eager to see what changes favorable to them will be brought about by China's vigorous participation in international politics.

Secondly, the underdeveloped small countries have experienced that China's relationship with them has changed. In the past, the relationship between China and those countries used to be one-way economic support from China and limited two-way cultural exchanges. Now China has supported several big projects in dozens of countries in the recent decades. In Nepal, I can recall several big projects like highways, the Kathmandu ring road, and large-scale factories constructed with Chinese support in the last seven decades. China was not a developed and wealthy country in those days. Yet, China provided immense economic and technical assistance to dozens of small and underdeveloped countries for decades without any political precondition.

With the proposal for a community of a shared future for mankind, the nature of China's relationship with small underdeveloped countries has changed. In addition to the one-way economic support from China, it has now proposed establishing partnerships with small and underdeveloped countries. For the effectiveness, China proposed developing partnerships under BRI's framework. A few years after the BRI was proposed, China signed a memorandum of understanding with dozens of countries: mostly underdeveloped small countries, for the partnership.

The partnerships with China are basically of two types. One of them is purely economic cooperation partnership for a particular project. Another was long-term economic cooperation and other strategically important issues.

The new type of partnerships with China witnessed more economic and business activities in underdeveloped countries. With the Chinese governmental investment, many projects in several underdeveloped small countries materialized, which were formerly considered impossible.

In the past, poor and underdeveloped countries would get loans for particular construction projects from international agencies like Asian Development Bank, World Bank, etc. The foreign loan was common in those poor and underdeveloped countries, but they usually did not take a loan from a foreign country for a particular construction project in the past. But after the promotion of the BRI, China came forward with partnerships and loans for construction projects in these countries.

Chinese investments have brought awe and confusion among scholars and people of small and underdeveloped countries. People were surprised why Chinese investments came so aggressively. Other international agencies spent several years conducting feasibility studies before investing in some infrastructure projects. Several meetings would be held to discuss its feasibility and viability before deciding to invest in a particular project. The investment agency would conduct those feasibility studies at least once. Many project proposals were rejected after the first or second round of meetings.

But the BRI project approvals were never delayed. In many cases, it is known that the feasibility studies of projects had been done only by third and fourth parties several years ago. China agreed to invest based on those feasibility studies. China has invested in dozens of countries at a fast speed in less than two decades. The amount of money invested in small and underdeveloped countries has exceeded the total loan from the world's largest financial agencies founded seven decades ago.

It is also equally amazing to find that more than ten small and underdeveloped countries have received Chinese investment exceeding twenty percent of their annual GDPs. One country has received Chinese investment, almost half its annual GDP. It is estimated that for the top ten debtor countries, it will take more than forty years to pay back the loan, provided all the projects and other economic conditions go fine in forty years to come.

It seems that people and governments in some small, underdeveloped countries have not grasped the difference between grants and partnerships. They are still under the illusion that all the Chinese projects in their countries are grant projects as they used to be a few decades ago. In reality, the projects carried out in partnership are not grant projects, and the governments of the small and underdeveloped countries have their liabilities to China.

While in most cases, the current leaders of the countries have tried to abuse Chinese investment for their political gain. By bringing large amounts of Chinese investment, they try to give their people the impression that Chinese investment is possible only because they are in office. In that way, they tried to convince their people that they should be elected as leaders for another term, and they would guarantee more Chinese investment in their countries. They did not clarify how they would pay back the loan to the public. The investors were not clear whether all projects proposed by the current leader benefit the country or only the current leader and his/her political party. In several circumstances, some of the projects they proposed and invested in were more beneficial to the current leaders and their political parties than to the country and people.

In this way, the unconditional and benevolent investment from China has been misunderstood by people of the concerned country as an interference in their country's internal affairs by supporting the current leader, who may not be popular among the citizens of the country, at the cost of national interest. Under such circumstances, nationalists of the concerned countries mistook ignorance of the Chinese side as to intention to help the current leader in office. They became negative to Chinese investment in their countries. It is a great diplomatic loss for China.

China is already aware that it should not get involved in the regional dispute among countries by investing in projects in those disputed regions. In most countries practicing the Western type of democracy, the leader or government may change every five years or earlier. And the succeeding leader or government may not follow the treaties signed by the preceding government. Consequently, the current leader will not take responsibility for repaying the loan after he/she is no longer in office. The succeeding leader may also not assume responsibility to repay the loan, declaring it against the national interest. It is the worst part of such investment in small and underdeveloped countries for China.

Some related politicians and media hold that The Chinese investment under the BRI has not been very transparent in several cases. Scholars with good attitudes toward China and the BRI have criticized the BRI projects' opacity. In most cases, the financial details of the projects and terms of investment of the BRI were not made public. When scholars looked for necessary data and figures on the BRI projects for benign purposes, they could not find them anywhere. When there is a lack of authorized information on projects, people turn to rumors and guesses, which produces distrust.

Partnership with China brings about a joint financial venture for infrastructure development and profit. In this way, it is a win-win game, but without proper feasibility and viability studies of such projects, those projects may not be a win-win game. On the contrary, it could become a lose-lose game. Unfortunately, there are already several such examples. In this worst condition, since the size of the economy of the small underdeveloped countries is incomparably much smaller than China, the equal loss of the two countries has different effects on their countries. That loss may not be felt in China, but for the small underdeveloped country, it could be seriously harmful, if not fatal.

What if the small underdeveloped countries could not repay the loan to China is a question many scholars and ordinary people ask. However, China has negotiated the debt with several countries for a more balanced outcome between the lender and borrower. China has written off some debts totally or partially. In some cases, China has extended loan terms and repayment deadlines. Refinancing or re-negotiations on the term has also been done. There have been more than fifty cases where China restructured or waived loan payments without seizing state assets. But these outcomes are not known to most of the people who are interested to know about Chinese investment under the BRI, again because of inadequate transparency. Asset seizures are rare, but they have been mentioned so many times by foreign media that all the people interested in the BRI know about them.

People of a long-term debtor country, usually small and underdeveloped countries, are concerned that the creditor country China may influence them diplomatically and politically, especially when those countries fail to repay their loan to the creditor. These countries have had a bad experience of becoming subordinate countries to lenders. Therefore, the outcome with the creditor China also worries them.

It is a financial partnership between any two parties, nothing special. While one nation borrows money from an international financial agency, the nation is always at risk of conditionality imposed by the lender. When the country cannot repay the loan, it may have to change its economic policies at the dictation of the lender, which may include devaluation of the currency, changes in internal banking systems, etc. There are no such risks while borrowing money from China, and the interest rate of Chinese loans is only nominally higher than those of other international financial agencies. On the other hand, the Chinese party is not as experienced as other international financial agencies. In some case it cannot assess whether the projects are viable and whether the debtor country can repay the loan. In this way, the small and underdeveloped countries are yet to clarify why it is more beneficial to work in partnership with China than with other international financial agencies.

Thirdly, the small underdeveloped countries have experienced their relationship with China becoming more complicated than before. A few decades ago, the relationship between small, underdeveloped countries and

China was quite simple. In most cases, it used to be one-way economic support from China and some two-way cultural exchanges between them. It did not involve a third party, or attract unnecessary attention from a third party. Of course, during the days when China supported other countries' revolutionaries, the concerned countries' leaders were cautious about relations with China. That was an exceptional situation in a few countries. Now the situation is not as simple as before in most small and underdeveloped countries that wish to develop relations with China.

When we review China's diplomacy after the establishment of the People's Republic of China, the Sino-Soviet Treaty of Friendship, Alliance and Mutual Assistance was signed in 1950 but not entended later.

Most of the small underdeveloped small countries were and are members of the Non-alignment Movement. China never joined the non-alignment movement as a member during the Cold War. China had once tried to form a political coalition in the third world which were mutual opposition to hegemony by supporting national liberation struggles in foreign countries and by close cooperative relations to shape the third world as a third force.

In those days, China observed the small underdeveloped small countries closely and was aware of possible bullying of those countries by bigger neighboring countries. In such cases, China stood for justice by supporting the bullied countries. There is a good example of China's support for a small, underdeveloped country, Nepal, bullied by a neighboring country. When the foreign interest and interference in Nepal kept increasing in the 1960s, China openly expressed that if anything happened to Nepal due to interference from other countries, China would support Nepal to fight back the external interference. The day of external military interference in Nepal never came in the contemporary history. Several senior politicians of Nepal consider that this timely and clear expression saved Nepal from the interference of foreign countries. During this period, China left a good impression on most small and underdeveloped small countries, although China was not a member of the Non-alignment Movement.

China is a large country with a huge population, and it has always had the potential to become a superpower in the world. As the Soviet Union was still a threat to another superpower, it approached China and developed good relations to balance the threat from the United States. China's economic development started to gain momentum, and triangular diplomacy had been prevalent in the international community for about twenty years.

Since the proposal of creating a community of a shared future for mankind, China has strongly opposed forming alliances. But China has not joined the Non-alignment Movement as a member either, and only retained the status of the observer in the conference of non-aligned countries. The foundational ideologies of the Non-alignment Movement at the initial stage, such as national independence, territorial integrity, and struggle against colonialism and imperialism, may not all be applicable today, and it does not have as big momentum as it used to have a few decades ago. But it is still a loosely formed organization of more than one hundred nations. Although divergence of agenda and allegiances of the member nations have been a fatal problem to taking any definitive actions since the early time of its establishment, it still emphasizes multilateralism, equality, and mutual non-aggression. It is realigned against Western hegemony and neo-colonialism. Apart from these, it opposes the foreign occupation, interference in internal affairs, and aggressive unilateral measures. Actually, all of these norms and ideals match with Chinese suggestions for solving the problems faced by humanity in the present day in the sector of international politics.

The miraculous economic development of China established it as a new superpower in the international arena. In the last eight years, more than one hundred and thirty countries joined the BRI and expressed their interest in cooperating with China. Although a few developed countries are also included, the majority of the countries in the list are small and under-developed countries. Even what is worth mentioning is that there are still more than fifty countries that have not joined the BRI. And the majority of them are developed and wealthy countries. The nations which remained away from the BRI may be skeptical and critical of the BRI and openly urged their allies not to join it. In several instances, those countries gave others the impression that one country had to make a choice between China and the US and its allies. Providing such a choice is, in fact, a gentle version of a threat to the countries interested in working with China.

The projects funded by China would be hindered by the anti-China parties in those countries, and these were not new practices. When China proposes cooperation projects, especially ambitious ones, some other countries develop similar projects with some connections with the Chinese projects, making the situation complicated. Those small countries are always at risk of economic sanctions or additional penalties and troubles from those countries when they want to decline the offer and cooperate with China. When Chinese investment increases in a country, that country may face political instability caused by the support of the anti-China parties and the cessation of all other foreign investment, aid, and loans.

Such things have happened not only in infrastructure construction but also in cultural projects. The China Cultural Centers, which operate in foreign countries independently and separately, have not faced such problems. But the Confucius Institutes, funded by the Chinese government, have faced several problems because Confucius Institutes are partnership projects, and affiliated to local universities. It indicates that the anti-China force considered the partnership projects with China as the symbol of China's growing political influence in the concerned countries.

This change in the attitudes of the anti-China forces toward China partnership projects in small underdeveloped countries is certainly due to the change in China's position in the international arena. China is becoming wealthy, powerful, and progressively important in international politics in recent years. China has always advocated plurality and opposed polarized global conditions, putting forward the idea of forming a community with a shared future for mankind. Consequently, China's partnership with dozens of countries has motivated the anti-China forces to look for some conspiracy behind it. And for this purpose, China has been portrayed as a "pole" of the international community. Along with describing China as a pole in the international community, the anti-China forces have started to target countries with an intimate partnership with China. In this way, the partnership with China would make a small country subject to the risk of being targeted by the anti-China forces.

Anti-China forces are making alliances openly, but China is always against forming alliances with other countries. Forming alliances is against the Chinese formula of international governance because the formation of alliances will eventually bring conflicts, which will, in turn, hinder the creation of a community of a shared future for mankind.

China was not able to suggest a better practical ideology or strategy to overcome the formation of alliances. Only AIIB has announced an MoU with the World Bank to deepen cooperation. Otherwise, China would also resist international involvement in the BRI projects, so all the BRI projects till now are only bilateral treaties between China and the concerned country. In this way, it has become an unintentional Chinese version of giving a choice to the BRI member countries between China and the US and its allies.

On the one hand, China always stands for small underdeveloped countries, always extending its hand of cooperation, support, and partnership. On the other side, there are anti-China forces, in alliances or as individual countries, which tend to threaten them against the partnership with China. Small and underdeveloped countries are naturally more attracted to China because they think they have more in common with China due to similar situations in the last few decades. China is facing economic sanctions and all kinds of troubles created by the anti-China forces. Under such circumstances, small underdeveloped countries are in a dilemma to further strengthen their partnership with China.

Finally, China will not forgot the so-called third world countries, poor and underdeveloped. It has kept its decade-old promise to maintain special relations with them, no matter how developed China is. China's advocacy for forming a community of a shared future for mankind may be viewed as a continuation of its past foreign policy based on world peace and development. China's development is an opportunity for all the underdeveloped countries, especially those along the Belt and Road. China has always encouraged these countries to take advantage of its development.

Now it is upon the underdeveloped countries to utilize that opportunity. No country has ever developed solely with foreign aid and investment. For the development of a country, the most important thing is, undoubtedly, good leadership and good governance with the right vision. China also developed quickly because of good leadership and governance with the right vision. But most underdeveloped countries still lack one or more of these traits.

The use of the opportunity provided by China is also not as simple as it used to be, as we have discussed above. Therefore, more wisdom is required for underdeveloped countries to develop partnership with China further. Only wise decisions while establishing a close partnership with China may help to avoid all the troubles faced by underdeveloped countries.

Sonia Bressler

A French writer and a Ph.D. in philosophy and epistemology and now teaching at the Advanced European Institute of Management (ISEG). She is the publisher of La Route de la Soie-Éditions (the Silk-Road Editions). Simultaneously, Sonia works as a reporter, writing reports and articles for *L'Humanité*, *Nouvelles d'Europe*, and *L'Observateur*. She loves traveling and photography and has been to Tibet, Xinjiang, and Gansu of China, where different ethnic groups inhabit. She has recorded the local people's daily life there with her pens and lenses.

China of Tomorrow

Many books introduce the profound history and splendid civilization of China[1]. At the same time, they are a guide for foreigners to do business in China and establish relations with this fascinating nation. Nevertheless, it seems that we, people from the West, can hardly have a thorough knowledge of China.

Such being the case, the West seems to have only two attitudes towards China: rejection or fascination. Soon, rejection turns into a fear of China—a nation which, as a matter of fact, has become awe-inspiring, for it can do everything[2]. On the other hand, there has emerged a view on what we call delicacy and art...with Chinese characteristics. Therefore, books have come out in large numbers which lay emphasis on the strength of China and idealized daily life of the Chinese people.

Today, I suggest you discard these two extreme views on China, for neither gives the true picture of the country. Actually, China is a country with a vast territory and wide regional differences. It is a country with many ethnic groups, languages, cuisines, and techniques. In this sense, China is a balanced body composed of many imbalances. It is an amazing country that has passed down its civilization through an ingenious integration of the past and the present. China is ever-lasting in impermanence. In fact, the strength of China lies precisely in the quality of infinity (the balance composed of imbalances).

---

[1] Take Henry Kissinger's *On China* (Fayard) as an example.

[2] Quoted from the following latest publications: Jean-Pierre Cabstan (2021), *Tomorrow's China: War or Peace?*, Gallimard; François Heisbourg (2020), The Predators' Times: China, The United States, Russian and We, Odile Jacob.

For this reason, I decide to talk about tomorrow's China in this article. So far, we cannot see its future clearly. However, it is in preparation with an eye on the future. To have a good knowledge of China in the future and the possibility of its existence, we must take off our colored spectacles. Moreover, we should not insist on the cliche in the West that China is a state under dictatorial rule.

I was born and brought up and received my education in France, so I know well how influential such a view is and how difficult it is for me to avoid it. Then, why do I begin to write this article? And why is this preface written to discuss the future of China?

The reason is very simple. In the first part of this article, I will try to explain the trap in which China is caught. It is a mirror trap set in the opinions of the West. Though this negative mirror results from conscious or unconscious racialism, it originates mainly from the flaws of the rational thinking of the West. It is a binary opposition-based ideology: good and bad. As a matter of fact, binary opposition hardly leaves any space between the two world outlooks: Utopia and Dystopia.

Second, I will state that China should follow the pattern of "Protopia." Therefore, I will give some examples in Chinese society (technology, science, and society) to see whether they will become a reality.

Third, I will stress that if China continues today's model, it will create a unique society featuring a balanced development of technology, nature, and human beings. Therefore, we may ask ourselves, "Can't China create an outlook of democracy in the future?"

Abandon Dualism of Utopia-Dystopia

In the West, whenever we try to think of the future or the prospect, our thinking is shackled by two extremes. They are two insurmountable props: Utopia and Dystopia.

From the perspective of etymology, Utopia refers to "an imaginary place that does not exist," the letter "u" and τόπος, tópos ("place"). For centuries, humankind has been looking for Utopia. Sometimes, they do so to avoid the pressure of subconsciousness. Sometimes, they intend to help consciousness to see further by imagining a possibility, an active evolution.

The other side is Dystopia. According to etymology, δυσ, dys means "bad," and τόπος, tópos means "place." "Dystopia" means literally "a bad place." It emphasizes the assumption of an autocratic government, which suppresses the individuals and turns them into slaves of machines and other things.

Then, are there only these two choices for the future of humankind? Will these two futures suffer the same fate as Sisyphus? This gigantic rock always rolls back to Dystopia, and then human beings push it towards Utopia again. It is impossible to have it stopped, so the task is repeated... Human beings restart tirelessly, trying over and over between Utopia and Dystopia. For a long time, I have viewed the inevitability of Utopia as a driving force, which makes me exhausted. I am wrong.

As a matter of fact, while envisioning the future of humankind, we should change this dualistic way of thinking. A new word has recently been coined that tries to offer another possibility. It is "protopia." It was coined by Kevin Kelly[3]. Based on this word, he put forward a progress-based outlook on the future. Indiscernible as it is, it evolves upwards, and every decade witnesses a better world than the previous one.

Take automobiles as an example. As early as the 1960s, there were cars with power-assisted steering. However, it was not until recently that most cars were equipped with electricity-assisted steering. Though electrocars are very popular, their history is dated back to the 1830s. Robert Anderson invented the electro-carriage, and Thomas Davenport created an electric locomotive (in 1835). In 1859, Gaston Planté invented a lead-acid battery. In 1884, Thomas Parker was seen sitting in the first electrocar[4].

---

[3] Cf. Pam Weintraub, "Utopia is a Dangerous Ideal: We Should Aim for 'Protopia'", *Aeon*, March 7, 2018, https://aeon.co/ideas/utopia-is-a-dangerous-ideal-we-should-aim-for-protopia

[4] See *History of the First Electrocars in Pictures 1880-1920*, May 29, 2020
https://photoshistoriques.info/lhistoire-en-images-des-premieres-voitures-electriques-1880-1920/

Pollution-free hydrogen energy automobiles are available, and they will play a dominant role in the future. But here, we adopt the viewpoint of "protopia." In 1804, François Isaac de Rivaz made the first batch of hydrogen engines, which took coal gas as the fuel of the internal combustion engines. In 1859, Étienne Lenoir applied for a patent for coal gas-fueled two-stroke internal combustion engines. The next year, he produced 400 "coal gas and expanded air" engines with a power of 2-horsepower. In 1861, these first hydrogen engines were used to power the first powerboat on the Seine. In 1867, Nicolaus Otto invented a 4-horsepower gas engine. However, it was not until 1970 that Paul Dieges registered a patent for improved internal combustion engines fueled by hydrogen. His goal was to produce energy by pollution-free means instead of oil.

Other examples may illustrate the point that we need to change our view. We are following in the footsteps of history. We are unaware that our society is advancing because of our actions (sometimes, our inaction). Of course, we should be concerned about technical progress and human rights. We should keep learning, maintain vigilance and pay close attention to some insignificant actions (for example, community meetings or self-help groups), which are likely to cause leverage effect in the long term.

When we think in the pattern of "protopia," we begin to interpret the evolution of our society in different ways. We realize that a trivial event may serve as a guide to development in the future. Finally, this way of thinking also means reviewing the history of China through its major inventions: gunpowder, the compass, printing, and many others. Suppose we review the development course of these inventions as I review the history of automobiles. In that case, we have to see China not only as a country with the most advanced technologies but also as a county that keeps pursuing a balance without affecting the elements of its development course.

Writing down these words, I can't help thinking of a line in *Tao Te Ching* (*Classic of the Way and Virtue*, the main classic of Taoism) which runs like this,

"If one tries to usurp the state, I can see that he is going to fail."[5] This is what the world is like. These small creations, insignificant or negligible as they seem, create the world of the future. However, we should know how to enable these invisible parts to play their roles.

Hypothesis on China's Tomorrow

From this perspective, we may observe China's today and hypothesize its tomorrow. In light of the potential development, we need to explain this research through several major typical examples. Here, I would like to choose the following examples: governance, intellectual revolution, and democracy.

New Governance

As for governance, we mean the physical system guiding the decision-making in some field, namely, governance system, especially governance structure and system dynamics (governance process, management activities, etc.).

Once this definition is given, we should look at current events objectively. The West is regressing in many aspects[6]: economy, industry, population, and research... Such retrogression shows itself in the decrease of strategic geographical regions. For Europe, this is not necessarily bad, for it should get out of the control of the United States and become an independent entity.

Realizing such regression of the West, China has found a new way of thinking to replace the pattern that the West dominates the world. This pattern does not mean substituting one rule for the other but building up a multi-polar world pattern. To this end, China puts forward this tool for new governance.

---

[5] Cf. Chapter 29 of *Tao Te Ching*.

[6] See the column by Jacques Julliard, "The Decline of the West", *Le Figaro*, September 6, 2021, https://www.lefigaro.fr/vox/monde/jacques-julliard-le-crepuscule-de-l-occident-20210905

This lever of change is the Belt and Road Initiative (BRI) Xi Jinping put forward in Kazakhstan in 2013. This multiform initiative involves land, railway, ocean, data, and space. Just as Fathallah Oualalou[7] said, this initiative gets the historically nonaligned countries together, creating a new prospect for exchanges between the African Continent, the Middle East, and China. To realize this great initiative, China has established a new institution.

In 2013, while paying a state visit to Indonesia, Xi Jinping proposed an initiative to establish an Asian bank to satisfy the needs of Asian countries in regional protection and development. In 2015, the Asian Infrastructure Investment Bank (AIIB) was founded[8]. Its goal is to promote the development of Asian countries and regional economic integration while satisfying the needs of infrastructure, establishing an international financial institution that does not rely on the United States, and enhancing the role of the main regional bodies in decision-making.

By 2022, AIIB will have had 89 member countries. Most are in the Asian-Pacific Region, but some are not, such as Algeria, Germany, France, Egypt, Luxembourg, Chile, and Cote d'Ivoire. Many other countries expressed their willingness to join the organization but have not submitted applications. They are Armenia, Iraq, Kuwait, Bolivia, Lebanon, Papua New Guinea, Djibouti, Kenya, Libya, Morocco, Nigeria, Senegal, South Africa, Togo, Tunisia, and Venezuela.

Take the establishment of AIIB as an example. It shows the possibility of new governance. AIIB operates based on three principles: sustainable infrastructure development, cross-border interconnection, and private capital flow. In terms of the standards for transparency, openness, environment, and society, it conforms to international standards. The motto of AIIB is "Lean, Clean, and Green." AIIB competes directly with the International Monetary Fund (FMI) in its operating activities. AIIB's business model is very likely to become the model of the future. As a matter of fact, with poverty elimination as

---

[7] Cf. Fathallah Oualalou (2021), *The Space Between China, Arab and Africa*, The Silk Road Press.

[8] https://www.aiib.org/en/index.html

its focus of operation, AIIB guides enterprises and its member countries while protecting the environment.

With new digitized governance, China's institution-based governance will double in the following decades. To understand this, we should keep a watchful eye on the transformation and the drawbacks of the current digitized governance.

New Digitized Governance: End of the GAFAMI Times

GAFAM refers to Google, Apple, Facebook, Amazon, and Microsoft. To be fairer, IBM should be added in, hence GAFAMI.

To be more exact, we should have added unicorn companies,[9] which dominate human activities for the time being. They are NATU (Netflix, Airbnb, Tesla, Uber).

In the West, these companies have absolute control[10] of our personal data. We unconsciously tell these companies our data (trip, step numbers, floor numbers, information exchange, telephone communication, photos, habits, etc.)[11]. However, for the sake of marketing[12], adjusting premium rate (cars, housing...), or monitoring, they sell our data to others[13].

Take the latest application Zenly[14] (its motto is "Your Map, Your Friend"). This app enables you to acquire the real-time locations of your "friends" and to check the electric quantity of their mobile phone batteries.

Through this "amusing" monitoring system, one may follow the tracks of others while covering up the fact with candy style, cartoon, and flaring colors.

---

[9] Unicorn companies refer to the enterprises whose value in science and technology exceeds US$1 billion (850 million euros). For example, unicorn companies in France include BlablaCar, Doctolib, Deezer, OVH...

[10] The definition from CNIL: "Personal data refer to any information of a natural person that has been recognized or is recognizable". - https://www.cnil.fr/fr/definition/donnee-personnelle

[11] This is why we should talk about "Capta" as Rob Kitchin stressed, cf. https://pdfs.semanticscholar.org/c5ff/796807fc22db9 037ae779e60b9e3c305909e.pdf

[12] Here, I would not like to review the data used in the movement, especially the event of Cambridge Analytica, refer to my article (2017) titled *Cambridge Analytica & Moi*, https://www.academia.edu/42063916/Cambridge_Analytica_and_moi

[13] See my article titled *AI and Human Rights* in January 2022 at: https://www.academia.edu/69408550/IA_and_Droits_Humains

[14] https://zen.ly/fr

Is this what the new social life is like?

Google has become Alphabet[15] and the game master in many fields: health, education, monitoring, digital tools, and optical fiber (communication network). For years, Google has established various "timelines"[16] for individuals. By doing so, you may find all the quantified data about the trip (walking, riding a bicycle, driving a car, taking a train or plane...). All have been calculated.

In an Internet-connected city in the West, data are used and analyzed ceaselessly to upgrade your life experience[17]. For example, lighting will become intelligent, reacting to your emotions and following your steps. Your health will be measured. If you do not feel well, an appointment with the doctor will be made, and proper treatment will be given to prolong your life. Moreover, public transportation will become more convenient because it will be custom-made for your mobility. Some intelligent vehicles may be used as offices and conference rooms, etc.

Therefore, we may imagine that Alphabet launched the "operating system for daily life and comfort" to maintain a comfortable living environment, teach people how to manage and save energy and keep healthy. Just a click, you may find a place to sleep. "Monetary exchange" will not be done in banks but finished through cryptocurrencies (like Binance we use today).[18]

In the West today, this viewpoint is seen as Dystopia. It is to enslave the individuals for the interest of private entities who determine the code of conduct.

In 2020, the legislature was faced with an urgent task: to make laws for the entities which seemed to have greater power than the state. In fact, the accumulative capital of Apple exceeded US$1.5 trillion (more than the GDP

---

[15] https://abc.xyz

[16] https://timeline.google.com/maps/timeline?

[17] See: https://www.objetconnecte.com/ville-connectee/

[18] https://www.binance.com/fr

of Spain). By the time when I am writing this article, its capital exceeds US$2 trillion19.

If we continue to study the data of these companies, we may feel confused and disoriented. The total value of GAFAM exceeds $6 trillion, equal to the world's third-largest economy in terms of GDP.20

Fragility of GAFAM

In our daily life, we feel GAFAM are insurmountable. However, as Olivier Ezratty[21] pointed out, these magnates may make mistakes. He listed several reasons: 1) the US predominance in the Internet can be traced back to the 1960s (therefore, such predominance had nothing to do with its application); 2) their strategic forces are relative; 3) the value systems of these enterprises are almost unchanged; 4) several acquisitions turned out to be failures; and 5) not all of their basic researches can be converted into commercial achievements. Charles-Édouard Bouée[22] made some complements to this viewpoint. He pointed out that if these magnates wish to survive, a major reform should be made in legislation. Especially in Europe, reform should be made in data acquisition and application. Though this lobby remained unknown several years ago, organizations such as Corporate Europe Observatory (CEO)[23] and Lobby Control have pointed out all this. According to these non-governmental organizations, Google spent 5.75 million Euros influencing the decision of Brussels. Facebook spent 5.5 million Euros and Microsoft 5.25 million Euros[24]. From the report, we find that these companies' operational measures and their

---

[19] From MarketCap website - https://companiesmarketcap.com/apple/marketcap/

[20] See the article titled *GAFAM is Equal to the Third Largest GDP Economy on the Globe: Facing Digital Economy, We Should Revise the Policy for Competition*. https://fr.businessam.be/videos/les-gafam-lequivalent-du-3e-pib-mondial-la-politique-de-concurrence-doit-se-reinventer-face-a-leconomie-digitale/

[21] Olivier Ezratty, "The Possibilities of GAFAMI Making Mistakes", *FrenchWeb*, February 13, 2020 https://www.frenchweb.fr/de-la-faillibilite-des-gafami/392429

[22] Charles-Édouard Bouée, *Confucius and Robots*, published by Grasset, 2014.

[23] https://corporateeurope.org

[24] Jean-Pierre Stroobants, "Gafam, King of Lobby in Brussels", *Le Monde*, August 31, 2021, https://www.lemonde.fr/economie/article/2021/08/31/les-gafam-rois-du-lobbying-a-bruxelles_6092811_3234.html

influence enable them to influence legislation[25].

We have good reason to make the following hypothesis: By exposing GAFAM's control over our daily life, we may guide the new generation to formulate an alternative scheme[26] that is good for human beings. Therefore, GAFAM will have to resort to restructuring, which centers on strong digitized morals. Otherwise, they are doomed to disappear.

From GAFAM to BATX

Digital technology plays a dominant role in the stake in geopolitics. Since the birth of the Internet, those countries have faced tremendous challenges. To continue their trade, they have to do transactions. To ensure these transactions, they should ensure digital technology is unhampered.

We can see this from the War in Ukraine. SpaceX, a private company led by Elon Musk, declared that it would provide Ukraine with Network Starlink to reestablish connections. For a country, this is the first time it has seen the Internet operating based on only satellites. This way, the Starlink company tested its products and exchanged them with Ukrainian engineers[27]. Apart from the promise from the same camp, this event makes us realize that private enterprises can organize a country.

Cogent[28] and Lumen[29], two companies offering Internet connection services, have decided to involve themselves in the conflict[30] by restricting Russia's Internet connection.

---

[25] See the complete report: *Big Tech's Web of Influence in the EU*, at: https://corporateeurope.org/sites/default/files/2021-08/The%20lobby%20network%20-%20Big%20Tech%27s%20web%20of%20influence%20in%20the%20EU.pdf

[26] Take Tristan Harris' works as the model, https://www.tristanharris.com

[27] See the article *Elon Musk Provides Ukraine with Starlink--But It Is Not Without Risks.* https://techhq.com/2022/03/elon-musk-launches-starlink-connectivity-for-ukraine-but-its-not-without-risk/

[28] http://www.cogentco.com/fr/

[29] https://www.lumen.com

[30] See Julien Lausson's article "Russia Lost Some Internet Connection", *Numerama*, March 9, 2022, at: https://www.numerama.com/tech/878235-la-russie-perd-une-partie-de-son-interconnexion-avec-internet.html

On the other hand, we have also seen changes in Russia's digital technology. In fact, the Russian government has declared closing the social network[31] of GAFAM. This news caused tremendous repercussions. However, there were precedents. For example, in 2016, LinkedIn was closed because it violated the relevant law that enterprises should store user data in servers in Russia.

In 2019, Putin proposed the *Sovereignty Internet Law of Russia* to the parliament, and voters approved it. This draft law suggested a specialized command post be set up in Moscow, through which the authorities could manage the information flow in Russia's cyberspace (also named Russian Internet). The task involved monitoring, restricting, or blocking up these information flows in the whole or part of Russian cyberspace. In addition, Russia plans to set up its domain name system, ensuring the operation once the Internet is disconnected from the World Wide Web.[32]

These events strengthened the idea that there emerged mutually independent sovereign Internets[33] to defend against a regional power. Of course, such sovereignty will influence education and understanding of other cultures.

Another minor change is that based on the number of users in the future and the improved real-time data handling capacity, we will see the predominance of GAFAM overthrown and give way to BATX (Baidu[34],

---

[31] See the article "Russia: With Lockdown of Social Network, Signs of 'Social Discontent'", *Courrier International*, March 15, 2022, at: https://www.courrierinternational.com/une/censure-russie-avec-le-blocage-des-reseaux-sociaux-le-presage-dun-mecontentement-social

[32] See Bastien L's article: "Runet: Russia Will Disconnect Internet and Test Its Own Network", Website: BigData.fr, February 15, 2019. - https://www.lebigdata.fr/runet-russie-internet

[33] Olivier Diebolt, "Sovereignty Internet, A Heavy Blow of Russia and The Confrontation Logic in Cyberspace", February 2020, on the website: École de Guerre économique, https://www.ege.fr/infoguerre/2020/02/internet-souverain-russian-bashing-logiques-de-confrontation-cyberespace

[34] Founded by Robin Li in 2000. It is the fourth largest website in terms of page views in the world. With the same functions (mail, calendar and video platform) as Google, it has begun to compete with Google in AI or automatic drive.

Alibaba[35], Tencent[36], Xiaomi[37]). Actually, H (Huawei[38]) should be added in. GAFAM, used mainly in the West, is declining. Years later, they can no longer satisfy the new generation's "ever-increasing demands" in technology and the virtual world experience. With the development of its operating system and China's quantum information science, BATXH seems to anticipate a new, interconnected and speedy world[39].

BATX is very inflexible. They don't negotiate with the local authorities but with the local market and adjust their quotations. This flexibility is a crucial trump card, enabling them to get closer to users[40] worldwide.

With disrupted habits and the powerful technology helping all people connect with the world, "China" links itself to nearly 100 countries, from the Indian Ocean-Pacific Region to Latin America, the Middle East, and some African countries. We may envision that in the global system, the African Continent has become independent through its cooperation and exchanges with China along the Silk Road. Taking advantage of their capacity for quantized data management, BATXH may promote the development of cities and regions that are more intelligent and environmental-friendly[41].

We know that the West and China have different views on the relations between individual digital data and collective ones. Therefore, China needs a great number of facts to demonstrate that its data management system may create a more beautiful world in which technology, human beings, and the

---

[35] Founded by Jack Ma in 1999, similar to Amazon.com.

[36] Tencent (Internet Service Provider) has developed APP "WeChat". It is a complete ecosystem for message-sending, payment and group-building.

[37] Xiaomi is Beijing-quartered electronics and computer company specialized in mobile phone and home appliances. https://www.mi.com/fr/

[38] Founded in 1987, Huawei is a leading global provider of information and communications technology (ICT) infrastructure and smart devices. https://www.huawei.com/fr/

[39] See Camille Macaire's "BATX, An Ambitious Internet Magnate", on the website INA, December 18, 2018, https://larevuedesmedias.ina.fr/les-batx-des-geants-de-linternet-aux-ambitions-contrariees

[40] See Olivier Marbot's article "Gafam VS BATX: Clash of the Titans", Jeune Afrique, August 16, 2018.
- https://www.jeuneafrique.com/mag/614209/economie/les-gafam-face-aux-batx-le-choc-des-titans/

[41] This is what we saw at the Boao Forum for Asia (FBA) on April 22, 2022. An exhibitor displayed digital technique to effectively use the energy of Boao. Refer to the article from Xinhua News Agency, entitled China: Green Elements at Boao http://french.xinhuanet.com/20220421/380a9f7ad53c4e58a41ccb2b43766ec6/c.html

environment exist in harmony. Moreover, China needs to formulate a code of ethics applicable to all relevant countries, and Chinese standards should be applicable outside its boundary line.

Intellectual Revolution and Democracy

In this part, we may immerse ourselves in novels, looking forward to the future without any anxiety. Etienne Klein suggested that we should seize the future with our thinking[42]. For example, we may have noticed that every era has science and technology-related outlooks on the future. Steampunk emerged[43] after the Industrial Revolution, and atompunk[44] during the 1950s, which may also be called Dieselpunk.[45] With the appearance of the Internet, people began to discuss cyberpunk. Today, Solarpunk has emerged.

Principles of Solarpunk-based Future

It refers to creating a species of human beings. In some bionics, they live in harmony with nature. One of its goals is to relieve the anxiety of ecological crisis to some extent by giving the vision of the coexistence of man and nature. It does not mean returning to the pre-industrial times but using science and technology and a rational social-economic structure.

Such an outlook on nature embodies the best wish human beings can realize: In a post-scarcity, post-class, and post-capitalist world, man thinks of himself as one part of nature, and clean energy takes the place of fossil fuel. It assumes that humans have overcome many challenges today, particularly global warming.

---

[42] Luc Debraine, "Etienne Klein: Does the Future Exist as the Past?", Le Temps, April 6, 2018, https://www.letemps.ch/lifestyle/etienne-klein-futur-existetil-autant-passe

[43] This is an outlook on alternating the world based on the mass use of steam engines in the early period of the Industrial Revolution and the Victoria Era, using such materials as copper, brass, timber and leather.

[44] https://aesthetics.fandom.com/wiki/Atompunk

[45] https://aesthetics.fandom.com/wiki/Dieselpunk

Therefore, human society can enjoy a high-standard life without going beyond the earth's limits. Recycling, a circular economy, strong local groups, and do-it-yourself are the essentials of solarpunk. This outlook on nature is very similar to John Rawls' justice viewpoint and his "behind the veil of ignorance."[46] It should be noted that Chongqing and Shanghai are Chinese cities where solarpunk may be implemented. It was precisely the hypothesis put forward at the Ninth World Forum on China Studies held in Shanghai in October 2021.[47]

Towards Digital Dictatorship (Beneficial)?

Everything around us may be digitized. We should have a good command of the law governing data size.

Moore's Law is an empirical law that has much to do with the computing power of computers and the evolution of hardware complexity. In 1965, Gordon E. Moore proposed the first law: If the price remains unchanged, the complexity of semi-conductor will double each year. Ten years later, Moore adjusted his prediction: the number of crystal valves on the microprocessor chips would double every two years.

We put this law and Kryder's Law together. Since 1970, Mark Kryder has studied hard disk technology for decades. Since 2005, Kryder's work has inspired Kryder's Law, saying that the storage density of disc drives increased rapidly during the past 60 years. On average, the storage capacity doubled every 13 months.

Apart from this, the third law should be added: Nielsen's Law. This mathematical model assumes that the volume demand of Internet users increases by 50% per year. In the past 20 years, this figure approximated 30%.

---

[46] According to John Rawls (1921-2002), the justice principle should be chosen after the "veil of ignorance". What Rawls imagines is the primitive equal condition instead of the natural condition. The condition features of this hypothesis are that no one knows his status in society, class status or social status, nor does he know the ability and the inborn nature distributed to him, such as intelligence and power.

[47] http://english.scio.gov.cn/scionews/2021-10/19/content_77818258.htm

To access more data and increase accessible data, relevant technologies must be developed. However, it will cost huge financial resources, so a state can hardly engage in the development for a long period. For this reason, a gap appears between the state, organizations, and private enterprises.[48]

Simply put, to have a good command of data analysis as quickly as possible, these data should be put together[49]. We must ask ourselves, "Will a completely digitized society become a centralized system? Will this centralized system lead to the establishment of a dictatorship, whether this involves an institution, a state, or a private company[50]?"

Here, we have entered a grey zone. It does not mean comparing democracy and dictatorship (such a comparison makes no sense in terms of AI). We should propel scientific and technological progress within the framework of the photocell to foresee tomorrow's China.

For the time being, we should ask, "Is digital dictatorship beneficial, and is it built on the Multivac Principle of Isaac Asimov? Just like most of the technologies described in Asimov's novels, the accuracy of the Multivac changes according to its appearance. However, in every case, it is a computer the government uses. For the sake of safety, it is deeply buried underground. However, Asimov never told its specific size, nor did he describe its peripheral devices.

Unlike the AI described in Isaac Asimov's *Robot Series*, Multivac's interface is mechanized and impersonal. Besides, its console panel is so complex that few people can operate it. The principle is that we may use it to solve the problems plaguing human beings, such as starvation and climate change...

---

[48] It should be noted that here, I would not like to talk about the quantum capacity of computer. In 2021, researchers from University of Science and Technology of China (USTC) claimed that their 66-qubit quantum computer, "Zuchongzhi 2", is 1 million times faster than Google's Sycamore processor, and 10 million times faster than the current fastest supercomputer. Cf. Mathilde Rochefort's article: *Quantum information science: China's New Achievements*, November 4, 2021. https://siecledigital.fr/2021/11/04/ordinateur-quantique-chine-zuchongzhi/

[49] Here, the concept of data lake needs to be introduced. Data lake is a method to store mass data used by big data. These data are stored in the unprocessed form nearly without any conversion. Through the cluster, the database gives priority to the rapid and mass storage of different kinds of data.

[50] In 2014, an article titled *Confucius and Robots*, by Charles-Édouard Bouée & François Roche, pointed out that Facebook, Google and other enterprises adopted strategies to amend the law and make it in their interest so that they could transcend the restrictions of data collection and task automation.

It is an authority that can answer all questions raised by all people and can manage the earth most effectively. Therefore, this is a centralized system with all the features of dictatorship, for everything is centralized. However, such centralization seems beneficial because it possesses all historical resources and knowledge. Undoubtedly, the AI of the head of a state (idealistically), given that he does not encroach upon civil liberty, enables most people to live a happy life to the greatest extent. I would not like to deal with such a grey zone here, nor do I want to go too far because of my idealistic inclination. Obviously, we may easily imagine that an AI with open codes will develop towards totalitarianism[51].

By researching "cutting-edge technology," China has begun to deal with these topics. The Five-Year Plan points out that "China's self-reliance and self-improvement in science and technology" are the strategic support of national development." Premier Li Keqiang stated that from 2021 to 2025, China's research and development expenditure will increase by 7% annually to propel "significant breakthroughs" in science and technology. China may develop into a society based on fairness and balance by deepening quantum studies. Undoubtedly, we may call it a society friendly to most people of the world.

Flowing Democracy Towards Friendship

For years, my study has laid a foundation for flowing democracy. I have realized the new usage of this term because, up to now, Zygmunt Bauman's works make us pessimistic about disorganizing our daily life. I suggest we look at tomorrow's future in terms of technological progress. The technological progress made when I was born is insignificant today and tomorrow, and later generations will think so, too.

---

51 Here, what I mean is "Tay". In 2016, it was forced off the line by Microsoft after the former went online on Twitter for less than 24 hours because this artificial intelligence robot became a racist and a Nazi...Refer to the article at France Info: https://www.francetvinfo.fr/replay-radio/france-info-numerique/tay-le-robot-intelligent-de-microsoft-devenu-nazi-en-24-heures_1779187.html

Therefore, when writing this article, I feel it imperative to make people realize that these technologies may be used and developed friendly, collectively, and humanistically. "No more interference, yet full of governance" (Chapter 48 of *Tao Te Ching*). This remark is very instructive in that "no more interference" means neither "being passive" nor "fatalistic," unconcern, or even giving up. In fact, we should seize the momentum. From China's "Protopia"-mode development, we have realized only friendly flowing democracy can become tomorrow's social model. Flowing democracy is sprouting in China itself. How to maintain diversity? For thousands of years, China has succeeded in this regard. It will benefit the countries[52] that have joined the Belt and Road Initiative.

Based on the lowest-level digitized morals, flowing democracy plays its role by putting current human beings or new humans again into the system's center. Its basic principle is "No harming others."

A flowing democracy or society is built only upon complete equality. Undoubtedly, it abandons any arrangement of the Mafia and places (once again) everyone in the center of the system. Therefore, everyone may determine his degree of engagement in society (very active, active, or inactive). Flowing democracy is an organization that is ready to listen to everyone. Moreover, it enables people to be more creative and ideas to communicate more easily. Don't forget: its goal is not to compete but to satisfy[53].

How to Give a Judgment on Tomorrow's China?

There is hardly any answer to this question because a more detailed study of these clues is to be conducted. Obviously, we are in a complex and chaotic world as if the 20th century were not inclined to hand in its technology, figures,

---

[52] Cf. Chris Devonshire-Ellis, "China's Belt and Road Initiative: Infrastructure Developments to Expect in 2021", *Silk Road Briefing*, December 16, 2020, https://www.silkroadbriefing.com/news/2020/12/16/chinas-belt-and-road-initiative-infrastructure-developments-to-expect-in-2021/

[53] Here, it reminds me of the two lines from Chapter 49 of *Tao Te Ching*：- "The Sage's heart is not unchangeable"; - "He takes the people's hearts as his heart."

information progress, and social reform to the 21st century. In this century, self-narration is both eternal and instantaneous. In any place, we may accurately tell our own stories. Therefore, everyone communicates with his group (this doesn't necessarily correlate with his birthplace). This super-communication and perpetual information overload have changed our cognition and understanding of the world.

We are experiencing dual realities (we call them "real" and "virtual"). The more our technology develops, the more deeply we go into the virtual world and the more we learn about our human nature.

The further we advance, the more we understand Nick Bostrom's ideas[54]. He proposed that at least one of the following propositions is correct:

1. Man is very likely to become extinct before the "post-human" times (the times with very advanced technology) arrive;

2. Post-human civilization can hardly simulate its evolutionary history (or its changes) on a large scale;

3. We are almost certainly living in a computer simulation.

Therefore, it is wrong to think that we are very likely to become post-human who simulate our ancestors one day unless we live in simulation for the time being.

If we follow this viewpoint, as Nick Bostrom pointed out, we will be subject to technical restrictions in data processing capacity. After all, we have not obtained sufficient computing power to create the consciousness that computer generates. Nevertheless, we have reason to believe we can succeed sooner or later. Some scientists even believe that this can be realized decades later.

Then, in this new world, where is China's place?

In *China, the Next Superpower*, a book by Selon Geoffrey Murray, he holds that with its economic, political, and military development, as well as a huge population and splendid civilization, "China is rising and becoming one of the superpowers in the 21st century."

---

[54] https://www.simulation-argument.com

This analysis is rational and realistic. However, I can see further. With a civilization of thousands of years, China has maintained contact with its past and present for centuries. After all, the deeper the root of a nation is, the farther its future will be. It is what China is striving for: advancing towards the future. As mentioned above, walking along its own road, it narrates, and in the mode of Protopia, China may create a new society: a flowing social democracy featuring the harmonious coexistence of technology, nature, and humanity.

To accomplish this heroic undertaking and carry out its concept of a "community of a shared future for mankind," China must step out of the trap set by the Western world: a trap with a twisted mirror[55]. The more China insists on developing itself while sticking to the principle of harmony and justice, and the more determined it abides by pacifism, the more capable it will be in creating a super-intelligent society, however, in the face of the old belligerent Western world that knows nothing but binary opposition.

---

[55] For this, I would not like to talk about my research, and I will focus on this in other articles. However, we should not forget that for centuries (from the 17th to the 20th century), the repeated and changeless narration has led to and will continue to lead to doubts about China and Chinese civilization

www.ingramcontent.com/pod-product-compliance
Lightning Source LLC
Chambersburg PA
CBHW041733200326
41518CB00020B/2581